DAT

The drug policy process in the United States is permeated with ideology, impervious to the lessons of history, and addicted to debating polar abstractions, such as drug decriminalization, rather than focusing on practical alternatives to current policy. The book aims to improve the way in which American government officials think, talk, and act in the area of drug control. The authors argue that a rational drug control policy depends on a sensible policy process and demonstrate that the current process is far from satisfactory. Their book offers concrete suggestions for making our drug policies better serve significant goals like the protection of youth and the reduction of street crime. It provides a foundation for long-range and coherent policies for dealing with America's chronic drug problem.

The search for rational drug control

An Earl Warren Legal Institute Study

The search for rational drug control

FRANKLIN E. ZIMRING
and
GORDON HAWKINS

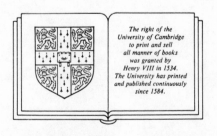

The right of the
University of Cambridge
to print and sell
all manner of books
was granted by
Henry VIII in 1534.
The University has printed
and published continuously
since 1584.

CAMBRIDGE UNIVERSITY PRESS

Cambridge
New York   Port Chester   Melbourne   Sydney

Published by the Press Syndicate of the University of Cambridge
The Pitt Building, Trumpington Street, Cambridge CB2 1RP
40 West 20th Street, New York, NY 10011-4211, USA
10 Stamford Road, Oakleigh, Victoria 3166, Australia

First published 1992

Printed in the United States of America

Library of Congress Cataloging-in-Publication Data
Zimring, Franklin E.
The search for rational drug control / Franklin E. Zimring and
Gordon Hawkins.
p.   cm. – (An Earl Warren Legal Institute study)
Includes bibliographical references and index
ISBN 0-521-41668-X (hardcover)
1. Narcotics, Control of – United States.   2. Narcotics, Control
of – United States – History.   I. Hawkins, Gordon, 1919–   .
II. Title.   III. Series.
HV5825.Z56   1992
363.4'5'0973–dc20   91-25035
                                                                         CIP

A catalog record for this book is available from the British Library.

ISBN 0-521-41668-X hardback

In fond memory of John Kaplan

Contents

Tables and figures

Tables

Figures

Preface

At the threshold of the 1990s, control of illicit drugs is the preeminent problem of criminal justice in the United States. Because a high level of public concern produces governmental action in a political democracy, the drug problem has already produced within five years two major federal legislative initiatives, the creation of a new special office headed by a federal "drug czar," and numerous antidrug campaigns at every level of American government. Although many of these governmental responses themselves increase public awareness of drugs as an issue, public anxiety and alarm about drugs seem to have been an authentic grass-roots phenomenon of the mid-1980s that has taken hold in the American landscape. Drug control seems poised for a long run as a high priority for political action.

This book is about the process of making drug control policy. How are policy choices identified, debated, and made in an atmosphere of intense concern? How are the consequences of governmental policy measured and evaluated? How, if at all, do we learn from our mistakes? We undertook this project convinced that just as much as we need new drug policies, we need a new drug policy process to create an environment in which alternatives can be rationally debated.

What is conspicuously missing from this volume is a neat solution to the complex of phenomena that Americans call the drug problem. The appetite for mood-affecting substances is universal, and it is a chronic condition of American life rather than an acute emergency that is likely to be quickly resolved. Like most chronic conditions, our drug problems can get better or worse, but they will not go away. The goal for the effective treatment of chronic disease is management rather than cure, a long-term and consistent program to minimize the damage and pain attributable to the disease process. A model of management rather than cure is the most appropriate drug policy goal for American government and society.

This book is divided into two parts. In the first, we try to establish a foundation for a more rational policy debate, by analyzing aspects of current policy processes and supplying the historical and definitional data necessary for responsible policymaking. Chapter 1 explores the ideological roots of the current drug control debate, contrasting what we call legalist and public health ideologies in drug control and demonstrating the pervasive legalist influence on the official *National Drug Control Strategy* published in late 1989.

Chapter 2 discusses issues of definition and measurement that are important to policymaking. One should not elect a drug control law enforcement policy without deciding what the term *drug* should mean, and yet that term is commonly not defined. The issues of measurement we address in Chapter 2 are critical to determining both the current conditions and the impact of countermeasures on drug use and its consequences.

Chapter 3 surveys the available historical evidence regarding four periods of prohibition policy in American history, searching for lessons about drug use and the results of drug control strategies. The state-level alcohol prohibition efforts of the 1850s, the Harrison Act's controls on opiates and cocaine, the national alcohol prohibition from 1919 to 1933, and the Marijuana Tax Stamp Act of 1937 provide four sources of data on the origins and effects of prohibition policies.

The final chapter in Part One deals with the history of ideas rather than of policies. In Chapter 4 we compare the current debate on drug decriminalization with the exchange in the nineteenth century between John Stuart Mill and Sir James Fitzjames Stephen. That exchange was more than a preview of coming attractions; it was the prototype of the "modern" debate, as our survey of current opinion illustrates.

We re-interpret the decriminalization debate in Chapter 4 as a clash of presumptions between an emphasis on liberty and a preference for continuity in social and legal policy. We also argue that the decriminalization debate should be regarded as a sideshow rather than the main arena of policy debate on drug control. The hard questions are not whether we should elect a criminal law of drugs but, rather, what kind of criminal controls we should choose, and at what price. In making these decisions, the broad strokes of a general policy are less useful than are specific judgments about specific problems. In our view, the most effective drug control policy is one constructed from the ground up, and an exclusive focus on the decriminalization-versus-prohibition issue only distracts from this task.

The second part of the book is designed to provide building blocks for a rational drug control policy. Chapters 5 and 6 discuss the two leading concerns associated with drug policy: children and child protection and the linkages between drugs and predatory crime.

Chapter 5 considers aspects of drug control policy toward young persons that we regard as nuts-and-bolts issues that any child protection policy must incorporate. We discuss the rationale for denying young persons access to psychoactive substances and distinguish between those substances allowed to adults and those generally prohibited. We survey the variety of strategies available to deny drugs to young persons and to control their consumption. The issues presented by the child drug offender – in which the young person is both the subject and object of a prohibition – are analyzed separately. Last, we explore the possible conflict between a prevention and a treatment emphasis as a child protection strategy.

What all these questions have in common is that each must be integrated into a coherent child protection package. No drug policy – from free availability to draconian prohibition – can make any sense unless these issues of child welfare have been considered in detail.

Chapter 6 shows that the complexity encountered when thinking about the relationship between drug policy and crime stems from the large number of possible relationships between drugs and predatory crime. But because so little is known about the magnitude of most drug–crime linkages, the impact of most of the shifts of drug control policy on rates of crime cannot be confidently predicted. Further, it is likely that drug–crime relationships vary significantly in different urban environments, making highly precarious any generalizations from case histories. Some policies, such as compulsory drug treatment for convicted offenders, merit repetitive trial. Little is known, however, about the extent of crime attributable to drug use, let alone the responsiveness of crime patterns to shifts in drug policy. Although the concern with crime is a justified aim of drug control policy, drug control turns out to be an experimental method of dealing with predatory crime that is by no means more promising than are alternative methods of using criminal justice resources to reduce street crime.

In recent years in the United States, the federal role in drug control – traditionally more extensive than that in other areas of criminal justice – has been expanding in scope and changing in nature. Chapter 7 examines principles that can be used to determine appropriate federal, as opposed to state and local, functions and discusses the allocation of federal responsibility, such as between the drug control office and other agencies of national government.

The last chapter in this book is drafted as a memorandum to an incoming head of the federal Office of National Drug Policy. Here we criticize the assumptions of the current national drug control strategy and suggest changes in emphasis and organization in American drug control.

In the 1990s, drug control policy has become a crossroads where many different disciplines and orientations meet. Our own interest in this topic is the product of work on the institutions and jurisprudence of the criminal justice system. It seemed to us that a study of drugs from that perspective was justified, both because drug control is an important aspect of criminal justice and because drug policy could benefit from the experience of three decades of reform and dissatisfaction in American crime policy. We view the current war on drugs as a lineal descendant of the war on crime and believe that drug policy can benefit from a measured examination of this family tree.

Acknowledgments

The debts accumulated in the preparation of this volume are substantial and diverse. To begin, the idea for this book was not ours. Our colleague Norval Morris first recognized the need for a book on drug policy and organized support for Gordon Hawkins's research at the Center for Studies in Criminal Justice in Chicago in May and June 1989. Professor Morris also participated in the planning of this book and read each chapter in early draft. In the best Mario Puzo sense of the term, he has served as the godfather for this enterprise.

The main institutional support for our research and writing came from the Earl Warren Legal Institute at the University of California at Berkeley. David Johnson and William Nelson provided first-rate research assistance. Karen Chin was responsible for every aspect of preparing this manuscript, and Rod Watanabe coordinated the administrative support.

Two professional colleagues, Professor Morris and Peter Reuter of the Rand Corporation, read and reacted to most of the book. Our other reader-critics included Sanford Kadish and Jerome Skolnick of Berkeley, Mark Moore of Harvard, James Jacobs and Graham Hughes of New York University, and Maury Zimring of Hilo, Hawaii.

John Kaplan taught us much of what we know about the drug policy process. Our dedication celebrates this and the gift of his friendship.

PART ONE

The drug problem

Introduction

The first part of this book concerns four different ways of looking at drug problems in the United States. Chapter 1 examines drugs and drug control as an ideology. Chapter 2 addresses drugs as an issue of definition and measurement. Chapter 3 analyzes the history of drug control in the United States, and Chapter 4 deals with drugs as an occasion for debating the proper role of the state in regulating citizen conduct.

Viewed together, these chapters reveal both contrast and similarity. Each view of drugs competes with the other perspectives for the status of dominant paradigm. Because the ideologically committed drug warrior has no real need for definition and measurement when deciding drug control questions and little regard for historical analysis, the significant issue in drug control is a question of values. Persons committed to the historical viewpoint often believe that the lessons of history should have a dominant influence on the determination of policy toward drug programs and thus tend to dismiss the ideologist as irresponsible.

One way to evaluate the significance and importance of each perspective is to review each claim in the context of the other perspectives. Accordingly, we hope that the whole is greater than the parts, in that the four chapters read together will have a cumulative value that exceeds the individual worth of any one of them taken on its own.

But if the four perspectives described and discussed in this part of the book represent a study in contrasts, there is one notable respect in which they are similar to one another: In all cases it is either implicitly assumed or explicitly argued that the drug problem is a unitary one. This assumption of conceptual unity in the discussion of drugs and drug control means that "drugs" are treated as a single topic and that drug control is more often than not treated as a single problem. In this respect, the four chapters in this part present a contrast with our discussion in the second part of the book. In this second part, different aspects of the drug problem are distinguished, and different components of drug control policy, such as child protection and crime, are given separate treatment.

1

Ideology and policy: A look at the *National Drug Control Strategy*

The *National Drug Control Strategy*, published in September 1989, is not, in several respects, an ordinary government document. Rather, it is a government report that is meant to be read – it is only ninety pages long, excluding appendices, with a fourteen-page introduction personally written by then-"drug czar" William Bennett that seeks to build a rhetorical and philosophical foundation for a multifaceted campaign against drug abuse. The goal is a comprehensive program involving not only national, state and local government but also employers, community groups, and the private sector. Budgetary figures and projections by fiscal year – usually the mother's milk of government planning documents – are relegated to the appendices of the white-on-red-covered document with the presidential seal on the cover. Indeed, the report is intended to serve as a manifesto for a long-term drug control strategy in the United States. By grounding its proposals in strategic rather than merely tactical considerations, this document helps illuminate the basic premises on which public policy is to be based.

Analysis of the *National Drug Control Strategy* is a window into the three competing schools of thought that divide those in our midst who support some version of a war on drug abuse. We aim in this chapter to illustrate the powerful role of ideology in drug policy choice in the United States, with a special emphasis on the ideological stance that dominates the current government program. After a brief description of the contents of the Bennett report, we outline three contrasting approaches to drug control – the generalist, the legalist, and the specifist modes. We then contrast each of these three schools of thought in relation to four issues of drug policy. We show how the Bennett drug program fits squarely in the legalist framework. The final section discusses the implications of adopting a hard-line legalist perspective on the degree of power that the government should be permitted to exercise and the theoretical justification for exercising such power.

I. The national strategy

In his letter to the speaker of the House of Representatives and the president of the Senate laying out his administration's 1989 drug control strategy, President George Bush described it as "a comprehensive blueprint for new directions and effort" focused on "the scourge of drugs." The national strategy proposed in the report takes the form of a "plan of attack" (Office of National Drug Control Policy, 1989, p. 13), outlined in five chapters dealing with the criminal justice system, public awareness and community prevention campaigns, international policies, and activities and efforts to interdict smuggled drugs.

Two further chapters discuss a research and intelligence agenda. These are followed by a number of appendices describing various quantified goals and measures of success; a federal implementation plan with budget tables; a package of recommended state antidrug legislation; possible federal designations of high-intensity drug-trafficking areas, as mandated in the Anti-Drug Abuse Act of 1988; and a proposed plan for improved automatic data processing and information management among the involved federal drug agencies.

The introduction by William Bennett, then the director of the Office of National Drug Policy, which prefaces the report, begins by reporting some "very good news." According to the most recent National Survey on Drug Abuse conducted by the National Institute on Drug Abuse (NIDA), there had been a "dramatic and startling" decline in the use of illegal drugs, in that the estimated number of Americans using any illegal drug dropped 37 percent, from 23 million in 1985 to 14.5 million in 1988. Moreover, use of the two most common illegal substances – marijuana and cocaine – had fallen by 36 and 48 percent in that period.

According to Mr. Bennett, this good news is "difficult to square with common sense perceptions." Americans, he states, have "good reason" for being convinced "that drugs represent the gravest present threat to our national well-being," for there is a wealth of other evidence that "suggests that our drug problem is getting worse, not better." The only specific evidence he actually cites is related to an increase in drug-related emergency hospital admissions between 1985 and 1988. But Bennett asserts that the "fear of drugs and attendant crime are at our all-time high"; "reports of bystander deaths . . . continue to climb"; "drug trafficking, distribution, and sales in America have become a vast, economically debilitating black market"; "drugs have become a major concern of U.S. foreign policy"; and that in every state in America, "drugs are cheap, and . . . available to almost anyone who wants them" (Office of National Drug Control Policy, 1989, pp. 1–2).

What is called "the intensifying drug-related chaos" is said to be largely explained by crack, which "is an inexpensive, extremely potent, fast-acting derivative of cocaine. . . . And crack use is spreading – like a plague." "Our most intense and immediate problem is inner-city crack use." Nevertheless, it also appears to be spreading "into the country at large . . . almost every week, our newspapers report a new first sighting of crack – in the rural South or in some midwestern suburb, for example." America is faced with an "appalling, deepening crisis of cocaine addiction" (Office of National Drug Control Policy, 1989, pp. 3–5).

But although cocaine use in the form of crack is defined as the principal current problem, the "drug problem . . . continues to involve drugs of every sort." Moreover, "anyone who sells drugs – and (to a great if poorly understood extent) anyone who uses them – is involved in an international criminal enterprise that is killing thousands of Americans each year." It follows that "we should be tough on drugs – much tougher than we are now" and "we should be extremely reluctant to restrict [drug enforcement officers] within formal and arbitrary lines" (Office of National Drug Control Policy, 1989, pp. 4, 7–8).

In short, the United States is facing "the worst epidemic of illegal drug use in its history – more severe than the heroin scare of the late 1960s and early 1970s; far more severe, in fact, than any ever experienced by an industrialized nation." Indeed, the suggestion that this should be met by a "shift of emphasis away from drug enforcement and toward instead treatment for addicts" and that the "money saved in reduced law enforcement could be more effectively spent on health care for addicts and on preventive instruction of the rest of us" is mentioned only to be peremptorily dismissed: "*Any* significant relaxation of drug enforcement – for whatever reason, however well-intentioned – would promise more use, more crime, and more trouble for desperately needed treatment and education efforts" (Office of National Drug Control Policy, 1989, pp. 5, 6, 7; emphasis in original).

It follows from this analysis of the problem that faced with "a crisis – especially one which has for so long appeared to spiral wildly out of control . . . tough and coherently punitive anti-drug measures . . . should be employed." The "essence" of the drug problem is the "use itself," and the "highest priority of our drug policy" must be an attack on "drug use nationwide – experimental first use, 'casual' use, regular use, and addiction alike." Moreover, the focus of the attack must not be on drug addicts but on non-addicted users of whom there are many millions, each of whom is "*highly* contagious" and represents "a potential agent of infection" (Office of National Drug Control Policy, 1989, pp. 7, 8, 11; emphasis in original).

It is acknowledged that "locking up millions of drug users will not by itself make them healthy and responsible citizens." But while "the search for long-term solutions" continues, "short-term reduction in the number of American casual and regular users will be a good in itself," and "because it is their kind of drug use that is most contagious . . . [it] will also promise still greater future reductions in the number of Americans who are recruited to join their dangerous ranks" (Office of National Drug Control Policy, 1989, pp. 7, 12).

The antidrug strategy document outlined in the five chapters immediately following this introduction discusses, in varying degrees of detail, the practical steps required to implement the policy that it proposes. The first chapter, "The Criminal Justice System," sets the tone in the first paragraph: "We declare clearly and emphatically that there is no such thing as innocent drug use." The criminal justice system, it is said, has suffered too long from the policies of "those who enthusiastically endorse plans for more parole officers but balk when it comes to planning new prisons" (Office of National Drug Control Policy, 1989, pp. 17, 32). It is evident that if "the war against illegal drug use" is waged along the lines indicated, planning new prisons may well need to be given priority as a part of the significant expansion foreshadowed in the introduction (Office of National Drug Control Policy, 1989, p. 7). Both "more police" and "more prisons" are said to be necessary (Office of National Drug Control Policy, 1989, p. 24). The estimated cost of the "many proposals advanced in this report" is considerable, involving a FY 1990 federal drug budget totaling $7.864 billion, "the largest single-year dollar increase in history" (Office of National Drug Control Policy, 1989, p. 13).

Four aspects of this national strategy document challenge us to examine the ideological roots of these policy prescriptions: First, the nature of the drug problem is never precisely defined. Not one sentence in a 153-page report is devoted to defining the terms *drug* or *drug problem*. Implicitly, therefore, all illegal drugs seem to be included, with alcohol and tobacco evidently excluded. Also apparently excluded are barbiturates, amphetamines, and other substances that are frequently obtained both legally and illegally for abusive use.

A second significant element of the report is its novel treatment of *all levels* of drug use as equally troublesome and threatening. The memorable phrase is "experimental first use, casual use, regular use, and addiction *alike*" (Office of National Drug Control Policy, 1989, p. 8; emphasis added).

The third striking feature of the report is the way in which all types of drugs – that is, illegal drugs – seem to be regarded as equally pernicious. Although the use of crack cocaine is described as "our most intense and immediate problem" (Office of National Drug Control Policy, 1989, p. 4), there is nowhere any suggestion of choosing priorities for the resource allocation in waging the war on drugs. "The highest priority" is said to be simply "to reduce the overall level of drug use nationwide" (Office of National Drug Control Policy, 1989, p. 8).

Finally, one of the most extraordinary features of this report is the characterization of the effort to control drugs as essentially a struggle between good and evil. "Drug use is a *moral* problem" (Office of National Drug Control Policy, 1989, p. 53; emphasis added). The report divides the United States into two parts. On the one hand are drug use and drug users representing the forces of evil, and on the other hand is "the vast majority of Americans who have never taken an illegal drug" (Office of National Drug Control Policy, 1989, p. 9), together with their government, representing the forces of good.

In this chapter, we shall describe the view of the drug problem presented in the *National Drug Control Strategy* as reflecting a legalist position, and we shall contrast that approach with two alternative schools of thought regarding drug control policy.

II.   Three schools of thought

We have found it helpful to distinguish among three schools of thought when sorting through contemporary discussion of drug control policy. All three approaches support some version of a "war on drugs" and thus can be contrasted with approaches that urge the across-the-board decriminalization of drugs considered in Chapter 4. But the policies supported differ as a function of different perspectives on why drugs constitute a societal problem.

Public health generalism

The public health perspective is principally concerned with reducing the harmful consequences produced by the consumption of psychoactive substances: problems such as health costs, time off from work, family problems, and a shortened life span. The public health generalist worries about these consequences no matter whether the drugs that produce them are legal or illegal. Usually the generalist believes that many different drugs produce the same type and extent of dependency costs and that in this respect most drugs have been created equal.

Thus, patterns of morbidity and mortality, rather than the statute book, are the standard used by the public health school to judge policy toward drugs. The presumption seems to be that most of the abusable substances can cause nearly equal harm. The proponents of this view commonly see the drug abuser as the victim of a disease, even if the user is generally viewed with the mixed feelings that we tend to reserve for those who suffer from self-inflicted wounds.

Legalism

The principal concern of the legalist school is the threat that illegal drugs represent to the established order and political authority structure. In this

Table 1.1. *Distinguishing features of three approaches to drug control policy*

	Generalist	Specifist	Legalist
Which drugs are problematic?	Licit and illicit	Licit and illicit	Illicit only
Are all drugs as defined equally problematic?	Yes	No	Yes
Is drug taking or its harmful consequences the primary problem?	Harmful consequences	Harmful consequences	Drug taking

view, it is the consumption of the prohibited substance rather than any secondary consequences that might ensue that is the heart of the matter. The taking of drugs prohibited by the government is an act of rebellion, of defiance of lawful authority, that threatens the social fabric.

From this perspective, all illegal drugs are similar to one another and quite different from drugs that are not prohibited. For the legalist, the harms and injuries that result from alcohol consumption are beside the point, because those who ingest alcohol are not affiliating themselves with enemies of the government. For similar reasons, the legalist regards as irrelevant any claim that a particular prohibited substance is nontoxic. If the harm lies in the rebellious nature of ingestion, then the chemical properties of the substance ingested are of little significance. According to this account, drug taking is a species of treason. That it might not harm the user – who is in effect a declared enemy of the state – is of no comfort to the legalist.

Cost–benefit specifism

The distinctive feature of cost–benefit specifism is the belief that all drugs of abuse have not been created equal. Specifists agree with public health generalists that drugs of abuse generate substantial individual and social costs, and they count those costs in the same way as the generalists do. They see drug policy as requiring a balance between the costs of abuse and the likelihood of reducing them by means of legal prohibition, and the manifold costs of enforcing those prohibitive laws. In regard to such a delicate balance, the specifist school insists that judgments about the appropriateness of drug prohibitions should be made one at a time, rather than with sweeping generalization, and that they should also be tied to the social context in which particular drugs are used.

Table 1.1 contrasts the three schools of thought in regard to their answers to three key questions: Which drugs are problematic? Are all drugs equally troublesome? Is the primary importance of the drug problem the consequences that flow from drug abuse or the drug taking itself? As this table illustrates, the legalist sees only illegal drugs as the problem, whereas both the generalist and the specifist see the drug problem as including legal substances as well. Both the generalist and the legalist think that most drugs, as they define them, are equally harmful, but each has a different definition of the term *drug*. Finally, the legalist sees drug taking itself as the major harm to be combated, and the other two schools are more concerned about the harmful effects of drug taking.

The public health generalist approach is the dominant viewpoint of the medical community that deals with the assessment and treatment of substance dependency. It is this "all drugs are created equal" philosophy that has led to the creation of treatment programs in which all drugs – from alcohol to cocaine to heroin to diet pills – are dealt with in the same type of twenty-eight-day inpatient programs. This "one size fits all" treatment design is a good example of a generalist approach to drugs of abuse. Prominent spokespersons for this approach include Lester Grinspoon of Harvard University and Arnold Trebach of American University. The cost–benefit specifists include a number of scholars of the criminal justice system whose expertise is drugs. The most prominent modern proponent of this viewpoint is the late John Kaplan of Stanford University, who balanced a call for the decriminalization of marijuana with the subsequent endorsement of the continued prohibition of heroin and cocaine (compare Kaplan, 1970, with Kaplan, 1983, 1988).

The legalist perspective is the dominant orientation of the law enforcement community in the United States, including the extensive specialized policy enforcement networks that have grown up around drug control. The *National Drug Control Strategy* is the charter of the legalist perspective on drugs and their control in modern American life.

This tripartite scheme cannot claim to cover every possible basis for supporting an antidrug campaign, and there are doubtless also variations and shadings of opinion among adherents to the three schools that the basic outline overlooks. Still, a surprisingly large proportion of U.S. attitudes toward illegal drugs is found in the generalist, specifist, and legalist rubrics, and as the next two sections illustrate, the essential orientation that the observer brings to these issues determines much concerning what policies will be supported.

III. Three views of drug programs

The general orientations discussed in Section II explain not only the shape of the proposals in the *National Drug Control Strategy* but also the character of much of the criticism that has been directed at them. This can be shown in a survey of the attitudes of the three schools of thought toward four different potential elements of a drug control strategy: supply reduction, treatment programs, prevention and drug education, and decriminalization.

Supply reduction

As the *National Drug Control Strategy* makes clear, the legalist perspective puts great stock in programs to reduce the supply of illegal drugs in the United States by means of interdiction and domestic law enforcement efforts. The logic of such support is straightforward: If a reduced supply results in a net decrease in the consumption of illegal drugs, the legalist will count the policy as a success.

The public health generalist sees the effort to reduce the supply of prohibited drugs as necessarily futile because nonprohibited drugs will still be available to inflict the same amount of damage. For example, diverting an abuser from cocaine to alcohol or amphetamines through supply reduction efforts directed at cocaine would create no net benefit for the generalist, but it would represent a total victory for the legalist. Both the legalist and the generalist believe that all drugs are created equal, but the legalist's definition of drugs includes only the illegal ones (hence the "victory" in our example), and the generalist's definition is much broader.

The hallmark of the specifist approach is that not all drugs are created equal. The specifist believes that in a social context some drugs are so much more destructive to the user and to the community that the costs of selective criminal prohibition can be justified. Because the possession of only these drugs should be made criminal, the diversion of users from illegal to legal drugs, such as from cocaine to alcohol, should reduce the aggregate social cost of drug use. Thus, the specifist would support the beneficial potential of supply reduction strategies only as long as the dividing line between legal and illegal drugs is correctly drawn. The specifist would expect the diversion from illegal to legal drugs to result in decreases in morbidity and mortality. Unlike the legalist, these benefits are the reason that the specifist supports supply reduction.

Treatment

In regard to drug treatment, it is the legalist who is the most suspicious of treatment interventions. The specifist and the generalist would invest larger resources in treatment, but for different reasons. Once the *National Drug Control Strategy* has defined drug use as a moral problem, and one involving a majority of nonaddicted and willful participants, it is hard to imagine a treatment regime suited to the task of their moral rehabilitation. In fact, the

conception of drug treatment in this report is a regimen in which the participants are forced or frightened into treatment programs and threatened into
abstinence during and after treatment. This radical restructuring of the treatment enterprise is necessary to fit the legalist conception of how drug users
can be changed into a conception of treatment and rehabilitation.

For the specifist, drug treatment competes on an equal footing for resources with supply reduction and other countermeasures. The specifist is
particularly anxious to target high-risk, active users for treatment because
these persons impose the highest per-person social costs, through crime and
needle-sharing disease (Kaplan, 1983, p. 230).

The specifist perspective is also particularly well suited to the substitution
of relatively benign drugs for more harmful ones. Thus the "lesser of two
evils" approach that maintains heroin addicts on methadone makes sense to
a specifist because this approach emphasizes loss reduction rather than victory over rebellion or the notion of a disease requiring a cure.

For similar reasons, the specifist is also likely to be sympathetic to supplying syringes to intravenous drug users as a policy of loss reduction, but the
legalist might not see this as leading to moral improvement. The legalist is
not highly motivated to protect drug abusers from bad consequences.

If treatment might be an attractive option to the specifist, it is the only
hope for the public health generalist, because reducing the supply of dangerous drugs is impossible as long as alcohol and tranquilizers are widely available.

The generalist assumes that destructive drugs are widely available to the
population and that the appropriate public policy is to treat those who become pathologically involved with psychoactive substances. Just as the legalist believes that the medical dimensions of drug use are of little consequence,
the generalist feels that any capacity of the system to turn users from one
drug of abuse to another makes little difference in personal or social cost.
Only the specifist can choose between treatment and supply reduction without a strong initial bias.

Prevention and education

Drug prevention and education seem to represent as close to a point of consensus as there is in the current drug control debate. But the consensus support for primary prevention does not extend to the content of drug education
messages, and the absence of any strong group of skeptics may also lead to
an unquestioned investment in antidrug messages that are not effective.

The legalist, specifist, and public health generalist all support drug abuse
prevention campaigns, but the sort of campaign that each would favor differs. The legalist endorses antidrug propaganda messages, distrusting pure

informational campaigns. The legalist is less concerned about fact content than either the specifist or generalist is. The legalist drug message to children is that illegal drugs are a bad thing and that drug takers are bad people. For the legalist, the most important target audience of these messages are those who have never taken illegal drugs and who are thus to be reinforced and congratulated. Because this view seeks to divide the population into good people (who never try drugs) and bad people (who do), there is no room on the prevention pulpit for either discussion of the continuity between licit and illicit drugs or for distinctions among different illicit drugs. Preaching against alcohol abuse may be problematic from this perspective because it blurs the sharp distinction between legal and illegal drugs that lies at the heart of the legalist brief.

The public health campaign stresses information and a high-priority target audience of those who probably will experiment with at least one illegal drug in their substance career. Information about potential misuse of both legal and illegal drugs is important to minimizing the deleterious impact of substance abuse. The generalist tries to build a course on drugs into a broader life skills or health education curriculum, whereas the legalist wants a freestanding course on the perils of illegal street drugs. The legalist wants antidrug sermons delivered to the young, and one function of such sermons is preaching for the benefit of the converted. The generalist wishes questions from the audience and factual answers to them. The conflict in these two agendas is obvious.

But the legalist agenda for drug education may clash even more clearly with the specifist program, because the specifist hopes that public programs can distinguish among illicit drugs in order to provide special warnings for the most dangerous drugs. A specifist might believe that a credible campaign against needle sharing or injectable heroin should issue from a source that does not overstate the dangers of marijuana, particularly if most of the persons in the audience at high risk for heroin use have acquired or will acquire firsthand experience with marijuana.

This sort of approach is rejected by the legalist because it comes close to condoning drug abuse and fails to chastise those who have used an illegal drug. From the legalist perspective, this undermines the gospel of absolute abstention from illicit drugs and tends to demoralize the faithful never-users who are the most important target audience of the legalist appeal.

Decriminalization

The contrast among the schools of thought regarding the function of decriminalizing currently prohibited drugs concerns both substance and tone. Both the generalist and specifist wish to approach questions of change in the criminal law concerning drugs with a dispassionate and pragmatic tone. In part because many of them come from criminal justice specialties, specifists tend to regard the scope of criminal prohibitions as a more important drug control topic than do generalists, with the latter group more skeptical that the number of prohibited substances or the substances on that list will have a large impact on the size of the substance abuse problem in the social system. Unless a society attempts to impose a general ban on mood-affecting substances, the profile of licit versus illicit substances should not matter much. Whereas it is an article of the specifist credo that where the law draws the line can have an effect that is significant enough to warrant the continual rethinking of the scope and justification of the criminal law. Accordingly, specifists invest much more time and energy than do generalists in discussing changing boundaries in the criminal law.

Rethinking is the last thing that legalists wish to encourage in regard to the scope of criminal prohibition, and they vehemently oppose decriminalization proposals. For the legalists, the proponents of decriminalization are the fellow travelers of the 1990s. Indeed, the legalists characterize proposals to decriminalize as "stupid" and "irrational," and they portray their purveyors as "naive," with the same sinister undertones to the adjective that used to be aimed at those who were accused of communist sympathies.

The *National Drug Control Strategy* amply illustrates the tone and substance of the legalist approach to this issue. The report speaks not of decriminalization but of what is called *legalization*, and it seems to suggest that a legalization process would represent a governmental seal of approval for drug abuse. "Exactly how under this scenario we would convincingly warn potential new users about the evils of drugs – having just made them legally acceptable – is not entirely clear" (Office of National Drug Control Policy, 1989, p. 6). The text of the report is unqualified in its condemnation of any decriminalization of any drug – "it would be an unqualified national disaster" – in rhetorical terms that could well have been used to oppose the repeal of alcohol prohibition ("would promise more use, more crime, and more trouble for desperately needed treatment and education efforts") (Office of National Drug Control Policy, 1989, p. 7).

The reason that the decriminalization of any currently illegal drug is anathema to the legalist position is that the vindication of state authority is the central value to be upheld in this version of the drug war. Changing the law thus would be literally surrendering to the enemy, by admitting that state authority has been inappropriately directed at drug users. The central inflexibility is that there is no way to change the terms of the criminal law regarding drugs without admitting defeat in the power struggle between good and evil that is the essence of this account of drug use and abuse. Thus, there can be no such thing as an unjust drug law, or the whole fabric of the legalist position would unravel. It is not that decriminalization might lead to bad things; it is, in itself, the bad consequence that the legalist most fears.

IV. A legalist manifesto

The legalist pedigree of the *National Drug Control Strategy* explains many of the curious features of the document that we have noted. Only illegal drugs are the concern of this strategy, and all illegal drugs are considered the natural enemy in the drug war. The subject of the war on drugs is therefore not defined because it is regarded as obvious: All, and only, illegal psychoactive substances are the target. What a drug is, is thus a question of the content of the criminal law at a given time.

On the question of whether the principal concern is drug use or the social and health consequences of drug use, the report is unambiguous:

First, we must come to terms with the drug problem in its essence: use itself. Worthy efforts to alleviate the symptoms of epidemic drug abuse – crime and disease, for example – must continue unabated. But a largely ad-hoc attack on the holes in our dike can have only an indirect and minimal effect on the flood itself. (Office of National Drug Control Policy, 1989, p. 8)

If crime and disease are only "the symptoms," what is the problem? Here the report is not explicit, but the inclusion of all illegal drugs and the failure to discuss the abuse of legal drugs implicitly makes the priority the threat posed to the government's authority. After calling the creation of "a Drug-Free America" an "admirable goal," the report goes on to say that "it is already a reality for the vast majority of Americans who have never taken an illegal drug" (Office of National Drug Control Policy, 1989, p. 9). By its own terms, this announcement includes some alcoholics and Valium users as members of "a Drug-Free America."

Indeed, the only concern with alcohol expressed in the report appears much later:

Though the legislated mandate of the Office of National Drug Control Policy excludes alcohol (since it is not a controlled substance under the law), it must be recognized that alcohol is still the most widely abused substance in America. *It is illegal for young people to purchase or consume alcohol.* Prevention programs must obviously take this fact into account. (Office of National Drug Control Policy, 1989, p. 48; emphasis added)

The choice of language in this passage speaks volumes: Even though alcohol is "the most widely abused *substance* [emphasis added] in America," it is not a drug viewed in the perspective of the *National Drug Control Strategy*. And the report seems not to be uncomfortable with this limited mandate for the Office of National Drug Control Policy, for nowhere is it suggested that the office's restricted jurisdiction is inappropriate or should be expanded.

Two other aspects of the *National Drug Control Strategy* make sense only in light of its legalist orientation. First, the report makes the same policy recommendations for all drugs. With respect to enforcement priority, the policy toward the casual user, treatment, and drug testing, the presumption is that all (illegal) drugs are created equal. This is so even though the report paints very different portraits of the threat posed by various drugs. For example, crack cocaine "is, in fact, the most dangerous and quickly addictive drug known to man" (Office of National Drug Control Policy, 1989, p. 3). Marijuana is worthy of prohibition mostly because it is a "gateway drug" leading to the use of more dangerous drugs (Office of National Drug Control Policy, 1989, p. 55). Some drugs apparently may be, in George Orwell's words, "more equal than others," but the priority and strategy are the same for each of these drugs and for all other illegal substances.

This lack of priorities is related to seeing the central harm of drug taking as defiance of the law. Whatever else their effects, all illegal drugs are equally illegal and, on that account, are worthy of equivalent treatment. While deploring the special costs of crack cocaine, then, a legalist advocate can never forget that all illegal drugs carry the same imperative for suppression. So the legalist must simultaneously argue that crack cocaine is the worst drug in human history and also that marijuana is just as bad as crack cocaine.

Another legalist sentiment animates the need to seek out and punish casual, nonaddicted drug users, and this is the most novel element in the *National Drug Control Strategy*. The justification for targeting casual users is that they present "a *highly* contagious" example to potential drug users (Office of National Drug Control Policy, 1989, p. 11; emphasis in the original). But the enforcement of laws against this group can also be justified because according to the legalist view, their deliberate infraction of the law is the central harm, the essential drug problem. That these persons are neither addicted nor collaterally criminal makes them even more dangerous role models. That is, their defiance of the legal authority of the state is more blameworthy and dangerous than that of addicts driven by their craving, for the addicts' "drug use is not very contagious" because they are "a mess" and make "the worst possible advertisement for new drug use" (Office of National Drug Control Policy, 1989, p. 11). It is the nonaddicted drug users who are most conspicuously thumbing their noses at the state authority. Both the priority of the nonaddicted users and the passion with which it is argued are salient aspects of the legalist perspective.

Indeed, it is hard to find departures from legalist priorities in the *National Drug Control Strategy*. Even when the report supports policies that do not flow from legalist premises, the qualifications that it imposes on them confirm the need to state all elements of drug control policy in the legalist mode. In this connection, the report's handling of the issue of drug treatment provides a significant example of the powerful influence of the legalist bias on the specific policies proposed in the *National Drug Control Strategy*.

As we noted in the last section, legalists do not place much stock in spending scarce resources on programs of drug treatment. Part of the reason is their distrust of medical models. But the legalists also view drug users as social and political enemies, and treatment programs therefore seem to represent a way of giving aid and comfort to the enemy, never a popular category of wartime expenditure. It is thus not surprising that the legalists prefer to invest resources in punishment and interdiction efforts. Yet this legalist document supports the expansion of treatment programs at an annual cost of over $600 million. Does this represent a deviation from legalist orthodoxy? Hardly. The drug treatment establishment contemplated in this document is permeated with the legalistic distrust of comfort to the drug users. Because the efficacy and patriotism of treatment programs are distrusted, their rigorous evaluation is required (Office of National Drug Control Policy, 1989, p. 102). But there is no such strict accountability for law enforcement efforts, education programs, or interdiction. The report also calls for mandatory treatment with confinement sanctions for treatment failures. It is thus the legalistic gloss of treatment-as-punishment that makes treatment initiatives palatable in the *National Drug Control Strategy*.

A final and striking example of the priorities of legalism can be found in the list of quantified objectives, at the back of the report, for reducing the extent of the drug problem. Nine quantified goals are presented, with eight of the nine relating to reducing drug availability or drug use. Only one, decreasing the number of drug-related hospital emergency room admissions, concerns the lessening of harmful consequences that flow from drug abuse. The report mentions lower domestic marijuana production as one of its nine specific goals. But fewer drug overdose deaths in the United States or fewer babies born drug addicted are not among the quantified objects of the national drug control policy as presented in the *National Drug Control Strategy*.

V. Legacies of legalism

It is important to consider some of the collateral consequences of a legalist emphasis for drug policy. In this section, we shall examine the impact of a legalist emphasis on a constitutional constraint on drug control policy, on the relationship between drug users and government-sponsored helping programs, and on the impact of government policy on how drug users respond to public opinion polls.

The state's motivation for action can carry implications for the kind of power that will be allowed in a limited government with constitutional constraints. In the coming years, the courts will face a substantial number of novel constitutional questions as new techniques for compulsory testing and for treatment for the purpose of controlling drugs become state policy. There are two respects in which a policy that emphasizes hostility to the drug user may be more strictly scrutinized for excesses of government power than would be the case for policies apparently motivated by the impulse to help. Procedures like civil commitment, traditionally justified more as compulsory assistance than as punitive isolation, may not be permitted when introduced as part of a legalist crusade against dangerously immoral drug users. If the medical model does not fit the apparent motives of state power, the exercise of that power may be more sharply curtailed. If the government's stance toward the targets of the program is unmitigated hostility, a constitutional court might conclude that the only legitimate arena for such warfare is the criminal justice system.

There is a second way in which the martial character of a drug war may limit the degrees of power exercised on its behalf. The courts are traditionally more vigilant in providing right-to-privacy and search-and-seizure limits in criminal law than in government intrusions that are justified for reasons of public health. The reason for this distinction may be a feeling that the government should be allowed more latitude when it is acting only, or principally, for the benefit of those citizens that it is inspecting. Also, the courts may feel that the offending citizen turned up in a public health search has less to lose than does the prototypical criminal defendant. Thus, for instance, the U.S. Supreme Court has been more amenable to inspections without probable cause made by health and building inspectors than to those made by police searching for the fruits of crime. Which analogy the judiciary applies to drug control strategies may be a function of the announced or imputed motive of the strategy.

Consider a program of universal, compulsory urine testing for drugs in secondary schools, patterned after the program currently in use in the U.S. military. The justification for such a program could not be based on the express or implicit consent of the schoolchildren or of their parents because education is compulsory. Thus, one key justification for military and employer drug test regimes would be absent. Yet the potential for identifying drug users would be more than substantial. How might a court resolve the novel constitutional question relating to such a program?

The point we wish to emphasize here is that the orientation of the government program could be a decisive factor in determining whether the program violated constitutional standards. A credible claim for public health justification based on finding out whether students are using any of a wide spectrum of legal and illegal substances and referring them to treatment and support programs that are avowedly nonpunitive might pass constitutional muster, whereas a drug-testing program aimed at suspending and expelling those with urine testing positive for illegal drugs could be viewed as overreaching either Fourth Amendment standards or the government's obligation to protect the young. In this way, ironically, a moral crusade on legalist premises may have to proceed from a narrower power base than would government programs with a more benign orientation to drug users.

A not-unrelated set of problems concerns the orientation of employer "employee assistance programs" that have been established to discover and facilitate the treatment of employees with alcohol and drug abuse problems. The mixed motives of such programs have always been inherent in the employer–employee relationship. Unlike drug and alcohol screening programs that operate before the establishment of such employment relationships, programs that involve workers with established employment relationships have usually been premised on employee entitlement. Yet an unmitigated legalist stance could drive a wedge between the perceived interests of employers and those of employees with a use history of those drugs targeted by legalist antidrug programs. Employees might well distrust the benign intentions of companies toward drug users. So might labor unions and employee associations, despite the upbeat narrative history provided by the *National Drug Control Strategy:* "As drugs have become more prevalent in the workplace, many corporations have begun to use drug testing as a means of identifying employees *in need of assistance*" (Office of National Drug Control Policy, 1989, p. 56; emphasis added).

In the view of the *National Drug Control Strategy,* the role of the employee assistance program is a combination of assistance and deterrence, in which the program simultaneously keeps "the workplace safe and productive by identifying those employees" using drugs and helps drug-using employees "by referring them to treatment, counseling, and rehabilitation." The *National Drug Control Strategy* favors a federal policy in which such programs are required to take punitive action in response to an employee found to be using illegal drugs (Office of National Drug Control Policy, 1989, pp. 56–57).

One problem with deputizing employee assistance programs to deter and ferret out drug use is the damage to the credentials of such programs as helping agencies for employees with drug and alcohol problems, at which they feel they can get confidential assistance. If employees attempt to conceal drug and alcohol problems, the resulting delays in treatment referral will have negative effects on workplace safety. And these could be compounded by the unwillingness of fellow employees to refer drinking or drug-using colleagues to an employer agency that has come to resemble a drug enforcement office. Finally, the attempt to keep alcohol and illegal drug policies on a separate track might well fail, and so one casualty of militant antidrug employer programs could be early intervention and treatment efforts for alcohol.

The way in which punitive orientations might discourage candidates from seeking treatment or their fellow employees from using the employee assistance program is nowhere considered in the document under review, and it is the lack of consideration rather than any substantive choices made in the report that concerns us here. The transformation of every institution relating to drugs in society into a branch of the criminal enforcement enterprise could have manifold effects that need more attention than has been provided in the *National Drug Control Strategy*.

One final example of the potential effects of a sustained legalist emphasis concerns the sensitivity of public opinion that the report uses to keep score for its nine quantified two- and ten-year objectives. No fewer than five of these benchmarks involve trends over time in survey responses of the population. One of the measures is the trend in student attitudes toward drug use, and four of the targets pertain to lowering the percentage of the population who tell the poll taker that they have taken illegal drugs in the previous month.

With the success or failure of a coordinated national campaign hinging on trends over time in survey responses, it is a matter of some concern that a campaign to censure and stigmatize drug use might reduce the willingness of citizens to respond candidly to strangers who ask whether they have ingested cocaine or other illegal drugs in the past thirty days. The more harshly focused a government campaign is, the more impact such a campaign can be expected to have on the respondents' candor about their drug use. The danger, then, is that of an antidrug campaign appearing to succeed because increasing proportions of the population conceal personal drug use from survey researchers. Yet even this artifact represents a substantial achievement for the dedicated legalist, because such a campaign would certainly reduce open defiance of the drug laws, even if it had zero impact on the levels of illegal drug use or the health and economic consequences that are associated with drug use.

Whereas the public health generalist and the specifist would regard any decrease in public support for drug taking or opinion poll reporting of illegal drug taking as illusory achievements unless they reflected real declines in the ingestion of drugs, the legalist would view such a trend as meaning that a growing segment of the population acknowledged the immorality of illegal drug taking. That the fear of consequences produced this acknowledgment is not the sort of thing that would offend legalist sensibility in the least. Nor would the fact that such a victory would be only symbolic be at all discouraging, because from the legalist perspective, symbolic adherence to legal definitions of right and wrong behavior is the most significant issue.

But this mode of analysis leads us to an important puzzle and a significant worry. The puzzle is that from a legalist perspective the late 1980s was by no means a peak period for illegal drugs as a national problem. The percentage of Americans who reported current use of illegal drugs did drop from double to single digits in the past decade, and this is, in the words of the *National Drug Control Strategy*, "very good news," whether or not the illegal drug use itself declined by any such margin. Some of the other social indicators that concern people – overdose deaths, AIDS infection, crack babies, and the like – seem to be viewed by the legalists more as the wages of sin than as indices of the seriousness of the drug threat to the law-abiding population. Why, then, was 1989 a more problematic period than the late 1960s or early 1970s? After all, from the legalist perspective, the more benign the social reputation of an illegal drug is, the larger its threat to the antidrug stance of the legal order will be. If drug takers are suffering more harmful consequences, so much the better for the deterrence of others.

Our worry is that many legalists saw the cocaine situation of the late 1980s as an opportunity rather than as an emergency. Drugs in the 1990s are a highly attractive target of authoritarian opportunity when compared with other issues and other time periods. Public support for extreme governmental responses to drugs is higher than for authoritarian countermeasures to any other social problem. In this sense, what the general public perceives as a drug emergency is a special opportunity to institutionalize the judgments and tactics of the legalist school. Indeed, the special opportunity for legalists may have arisen only because of the declining popularity of drugs among the general population. Just as the anti-Left witch hunts of the 1950s took place when the Left's popularity was waning, the lessened public support of drug use may be more of a cause of the legalist crusade against drugs than a consequence of it. The climate of opinion of the 1990s may thus be seen by the legalist as an opportunity to take revenge on earlier errors of permissiveness in American drug policy.

One problem with all this is its essential lack of relation to the public health costs of substance abuse in the United States of the 1990s. The lower priority accorded to illness, debility, and death in the legalist drug scheme is a matter of some concern when conflicting goals compete for scarce public resources, as is the warping effect produced by an overemphasis on punishment in treatment and rehabilitation processes. But the largest concern about ideological overkill in the current debate should be reserved for the potential exploitation of the drug problem as a rallying point for authoritarian sentiments in American society and government.

2

What is a drug? And other basic issues

This chapter deals with questions that many will regard as not only boring but also as unconnected to the real issues for decision in drug policy. Questions of definition and measurement strike most readers as procedural preliminaries to the discussion of important questions, as niceties to be relegated to a footnote or ignored altogether. But in drug control policy, what we do not define carefully we do not know, and what we do not know can cripple the capacity of policy to confront problems.

One of the hallmarks of an academic treatment of a subject is a concern with questions of definition and scope, with exactly those terms of reference that most people regard as obvious. So our preliminary insistence on the importance of definition here may mark us as hard-core academics. In fact, however, even those academics concerned with drug policy commonly ignore such matters, fearful perhaps that attention to them would be regarded as scholastic quibbling in the face of urgent social problems. But we think that it is worth time and attention to define the term *drug* and to discover to what extent different parties to the contemporary debate about drug policy define that key term in the same way. We shall show that a basic knowledge of the range of meanings assigned to key terms in the drug control debate is necessary to understanding the policy choices.

In a similar vein, we shall demonstrate that there are not only different estimates of the seriousness of "the drug problem" in the United States but that there are also divergent conceptions as to what aspects of drug taking make drugs a contemporary societal problem. It should come as no surprise that disagreements about what is harmful about drug taking lead to sharply contrasting estimates of the social damage attributable to drug use in modern American life.

Related to different definitions of the negative aspects of drug use are different methods of measuring the extent of the drug problem and comparing the magnitude of drug problems over time and among different areas. The second section of this chapter will discuss different measures of the extent and seriousness of drug taking and its consequences. The third section will look at one especially important method of attempting to compute the extent of the drug problem: efforts to express in monetary terms the cost of the problem and to establish criteria for determining whether or to what extent drug control measures are "cost effective." A concluding note will explore the relationship between the costs of drug use and public fears about drugs. By almost all measures, the peak of concern with drugs in the late 1980s came when the proportion of citizens using drugs and the direct costs of drug use had declined from earlier levels. Yet fears associated with crack cocaine were at historically high levels. We shall suggest some explanations for this disjunctive pattern.

I. Definitional issues

In this section we survey previous attempts to define four key terms in the drug area and then state our preferred approach to defining the relevant terms. Our objective is not to provide an exhaustive analysis of basic definitional issues but to profile issues of definition that we regard as necessary for understanding policy debates.

What is a drug?

On the first page of the *National Drug Control Strategy*, it is said that "drugs represent the gravest present threat to our national well-being," that "our drug problem is getting worse," and that "the threat drugs pose to American public health has never been greater." On the same page, there are also references to "drug abuse," "drug use patterns," "fear of drugs," "drug users," and "intravenous drug use." On the next page, there are further references to "drug trafficking," "drug use," "drug-inspired violence," and "the challenge of drugs." It is said that "drugs are potent, drugs are cheap, and drugs are available to almost anyone who wants them." What is not offered, however, on either those opening pages or anywhere else in the entire document, is a definition of the term *drug*. Although it is clear that the primary dictionary definition – "a substance used in medicine" – is not what the authors had in mind (Office of National Drug Control, 1989, pp. 1–2), the central term in the report is never defined.

In their disregard for definition, the authors of the *National Drug Control Strategy* cannot be seen as pioneers. On the contrary, their attitude reflects a long-standing tradition generally respected throughout the available literature on drug abuse and most clearly evident in previous reports on the subject published by federal departments and agencies. To that generalization there are only a few notable exceptions, which are the subject of this section.

The National Commission on Marijuana and Drug Abuse, established under the Comprehensive Drug Abuse Prevention and Control Act of 1970, broke with all precedent in its second and final report, *Drug Use in America: Problem in Perspective*, published in 1973, and dealt in the first chapter with such matters as "the vocabulary of the drug problem" and "the way in which the drug problem is presently defined" (National Commission, 1973, p. 8). The chapter begins by noting that "the meaning of the word drug often varies with the context in which it is used" (National Commission, 1973, p. 9). Indeed, the definition of the term *drug* provides an excellent example of that "large class of cases" for which, Wittgenstein noted, "the meaning of a word is its use in our language" (Wittgenstein, 1968, p. 20). Thus in a narrowly scientific context the word *drug* may be used to refer to any substance other than food that, by its chemical nature, affects the structure or function of a living organism, including also in this sense some agricultural chemicals.

A physician might define a drug as any substance used as an ingredient in a medicine or medicament. A wide variety of drugs are used in medical practice because of their analgesic or curative properties. Moreover, in the context of treating physical or mental illnesses the lay public often uses the word *drug* in the same sense, and the National Commission report refers to this as "the therapeutic meaning" of the term (National Commission, 1973, p. 10). In the report itself, the word *drug* is used more narrowly, being described as "intended to encompass only psychoactive drugs or those which have the capacity to influence behavior by altering feeling, mood, perception, or other mental states" (National Commission, 1973, p. 11). Psychoactive drugs are, of course, used widely in medical practice for therapeutic purposes, especially in the treatment of depression, anxiety states, and mental illnesses. But these drugs are also consumed for recreational purposes, and they include such commonly used psychoactive substances as alcohol and tobacco.

The report points out that

the use of psychoactive drugs is commonplace in American life. Distribution of these drugs is an integral part of the social and economic order. In 1970, 214 million prescriptions for psychoactive drugs were issued, representing annual retail sales of approximately $1 billion. The alcohol industry produced over one billion gallons of spirits, wine, and beer for which 100 million consumers paid about $24 billion. (National Commission, 1973, pp. 8–9)

The truth is, as the 1967 Presidential Commission's Task Force on Narcotics and Drug Abuse pointed out: "In terms of drug use the rarest or most abnormal form of behavior is not to take any mind-altering drugs at all. Most adult Americans are users of drugs, many are frequent users of a wide variety of them" (President's Commission, 1967, p. 23). What, then, does the assertion in the *National Drug Control Strategy* that "the majority of American city residents – rich or poor; male or female; black, white, or Hispanic; well- or poorly-educated – do not take drugs" mean (Office of National Drug Control Policy, 1989, p. 4)? It is by no means clear, nor is it clear what is meant by a reference to "recent reductions in most use of most drugs by most Americans" (Office of National Drug Control Policy, 1989, p. 5). But both meanings must rest on a definition of drugs far different from that of the 1967 and 1973 commission reports.

It seems to us that the 1989 document's failure to define the subject of "the war on drugs" is quite deliberate. For, according to the *Strategy* document, "the highest priority of our drug policy must be the stubborn determination further to reduce the overall level of drug use nationwide." And any definition of the term *drug* would call for an explanation of the disregard in that policy toward alcohol, which is in the same document acknowledged to be "the most widely abused substance in America" (Office of National Drug Control Policy, 1989, pp. 8, 48). In this document, a "substance" is different from a "drug" in ways that can only be surmised, as neither term is defined.

The National Commission report refers to the "social meaning" of the word *drug* as having a "value component" (National Commission, 1973, pp. 9–10). Even though this value component is pejorative and derogatory, it seems clear that it is in this sense that the word *drug* is most often used in the *National Drug Control Strategy*, such as when referring to "the threat drugs pose," "the challenge of drugs," "the evils of drugs," and "the best way to fight drugs and drug use" (Office of National Drug Control Policy, 1989, pp. 1, 2, 5, 6). The term *drug* is also used in a variety of combinations with a pejorative connotation, such as drug abuse, drug habit, drug peddler, drug pusher, and drug trafficker.

This pejorative component of the term *drug* in common social understanding has caused scientific bodies to avoid the term when discussing the subjects of drug policy debate. For example, the *Diagnostic and Statistical Manual of Mental Disorders-III-R* (DSM-III-R), published by the American Psychiatric Association, does not use the term *drug* to describe the class of recreationally used substances referred to by the National Commission. Instead, the term *psychoactive substance* is used to cover a wide range of substances, including opiates, alcohol, cocaine, nicotine, sedatives, and marijuana. The manual then discusses as separate processes the patterns of dependency and abuse associated with specific substances such as sedatives or nicotine (American Psychiatric Association, 1987, pp. 165–85). The advantage of this approach is that both the therapeutic and the pejorative components of the term are avoided in the taxonomy of psychoactive substances. All substances that affect mood and perception are presumably covered by the term *psychoactive*, although among the foodstuffs, only caffeine is mentioned in the two sectors of the manual that deal with psychoactive substance disorders. And major tranquilizers with profound psychoactivity but little appeal as recreational substances are not singled out for discussion in the sections dealing with psychoactive substance disorders.

The primary drawback to this approach is the gulf between lay and legislative definitions of drug and the psychiatric nomenclature. Most Americans do not think of their government's current policies as the "war on psychoactive substances." It is worth special note that the "psychoactive substance" approach of the American Psychiatric Association encompasses many more substances than definitions that restrict the term *drugs* to "narcotics" and "dangerous drugs" (see, e.g., President's Commission, 1967, p. 1). That is, the extent and costs of the use of major psychoactive substances far exceed the magnitude of drug use that is more narrowly defined.

Drug abuse

The expression *drug abuse* has been variously defined but is generally used to refer to the excessive use of a drug, to the use of a drug that causes unjustified problems, to the taking of a drug solely for its stimulant effects, or to the taking of a drug for any purpose other than a therapeutic one. "Now immortalized in the title of federal and state governmental agencies," the National Commission reported, "this term [drug abuse] has the virtue of rallying all parties to a common cause: no one could possibly be *for* abuse of drugs any more than they could be *for* abuse of minorities, power, or children." On the other hand, "neither the public, its policy makers, nor the expert community share a common understanding of its meaning or the nature of the phenomenon to which it refers" (National Commission, 1973, p. 11). It has been rightly said that "the most cursory examination of policy-oriented literature on drug 'abuse' shows a veritable fog of confusion, of much potential mischief" (Culyer, 1973, p. 449).

The commission sponsored a national survey carried out by response analysis, in which a random sample of adults and young persons were asked to list what substances they regarded as drugs and to give a free-response explanation of what drug abuse was. An analysis of their responses revealed that "psychoactive substances such as alcohol and tobacco, are generally not regarded as drugs at all" and, moreover, that "drug abuse is an entirely subjective concept. It is any drug use the respondent frowns upon. . . . It is an eclectic concept having only one uniform connotation: societal disapproval" (National Commission, 1973, pp. 10, 13).

The DSM-III-R defines the concept of "psychoactive substance abuse" as a "residual category for noting maladaptive patterns of psychoactive substance use that have never met the criteria for dependence . . . applicable to people who have only recently started taking psychoactive substances." Because a "maladaptive pattern" is present when an individual continues to use a substance "despite knowledge of a social, occupational, psychological, or physical problem that is caused or exacerbated by use of the psychoactive substance" (American Psychiatric Association, 1987, p. 169), the criteria for abuse seem both open-ended and quite sensitive to the judgment of the diagnostician as to what constitutes a significant social or occupational problem. The American Psychiatric Association's standards cover all substances in their scope, so that alcohol and narcotics abuse are treated as separate diagnostic categories.

Drug addiction and dependence

The President's Commission on Law Enforcement and Administration of Justice Task Force on Narcotics and Drug Abuse reported in 1967 that

there is no settled definition of addiction. Sociologists speak of "assimilation into a special life style of drug taking." Doctors speak of "physical dependence," an alteration in the central nervous system that results in painful sickness when use of the drug is abruptly discontinued; of "psychological or psychic dependence," an emotional desire, craving or compulsion to obtain and experience the drug; and of "tolerance," a physical adjustment to the drug that results in successive doses producing smaller effects and, therefore, in a tendency to increase doses. Statutes speak of habitual use; of loss of the power of self-control respecting the drug; and of effects detrimental to the individual or potentially harmful to the public morals, safety, health or welfare.

Nonetheless, the task force noted that the term *addiction* was "deeply embedded in the popular vocabulary" (President's Commission, 1967, pp. 1–2).

Just as it was said in the early nineteenth century that there was no safe distinction between the moderate and the immoderate use of alcohol because moderate use led inexorably to immoderate drinking (Lender and Martin, 1987, p. 69), so in the twentieth century what John Kaplan called "the inevitability of addiction myth" has been attached to both heroin and cocaine. In fact, as Kaplan pointed out, the available evidence suggests that "the number of controlled heroin users probably matches and may even exceed the number of addicts at any one time" (Kaplan, 1983, pp. 33–34). Although "no one has studied the kind of cocaine use that is analogous to social drinking," there is no doubt that by many citizens today "it is accepted as a relatively innocuous stimulant, casually used by those who can afford it to brighten the day or the evening" (Grinspoon and Bakalar, 1976, pp. 64, 129).

The notion of addiction that has provided an implicit or explicit justification, or rationale, for all drug prohibition movements and legislation is the product of a remarkable degree of conceptual confusion and factual error. Indeed, it is "a monstrous tangle of social, psychological and pharmacological issues" (Grinspoon and Bakalar, 1976, p. 176), which we shall not attempt to unravel here. It is, however, necessary to indicate briefly the crucial issue.

The concept of drug addiction – or drug dependence as it is often called – involves the implication that some substances are addictive in that they "have a mysterious power over the will that only coercive authority can cope with" (Grinspoon and Bakalar, 1976, p. 187). Studies of voluntary self-administration of drugs by laboratory animals are sometimes cited as evidence that some drugs do have this irresistible attractive power. The study most often referred to in this context is Tomoji Yanagita's work on the evaluation of dependence liability of various types of drugs in monkeys (Yanagita, 1973). What Yanagita's experiments and others of a similar character demonstrate is that drugs like the opiates and cocaine have a powerful drug-seeking, behavior-reinforcing effect on animals in controlled laboratory conditions.

A number of comments are relevant both to these experiments and the extrapolations from them. The principal point is that the conditions of these studies bear very little relation to the situations encountered by human beings in society. Indeed, as Zinberg and Robertson noted, the more carefully controlled the laboratory environment is, the less it resembles the real world (Zinberg and Robertson, 1972, p. 97). There are in fact many considerations that place a substantial barrier in the way of drawing conclusions from these experiments about the consumption of drugs in a normal human environment.

Grinspoon and Bakalar make the point that even in regard to the animals used in these experiments, it is questionable how far the drug dependence or addiction can be attributed solely to the neurophysiological effect of the drug's chemical action. "In Yanagita's experiment," they observed,

the animals were caged and under restraint. They had few sources of satisfaction except pressing the lever for drugs. Would they act in the same way if the situation offered a variety of dangers and opportunities? Is the conditioned pattern more than a laboratory artifact? . . . Caged monkeys pressing levers for drugs are in an artificial environment free from the dangers and exigencies of ordinary animal life and also free of competing interests or temptations. They are dependent on drugs in the sense of having few other resources. Can it not be said that they are "culturally conditioned" to crave the drugs or that the situation they are in makes them "psychologically disturbed"? (Grinspoon and Bakalar 1976, pp. 195, 197)

The broad public understanding of addiction is reflected in the *National Drug Control Strategy:* There are "a large number of Americans whose involvement with drugs develops into a full-fledged addiction – a craving so intense that life becomes reduced to a sadly repetitive cycle of searching for drugs, using them, and searching for them some more." Moreover, "casual or regular use . . . may always lead to addiction" (Office of National Drug Control Policy, 1989, pp. 10–11). This conception of addiction is usually linked to a category of substances classified as "addictive," in that physical symptoms of withdrawal develop when the blood level of one of these substances falls below a minimum. This dichotomized notion of addiction and its restriction to substances that produce withdrawal symptoms has been criticized in medical circles for several decades, and much of this criticism has lately been endorsed by drug enforcement and prevention personnel.

One central problem is the use of a physical addiction as a double-edged sword. If a drug is not addictive, many people will conclude that it is either harmless or at least susceptible to substantial personal control even in the context of persistent use. Indeed, the use of the status of "nonaddictiveness" as a *Good Housekeeping* Seal of Approval for recreational use was one reason given for the street popularity in the 1970s and 1980s of not only marijuana but also cocaine. For this and other reasons, medical definitions no longer focus on the physical processes that characterize addiction and instead have replaced that term with the notion of "psychoactive substance dependence": "a cluster of cognitive, behavioral, and physiologic symptoms that indicate that the person has impaired control of psychoactive substances use" (American Psychiatric Association, 1987, p. 166). The concept of dependence is more open-ended than that of addiction, but it seems to carry the same connotations of limited control. The key difference is that the explanation for limited control is no longer restricted to physical dependence; the degree to which dependence implies involuntary craving is not specified.

Drug problem

When observers speak of a drug problem, they are usually referring to the social aggregate of individual use patterns of either one or a number of drugs. This collective measure of the harm caused by drugs is the most common compound term in the drug debates and the most uniformly imprecise concept in the field. The use – and abuse – of drugs has been an integral part of the fabric of American social life ever since what has been called the "veritable national binge" took place between 1790 and 1830 (Rorabaugh, 1979, p. ix). It has also been seen as a social problem, one that afflicts the national community, although the nature of that problem has been the subject of a vertiginous degree of metamorphosis over the years. "For now," according to the *National Drug Control Strategy,* "our most intense and immediate problem is inner-city crack use" (Office of National Drug Control Policy, 1989, p. 4). Less than two decades ago, heroin was regarded as our most intense and immediate problem, and "cocaine, the use of which is relatively well-controlled within the present social policy framework" (National Commission, 1973, p. 36), was seen as of little social concern.

When President Lyndon B. Johnson delivered his State of the Union address in January 1968, it is said that his greatest applause came after proposals for suppressing crime and the traffic in LSD (Blum, 1969b, p. 326). Five years later, the final report of the National Commission on Marijuana and Drug Abuse stated that LSD had "a low dependence liability," that its use "tends to be age-specific and transitory," and that individuals under the influence of LSD "do not generally act in ways qualitatively different from their normal pattern of behavior" (National Commission, 1973, pp. 164, 224). Earlier in the century, alcohol, which "can legitimately be classified as a 'narcotic' in a very specific sense of that term and is surely a 'dangerous drug' as well" (National Commission, 1973, p. 18), was the main focus of alarm and concern. Today it is the most widely used psychoactive drug in America and, by most citizens, is not regarded as a drug at all. Just as subjective judgments are necessary at the individual level to determine whether someone is abusing a particular substance, a wide variety of subjective judgments influence the determination that a community has a drug problem and bear on how seriously the problem is regarded.

One thing that seems clear is that whatever "the drug problem" may be, it has a tenuous and variable relationship to both the pharmacological properties of the substances we call drugs and their effects. As the National Commission on Marijuana and Drug Abuse pointed out, all the psychoactive drugs "act according to the same general principles. Their effects vary with dose. For each drug there is an effective dose (in terms of desired effect), a toxic dose, and a lethal dose. All drugs have multiple effects" (National Commission, 1973, p. 11). In fact, "none of the mind-altering (psychoactive) drugs is inherently harmless, vicious, or magical in its properties." At the same time, all of them can be, have been, and are used by some individuals to a degree that "is damaging to [that] person's social or vocational adjustment or to his health, or is otherwise specifically detrimental to society" (Fort, 1969, p. 230). That is what constitutes the drug problem and the reality behind what Peter Reuter called "the devil image of drugs" (Reuter, 1984, p. 142). The crucial question, however, relates to the extent of that problem. To that question, the National Commission on Marijuana and Drug Abuse gave a singularly candid answer:

At the present time we have no firm knowledge of the number of people who use various drugs, or the incidence of different drug-using behavior patterns. Even in the area where concern and curiosity have been greatest, heroin use and dependence, the estimates rely on questionable extrapolation, based on tenuous hypotheses, from elusive data. (National Commission, 1973, p. 371)

Over a decade later, Peter Reuter of the Rand Corporation carried out a detailed analysis of the official estimates of such things as the number of heroin addicts and the total income from illegal drug sales. He concluded that they belonged to what he referred to as "a class of 'mythical numbers' that is becoming the routine product of government agencies." The estimates of the number of addicts made by the National Institute on Drug Abuse, he said, were devised by unsound statistical methods from data that were the product of "very questionable, but unquestioned, data collection." "At this stage," Reuter, suggested, "the only respectable stance is pure agnosticism" (Reuter, 1984, pp. 136–7, 142). He was equally critical of estimates of the total income from illegal drug sales published by the National Narcotics Intelligence Consumer's Committee, consisting of representatives of eleven federal agencies. Those estimates, he pointed out, were "without plausible foundation. The data on which they are based do not support them, and are themselves of dubious origin . . . the government's claim to have even a rough estimate of the level of expenditures on illicit drugs is simply unreasonable" (Reuter, 1984, pp. 142–3).

The distinction drawn in the *National Drug Control Strategy* between viewing drug use in America as "isolated self-indulgence" or as a major social problem, a "social, medical, and economic catastrophe" (Office of National Drug Control Policy, 1989, p. 2), must depend on such things as the incidence, prevalence, frequency, and intensity of drug use in the community and on both national and local drug use patterns. Yet even for these matters, which might be regarded as objective criteria of the problematic character of drug use, the essential data are not available.

Toward a principled definition

We think that significant progress can be made toward a principled definition of two of the key terms under discussion here: drug and drug addiction or dependence. We offer what have been called "stipulative definitions," whose advantages are that they remove any ambiguity (Robinson, 1950, p. 66). The object is to give some degree of precision and univocality to concepts that are, in ordinary usage, unclear and equivocal. On the other hand, the problems of achieving unambiguous definitions of drug abuse and a societal drug problem are more intractable, and they will certainly not be resolved in these pages. Indeed, attempting to resolve the definitional differences associated with those terms may not even be worth the cost.

Drug. For the purpose of this discussion, we will define a drug as a psychoactive substance capable of being used recreationally. In this definition, we intend the concepts of both psychoactivity and recreational use to be objective and susceptible to specification and measurement. This definition does not distinguish between illicit and licit substances, nor does it exclude substances, such as prescription drugs, whose licit use is restricted to special use by specific subpopulations. Rather, all of these substances are drugs within the scope of this definition. This is not to deny that there are important distinctions among these drugs. But there is, in our view, no advantage to be gained by employing a definition that restricts the application of the term *drug* to substances treated as illicit in a particular place at a particular time. In fact, there is considerable confusion inherent in attempting to make legality a criterion for classifying a substance as a drug.

One unavoidable ambiguity in our definition concerns how psychoactive a substance must be before its properties qualify it for inclusion in the drug category. Large numbers of substances not thought of as recreational drugs – including many foodstuffs – have, at ordinary levels of dosage, an impact on the moods of consumers. Our restriction to substances capable of being used recreationally restricts the field of drugs somewhat but still leaves a wide variety of substances with different levels of psychoactivity to be presumptively subsumed under the drug category. At the margin are substances like tobacco which, though powerfully addictive, have a relatively modest impact on the moods of nonaddicted users. Caffeine beverages are another set of substances that would be considered mild drugs. Excluded from this definition are some substances that may be physiologically addictive but are not psychoactive or are not capable of being taken for recreational purposes. The absence of either of these dimensions is a basis for exclusion.

Drug addiction and dependence. With respect to addiction, there is an extensive literature that explores the different concepts of addiction and their respective conceptual and functional utility. With regard to drug addiction, what we define as addictive behavior is drug use that is habitual and assumes a functional importance for the individual concerned, such that it renders his or her other social roles and preferences increasingly unimportant. Whether or to what extent there must be physiological correlates of the overriding desire for a particular drug before addiction takes place is a much-debated question. By ignoring this physiological dimension, our definition includes as addictive that behavior that others may regard as compulsive or obsessive or simply as habitual.

After acknowledging all these ambiguities, why do we regard the concept of addiction as susceptible to principled definition? Our answer is that according to this definition the behaviors that look like addiction can be objectively measured in most instances and that in most instances the behavioral pattern is one that observers would agree conforms to this definition of addiction. We argue that by contrast, there are fundamental difficulties in the concept of drug abuse and in the elements of the concept of a drug problem that render extremely remote any prospects of consensual definition in those cases. By comparison, much more widespread agreement seems possible in regard to what constitutes drug addiction or dependence than in regard to what constitutes drug abuse.

Drug abuse. There is thus a difference between objective and subjective definitions of drug abuse that cannot be conclusively resolved. Ideally, drug abuse could be subjectively defined by referring to those behavior patterns that significantly trouble persons who follow them. Moreover, few would disagree that persons whose drug use produces effects that substantially trouble the users themselves can be considered to be using drugs abusively. The problem with this subjective definition is that it excludes from the abuse category those persons whose patterns of drug use do not lead them to regard their behavior as problematic, no matter how many personal and social costs ensue from that behavior. Some people, therefore, manifest patterns of drug use that preclude them from realizing the harmful or even disastrous consequences of their behavior. Other people regard any perceived deleterious effects on their health, employment, or family situation as a relatively modest sacrifice in relation to the satisfaction derived from their drug use, and so they contrive to deny that their habitual or even addictive behavior is seriously damaging them. This behavior pattern is referred to as *denial* in the drug addiction treatment literature and is regarded as commonly, if not universally, found in the case of seriously affected habitual users.

The temptation to apply external standards when defining what constitutes drug abuse is considerable. But once external standards of the costs of drug use are applied to the definition of abuse, there is no principled limit to the kinds of costs that may be included. Nor is there any objective calculus that can be applied when judging whether or not particular behaviors or patterns of behavior constitute drug abuse. Drug use behavior that is experimental or transitory can nevertheless be regarded as abusive if it involves substantial risks of harm or produces no beneficial effects in the view of the person making the judgment. In these circumstances, what constitutes drug abuse is wholly in the eye of the beholder. Only a consensus on the boundaries of abusive behavior can shield us from the conceptual bankruptcy of judgments based on external standards of behavior.

The plasticity or open-ended character of the concept of drug abuse constitutes, of course, a large part of its appeal. The characterization of behavior as drug abuse permits us to avoid coming to terms with the restrictions associated with either the physiological or the behavioral criteria for the application of the term *addiction*. Thus, the main defect of the expression *drug abuse* has also been regarded, and continues to be regarded, by many of those who employ it, as its primary attraction.

Drug problem. All of the ambiguities we encounter at the individual level when discussing drug abuse we encounter again at the community or societal level when defining and measuring a "drug problem." The typical method of judging the seriousness of a drug problem is to sum up the measurable negative aspects and consequences associated with using a drug and to present that aggregate as a measure of the problem's seriousness. This procedure itself contains problems of definition, problems of causal attribution, and problems of measurement, of which we shall consider the first two here and the issue of measurement in the next section.

The definitional problems associated with summing up negative consequences as an index of the seriousness of social problems are manifold. First, there is the matter of deciding when an attribute is negative. Counting deaths and injuries as evidence of the impact of substance abuse is reasonably straightforward. However, the most common measured cost of alcohol abuse is "lost productivity," and part of that is due to the "failure to get promotion" (Barnes, 1988, p. 1731). But is forgone job promotion always a social cost? If so, the measured social costs of religious belief, familial ties, and a wide range of recreational activities other than drug taking must be substantial.

A second problem associated with this kind of aggregation is that arising from measuring the seriousness of problems by taking account only of the costs and ignoring any possible benefits. In such circumstances, the more extensive a practice is, the larger its costs will be, even if most users feel that the benefits derived from using a substance are larger than any costs incurred. A calculus of cost that operated in this fashion could arrive at some surprising and alarming conclusions about spectator sports, bridge, and dancing.

A third problem is the assumption that substance use is both the necessary and a sufficient cause of all the ill effects that are attributed to it. If ten thousand people miss work because of the aftereffects of using Substance A, then counting all that as a cost of using Substance A will assume that the absence of the substance would result in no substitute drug use or any residual of absenteeism. But because these assumptions are implicit, they are almost never considered or examined, let alone empirically tested.

If drug use is not always a necessary cause of some of the consequences that are attributed to it, it is also the case that causal attribution in the drug-abuse-as-a-social-problem industry is a task that is frequently achieved too easily. For example, if Smith commits suicide after twenty-five years of heavy drinking and its consequences, it is highly probable that that event will be assumed to be an effect of his pattern of alcohol consumption. On the other hand, if Smith's suicide follows twenty-five years of inveterate contract bridge playing, that is much more likely to result in a search for causes among other life events or characteristics of the decedent.

Recent disputes over the impact of rock music on adolescent behavior provide a nice illustration of the way in which preconceptions about the nature of a stimulus can lead to facile causal attribution. Those troubled by rock music seem too easily able to convert *post hoc* sequences into *propter hoc* conclusions. Aficionados of that type of music, on the other hand, and those of a more skeptical cast of mind, stress the lack of evidence of sufficient cause and the complexity of other factors that might determine aberrant adolescent behavior.

Two points are worth noting about the kinds of inference that are too commonly drawn in this context. First, causal inferences are often conditioned by extrinsic evaluations, so that, for example, those who regard alcohol as the "beverage of hell" are more likely than are those who see it as the "good creature of God" to regard its consumption as detrimental. Moreover, they are likely to arrive at higher estimates of the negative consequences and social costs of alcohol consumption than would result from a more skeptical appraisal of the supposed causal connections between the consumption of alcohol – or any other drug, for that matter – and whatever happens after the alcohol has been consumed.

Second, there is a systematic tendency for estimates of the seriousness of drug problems to be conditioned by current social attitudes toward particular drugs. Fifty years ago, few people would have regarded J. M. Barrie's description, in *My Lady Nicotine*, of his favorite tobacco as "that exquisite health-giving mixture" (Barrie, 1912, p. 17) as being in the least incongruous or absurd. That is, if a particular drug is regarded as innocuous, then any harmful or injurious thing that happens to people who use it are rarely, if at all, attributed to their use of the drug. But social evaluations change, and when a drug acquires a negative reputation, the ill effects that observers are willing to attribute to its ingestion tend to multiply.

Thus, the evolution of social attitudes toward cigarette smoking has probably contributed as much, if not more, to public perceptions of the high costs of cigarette smoking than have the results of scientific research into the effects on health of the ingestion of tar, nicotine, and carbon dioxide. This is particularly likely in relation to such things as the impact of passive smoking, for which the scientific data are by no means firmly established. In short, the size and seriousness of the problem attributed to the consumption of a particular substance vary over time and are linked to the social reputation of that substance, in a manner analogous to a self-fulfilling prophecy.

II. Measurement issues

A section on measurement in a book on drug policy is something of a novelty, yet measurement issues are of substantial importance in the design and evaluation of drug control strategies. And recent years have seen a significant investment of public resources in constructing measures of drug taking and its impact.

We begin this section with an overview of why reliable measures of drug taking and its impact are necessary in order to construct policy. We then survey the existing resources for measurement across the widening spectrum of drug indicators in the United States.

The uses of benchmarks

One advantage of having standard measurements for drug use and drug problems would be the capacity thus available for comparing drug behavior and its social costs at different times and in different places. The lack of standard measures of drug use and abuse makes that kind of comparison difficult, if not impossible. With respect to alcohol, estimates are available of per capita alcohol consumption at the national level in America going back to the late 1700s, and estimates of per capita alcohol consumption are also reliably reported in many other Western nations. For illicit drugs, however, there is no historical record and no public record-keeping system that provides reliable estimates of their consumption. In regard to cross-sectional measurement, we are only beginning to experiment with both survey research and drug test data.

There are two other respects in which it would be useful to make comparative assessments of drug use and costs. First, it would be helpful to have, on either a historical or a contemporary basis, the ability to compare both the uses and the costs of different types of drugs. Some estimates are now possible of the segments of the population using drugs at particular times. But we cannot make a comparative assessment of the problems presented by different drugs. For instance, to ask whether heroin presents a larger or a smaller problem in New York City as compared with Chicago would require estimates of the numbers of both users and addicts, as well as standard measures of addiction, which are currently not available. At this time, only very imprecise and uncertain judgments can be made, and they are best made in relation to such matters as large differences in the proportion of a population using particular drugs – for example, cocaine versus "ice" – or instances in which different drugs present grossly different health and dysfunction risks – for example, marijuana versus heroin.

Second, it would be helpful to have some basis for comparing the problems posed by different kinds of recreational drugs. The most common comparative statements about drug problems concern the costs of alcohol as compared with those of illicit drugs and are usually made by proponents of the decriminalization of illicit substances. Comparative morbidity and mortality statistics relating to illicit drugs are rarely presented and infrequently analyzed.

Finally, there is a need to compare drug problems, however they are measured, with other social problems that threaten the collective welfare of the people and compete for governmental resources. What we have in mind here is the kind of calculus that could be used to compare, say, cocaine abuse as a social problem with such things as health care needs, nutritional deficiencies, air and water pollution, or armed robbery. In theory, some such comparative assessment should be the precursor to judgments about the level of resources to be committed to drug control. But in public dialogue, explicit comparisons of this nature are conspicuous by their absence. Politicians commonly speak of the costs of drug abuse as "appalling" or "intolerable," or as higher now than at any previous period in American history. The nation's drug abuse problem, they say, has reached crisis proportions, represents the greatest present threat to national well-being, and even constitutes our gravest domestic problem. What is invariably missing, however, is any reference to the criteria to be used to measure the extent of drug abuse as a social problem and to compare the losses attributed to drug abuse with the costs of other competing social problems.

Drug measures

We briefly discuss in this section the expanding list of ways in which drug use and its consequences can be statistically measured. The Appendix contains a more detailed exploration of the specific methods currently used to estimate illicit drug use. Which of the various measures now employed are considered useful depends not only on the reliability and validity of the particular measure but also on the relevance of that measure to the observer's ideas regarding the importance and significance of the drug problem. Deaths attributable to drug overdose represent a good measure of the cost of drug abuse only to the extent that observers regard the loss of life in such circumstances as a significant loss. Similarly, indications of the widespread use of a particular drug may be viewed with alarm if the drug use itself is seen as the problem. Or they may be cited to buttress arguments about the safety of the substance in instances in which a relatively small mortality or morbidity rate results from large numbers of users in the denominator. It is evident, therefore, that questions regarding the measurement of drug use are closely related to the definitional issues covered in the previous section.

In this section, we do not sharply distinguish measures of drug use from measures that relate to the consequences of drug use. For some observers, the level of drug use in a population is an independent variable, and the consequences of drug use are considered dependent variables. But as we noted in Chapter 1, for many other observers it is not the fact that drug use can cause problems that is the source of concern; it is, rather, the drug use itself that is the problem. This approach, which is quite prevalent in the United States, classifies levels of drug use as a dependent variable in the same category that contains morbidity and mortality rates and other pathological phenomena.

The principal measures of drug use and its consequences that are currently used include (1) production and sales figures; (2) a variety of health indices, including morbidity and mortality rates and hospital admissions; (3) various indices derived from surveys covering such things as drug use and drug problems; (4) criminal justice statistics relating to drug convictions, parole violations, and the like; and (5) data relating to drug tests in the civilian sector.

Historically, the contrast between our capacity to measure the use of licit and illicit drugs is almost complete. Most psychoactive substances not prohibited by law are either taxed or regulated in ways that facilitate close estimates of trends in their production and use. But there are no parallel methods available to measure the production of illicit drugs, and for most of American history, there have been few reliable data on the incidence or prevalence of the use of various prohibited substances. The past fifteen years have witnessed sustained attempts to construct indices of illicit drug use by studying health statistics, population surveys in which questions about illicit drug use were asked, trends in drug offense arrests, and chemical evidence of recent drug use for arrested populations, as well as trends over time in the results of chemical tests of recent drug use among groups like members of the military and civilian job applicants.

The discussion of these various indices in the Appendix shows that no single measure of illicit drug use currently employed is sufficiently reliable for confidently estimating the proportion of the population using illicit drugs or the intensity of this drug use. However, the careful comparison and analysis of a variety of different indices of drug use can provide serviceable estimates of the extent of drug use for the policy analyst.

Trends in cocaine deaths and emergency room mentions of cocaine are not good direct measures of the incidence of cocaine use among the general public. Chemical evidence of recent cocaine use among persons arrested is equally flawed as an independent measure of general patterns of drug use. But if City A has more overdose deaths and, in addition, has a much larger proportion of its felons testing positive for cocaine than City B does, the inference that City A's proportionate cocaine use is higher than that of City B would seem to be warranted. Moreover, when survey data can be added to health and arrests statistics, an estimation of patterns and trends in illicit drug use becomes more plausible.

Two points about our ability to measure illicit drug use at the beginning of the 1990s deserve special mention. First, our capacity to consider multiple indices of drug use is relatively recent. The bad news here is that we cannot project the currently available measures back in time to construct historical comparisons anywhere near as reliable as the kinds of drug use estimates that can be made today. The good news is that our indices of illicit drug use are improving with our increased investment in measurement and with our accumulated experience in such programs as drug use forecasting (arrestee drug tests) and the Drug Abuse Warning Network (hospital emergency room drug mentions). It is reasonable, therefore, to expect both further progress in the development of indices of illicit drug use and more reliable indices of trends in drug use.

Our second point is that our current capacity to measure variations in drug use over time or among different areas has not yet been extensively used to investigate the relationship between patterns of drug use and social phenomena like crime and violence. A major expansion in the employment of illicit drug use indices in social science research is expected and should be encouraged.

III. Cost issues

One frequently used measure of the seriousness of a social problem is its economic cost. Although there has been some research on the cost aspects of drug taking and drug control, economic analyses of the social costs of drugs have been surprisingly rare, and they have not played a prominent role in drug policy debates. A review of some of the problems associated with published cost estimates suggests that the obscure role played by cost studies in drug policy discussions is not altogether undeserved.

Table 2.1, constructed from a federally funded study of the costs of drugs and alcohol, gives the total cost estimate for all illicit drugs and for alcohol, based on 1980 dollars and experience. The cost estimates contained in this table are not based on any explicit economic theory regarding the social cost of the substances. Rather, they are simple accounting categories representing sums of money lost or spent by individuals or governments.

With respect to alcohol, the major cost component is the economic cost of reduced work-force productivity. Sixty percent of all estimated dollar costs are reduced productivity from working adults suffering from alcoholism. This category so dominates the total that the plausibility of the aggregate estimate can be no better than that of its "productivity" component. When illicit drugs are added to this major category of cost, it must include a substantial aggregation of crime-related costs, as well as the total expenditure for drug law

Table 2.1. *Economic costs of drug abuse, 1980*
($ in millions)

Principal components	Alcohol abuse	Drug abuse
Treatment/support	10,471	1,443
Mortality	14,456	1,980
Morbidity*	54,680	26,028
Motor vehicle crashes	2,185	—
Crime	2,347	5,910
Social welfare/other	2,950	539
Incarceration	1,801	1,466
Crime careers	—[a]	8,725
Other	636	845
Total	89,526	46,936
*Reduced productivity	50,575	25,716
Lost employment	4,105	312

[a] Data not provided.
Source: Adapted from Table III-1 in Harwood et al., 1984.

enforcement in the United States. Why such expenditure should be attributed to drug use rather than drug use prevention is not explained, and it
is far from clear.

Three characteristics of these cost estimates limit their usefulness in social
cost analysis. First, these figures do not purport to represent the net costs to
society and cannot be so regarded unless it is assumed that drug and alcohol
use generate no benefits to offset any of the social cost items. Such an assumption violates not only common sense but also the fundamental tenets of
economic theory, unless all substance use is exclusively the product of addiction. Even then the economic consequences of a compulsion-induced utility
are not self-evident. It could be argued that when a drug is illegal, an analyst
is justified in presuming that no benefit can flow from its use and, therefore,
in assuming that the total costs attributed to the use of that substance are also
the net social costs of its use. But there are two problems in making this
assumption: First, it makes the social cost of drug use totally dependent on
its legal classification, and second, it assumes that none of the costs incurred
by using illicit substances would be experienced if licit substances were used
as substitutes.

A second limitation of the kind of economic cost analysis reflected in Table
2.1 is that it ignores the unquantifiable aspects of drug use, for example,
immorality and the damage to community morale. The exclusive focus on
quantifiable aspects is inevitable in calculations of this nature. But it would

trouble many observers if cost considerations were advanced as a major justification for policy choice.

The third problem, which is related to the first, is the moralistic equation
of the losses incurred by individuals in the form of the prices they are willing
to pay to use drugs with social costs. For example, if Jones forgoes $100,000
in additional income to pursue his taste for wine or cocaine, it is treated as a
net loss to the larger community, even if Jones is perfectly happy with the
bargain he has struck.

The principal use of cost estimates of the kind displayed in Table 2.1 is to
provide an economic context for evaluating the effectiveness of treatment
programs. Measures of the costs associated with the use of a substance are
compared with the cost of treatment programs. By estimating various programs' efficacy, evaluators hope to determine whether treatment intervention
is cost effective. Yet the consensual and conjectural nature of major cost categories like diminished job efficiency and health-related earnings loss undermines even that limited use.

There is a further implication of this kind of cost accounting that has a
substantial impact when dollar cost figures of this nature are used to measure
the severity of a particular drug problem. Because the estimates use gross
aggregate cost figures, they are quite sensitive to the number of users in a
society. Any substance that is not completely innocuous will generate huge
gross costs if fifty million Americans are regular users of it. Thus, the 20 to
30 percent reduction in prevalence of cigarette smoking in the United States
over the past two decades would overwhelm a doubling or even a trebling of
the costs associated with the use of illegal drugs, if only because the intensive
use of illegal drugs is far less frequent. Under these circumstances, the total
cost associated with both sets of substances would have decreased over the
period even if illegal drug use had doubled. The failure to stress the risk or
cost per user and to offset the use cost with any notion of the use benefit
reinforces the high leverage of the most commonly used substances.

Because the use of licit substances is far more widespread than is the use
of illicit substances, the economic magnitude of drug use varies dramatically
according to the definitional breadth of the classification of drugs. Thus, the
inclusion of alcohol in the costs attributed to drugs in Table 2.1 yields an
aggregate total almost triple that of illicit drug costs. The addition of tobacco
would at least double that total again. This definitional point also has an
application to historical comparisons that is not insignificant: Even if the
costs associated with illicit drugs had tripled in the United States between
1965 and 1990, the reduction in adult cigarette smoking, if tobacco were
included in the definition of drug, would probably have produced a declining
total cost of substance use.

For interdrug comparisons to be meaningful, some notion of individual unit or user cost is essential. This is particularly necessary when, in the case of a substance of high unit cost or risk, there is available a substitute with lower unit costs and risks. Using the analysis employed in the construction of Table 2.1, the least harmful substance would appear as the most costly if it attracted a large enough number of users.

The costs of drug control

In regard to the rather important question of the economic cost of current drug control, what we do not know could fill a book. The aggregated cost of governmental programs to control illicit drugs is not known. The federal government's expenditures in the field total $10 billion, but the outlays by states and localities have not been compiled. Because state and local governments account for more than two-thirds of all drug control law enforcement activity, this is no small matter (see Chapter 7). The business of drug control in the United States may be a matter of $15 billion in government expenditure, or $20 billion, or more. Our ignorance of drug control costs is not confined, however, to aggregate expenditures. Little attention is paid to the costs of the different police tactics used in antidrug operations. Further, we do not know what the comparative cost consequences are of different government agencies performing the same function, as when both the federal Drug Enforcement Administration (DEA) and the local police maintain a capacity to conduct "buy and bust" operations.

The current lack of cost data is disheartening for three reasons. First, we cannot compare the costs of different functions if we do not know the basic cost of each. In the federal government, for example, seven different agencies, ranging from the Coast Guard to the Defense Department to the Federal Aviation Administration, say that they are involved in drug interdiction. And fourteen different federal agencies conduct criminal drug investigations, but little is available to tell us anything more than the aggregate program expenditures of each agency (Office of National Drug Control Policy, 1990, p. 9).

Second, we take it as axiomatic that one cannot compute the cost effectiveness of a drug control strategy without knowing the cost, particularly when several different means are available to produce a single result such as the reduction of drug supply. One would think that much attention would be devoted to the cost effectiveness of the various alternatives. In fact, however, one throwaway paragraph in the 1990 document discusses cost–benefit research (Office of National Drug Control Policy, 1990, p. 76), and the cost data available will not support such research.

But more than serving as an impediment to specific lines of cost–benefit research, the lack of attention to cost is a symptom of the indifference by program planners to questions of cost and cost effectiveness. Resource scarcity is not mentioned in the *National Drug Control Strategy* documents, perhaps because resources are not yet scarce in this isolated program area. But no multibillion dollar program can long sustain such euphoric unreality. And the invitation to waste contained in the current policy atmosphere is regrettable.

IV. Conclusion: Of drug costs and drug fears

By almost all measures of cost, drug abuse in 1992 is a smaller problem in the United States than was the case five or ten years ago, and the costs of drug use in the United States in 1992 are probably smaller than those incurred a generation ago. Yet the public fear of illicit drugs and their consequences is higher at this point in the United States than at any time in recent history. Why is this, and what can it tell us about the relationship between conventional measurements of costs and those elements of drug use that raise the level of fear?

One approach would conclude that there is no direct link between objectively measured costs of drugs and the level of fear regarding drugs and drug abusers. Failing to find a direct connection, many would then be tempted to concentrate on the objective-cost criteria, to the detriment of those elements that might better predict levels of public concern. Yet public concern and fear are themselves costs associated with drug use, as well as a major influence on the character of governmental policy toward drugs. We think that the relationship between social costs and public fears needs to be explored rather than characterized as an antirationalistic folk element in American culture. The public reaction to crack cocaine in the 1980s provides a case study for exploring the determinants of public fear worthy of sustained attention. Our preliminary thoughts on the issue are put forward in the hope that they will stimulate greater scholarly attention.

Why did the public alarm focus on crack cocaine in the 1980s when there were more substantial social costs associated with cigarettes and whiskey? One helpful distinction in sorting through public reactions to drug threats is between externalized and internalized drug costs, a rough parallel to John Stuart Mill's distinction between harm to self and harm to others. The great majority of the costs associated with tobacco use are borne by smokers and those who live in intimate relationship with them. By contrast, however, the predatory crime and community disorganization that the public associates with hard drugs are costs imposed on nondrug users. It is the costs imposed on nonusers that correctly arouse high levels of fear, because these risks are not subject to personal control by choosing not to use the drugs. Further, this sort of harm to others is regarded as a more appropriate occasion for the use of coercive mechanisms of the criminal law in Western society. So with respect to the level of public fear associated with demands for the use of the criminal law, it is probably the externalized costs of drug use rather than the total costs absorbed by society that should be counted.

There is a second sense in which the costs imposed by illicit drugs are regarded by many members of society as both external and threatening to the social mainstream: The use of illicit drugs is a socially deviant practice challenging established norms, and the people who use these drugs are threatening social arrangements in ways that the use of alcohol and tobacco do not. This is an important explanation for the high level of public anxiety regarding illicit drug use, but it is an incomplete account of why crack cocaine was a particular focus of public fear in the mid- and late 1980s.

We believe that the case study of crack cocaine suggests three additional dimensions that can heighten public fear of illicit drug use: novelty, immediacy, and concentration. The fear of the unknown is one reason that reactions to socially novel drugs may be particularly pronounced. Any new psychoactive substance will be the object of exaggerated claims, both positive and negative, in ways that we shall consider in the next chapter. A new illegal drug will thus be advertised as being both more wonderful and more terrible than other illicit substances for which the social history of their use puts some upper limit on the level of public anxiety about harmful consequences. There is no sense of an upper limit from history to the damage that a particular drug threatens to impose on the social order until there is social experience with that drug.

The immediacy of harm is a second element that may explain our various reactions to the risks presented by different drugs. The worst things that cigarettes can do to our children are decades removed from their present lives, and all but the most anxious parents probably discount a substantial amount of this future harm from their current worries. The threat posed, however, by drunken drivers, as well as by the potentially lethal overdose of cocaine, is an immediate one. We think it likely that the most immediate negative aspects of drug use are also the most feared and that those substances that are perceived as posing the most substantial immediate risks therefore garner more than their eventual-cost share of public worry.

Recent experiences with the public's reaction to crack suggests one final aspect of the harms related to a drug that may make it a public worry: the extent to which the drug's effects are concentrated in certain areas or segments of society and are thus more visible in their impact. When illicit drug use is concentrated in particular places, it is much more likely that negative aspects of drug use will become a more visible part of the community areas where they take hold. The most palpable and concentrated damage done in the most drug-affected areas may generate levels of public fear greater than when the substances have large aggregate costs that are spread evenly and less visibly across larger segments of the social landscape.

3

Prohibitions and the lessons of history

It is a standard complaint that modern policy discussions, though replete with references to cost and benefit, lack the dimension of historical example and understanding. From the energy crisis to the progressive income tax, it is difficult to find a policy debate in which it has not been claimed that the lessons of history are being ignored. The patron saint of this kind of incantation is, of course, the philosopher George Santayana and the canonical text in his observation that "those who cannot remember the past are condemned to repeat it" (Santayana, 1906, p. 284).

Writing about drug abuse in the *New York Times* in 1970, Gore Vidal remarked that America had "always existed in a kind of time vacuum: we have no public memory of anything that happened before last Tuesday" (Vidal, 1972, p. 374). But even given the dismal norm for historical awareness in policy debates, the immunity to historical evidence that characterizes the contemporary discussion of drugs in the United States is peculiarly pervasive. In recent years, historians have begun to compile some accounts of America's adventures with psychoactive substances and their control. But for the most part their work stands unrecognized or ignored by participants in policy debates. So even though the historical record is incomplete in a number of respects, the knowledge base available for those formulating policy is far more adequate than the degree of historical sophistication displayed in either the political arena or most scholarly discussions would suggest.

It is beyond both our ambition and our competence either to summarize the history of drug control in the United States or to add to the emerging social history of drugs and drug control. Rather, our purpose is more limited: to illustrate the use of historical insight in drug policy analysis. In the first section of this chapter, we shall demonstrate how the failure to consult or to learn from the historical record leads, in the political arena, to an almost-verbatim repetition of sentiments and standpoints that each succeeding orator seems convinced are being uttered for the first time.

This lack of historical awareness is not confined to politicians but also pervades policy discussions among experts in the drug field. Moreover, there is a recurrent feature that we shall highlight: the way in which each new chemical found in America's recreational drug cabinet is treated like an inscription on a tabula rasa – a radical innovation, to which none of such wisdom, as has over the centuries been accumulated about psychoactive substances, has any relevance at all.

In the second section, we shall provide a capsule history of four separate episodes of legislative prohibition of psychoactive drugs in American history: alcohol prohibition twice, in both the nineteenth and twentieth centuries, the Harrison Act efforts since 1914, and the Marijuana Tax Act of 1937. We argue that whatever "the lessons of Prohibition" might be, they are best derived from all four of those episodes rather than from a single experience spanning one specific period. In the third section of the chapter, we shall explore seven of the lessons regarding drugs and their control that we believe can be derived from the available historical evidence on prohibition. In the concluding section, we shall list some of the key issues in the current drug control debate, about which we think that historical evidence can increase our understanding.

I. Santayana's revenge

In the past twenty years, three American presidents have successively made virtually the same speech approving essentially identical programs for dealing with drug problems. When read consecutively, their words display an almost echoic similarity. But a remarkable feature of the sequence, which begins with President Richard M. Nixon's Special Message to the U.S. Congress on Drug Abuse Prevention and Control on June 17, 1971, is the way in which the two subsequent contributors appear both oblivious of the nature and outcome of their predecessors' initiatives and untroubled by the possibility that familiar phraseology might arouse in their audiences an awareness that they had heard it all before.

In 1971, striking the chord that was to reverberate over the next two decades, President Nixon referred to "the tide of drug abuse which has swept America in the last decade" and spoke confidently of ending the flow of drugs into this country "by literally cutting it off root and branch at its source." He talked of the need for a coordinated federal response and stated that he was setting up a central authority to be known as the Special Action Office for Drug Abuse Prevention within the Executive Office of the President, "with overall responsibility for all major Federal drug abuse programs in all Federal agencies." He concluded that "the final issue is not whether we will conquer drug abuse, but how soon" (Nixon, 1971, pp. 739–49).

Those who assumed that the conquest of drug abuse was imminent were to be disappointed, however. For a decade later, drug abuse appeared to be little if at all diminished and was still widely regarded as one of the gravest domestic problems facing the nation. As a presidential commission later reported, "the extent of the Nation's drug abuse problem at the end of 1980 was as great, if not greater than, the problem in 1970" (President's Commission, 1986, p. 258).

Yet President Ronald Reagan in his address to the nation on federal drug policy on October 2, 1982, appeared to be no less confident than his predecessor had been over a decade before. He did, however, seem to feel that his sanguine mood required some explanation. "Now, you probably wonder why I'm so optimistic," he said. He went on to explain that it was because the era of "sit-on-your-hands kind of thinking" in relation to drug abuse in Washington was over and that "for the very first time, the Federal Government is waging a planned, concerted campaign [against drugs]. . . . Drugs are bad, and we're going after them. As I've said before, we've taken down the surrender flag and run up the battle flag. And we're going to win the war on drugs" (Reagan, 1982, pp. 1252–3).

But history once again proved recalcitrant toward presidential authority. For when the President's Commission on Organized Crime reported to the president and the attorney general in 1986, the situation under the battle flag seemed little different from that under the surrender flag. "The situation confronting us," said the commission, "is a crisis both nationally and internationally." Even though "our law enforcement and other government agencies, particularly on the Federal level, are deployed with a degree of determination, imagination and resource commitment unparalleled in American history," it appeared that drug abuse still "ruins individual lives, drains billions of dollars each year from American society and erodes the nation's quality of life." According to the commission, "drug trafficking accounts for almost 38 percent of all organized crime activity across the country and generates an income estimated to be as high as $110 billion."

The demand for drugs continued at a "voracious level," and there was once again a "need for . . . fully coordinated governmental action . . . a thoroughly coordinated national attack on every aspect of drug trafficking and abuse . . . we are in a fight for our lives." But the commission promised that "the curse of drug abuse will be broken." It even "adopted a definition of victory ('in this war on drugs'): the dramatic reduction, if not complete elimination of drug abuse in this society" (President's Commission, 1986, pp. 6, 7, 8, 10–11, 12). Only the implication that citizens might perhaps have to be satisfied with a dramatic reduction, rather than the complete elimination, suggested any qualification of earlier presidential rhetoric.

In such circumstances, it might have been hoped that when the time came for yet another president to take office, some awareness of the discrepancy between his predecessor's confident rhetoric and his commission's report would have induced a degree of wariness in approaching the drug problem. Yet in his inaugural address, George Bush quickly defeated any such expectation. Referring to the way in which drugs had "hurt the body and soul of this country," he asked the nation to take his word for it that "this scourge will stop" (Bush, 1989, p. 10). Moreover, seven months later in a televised address from the Oval Office when he launched his administration's plan for dealing with the scourge, he did so in terms that simultaneously duplicated and disregarded his predecessors' initiatives. Once more there was to be an unprecedented effort to curb illegal drugs. "This plan," President Bush observed, "is as comprehensive as the problem. With this strategy, we now finally have a plan that coordinates our resources, our programs and the people who run them" (Weintraub, 1989, p. B7).

The *National Drug Control Strategy* outlining the plan seemed equally oblivious of any previous governmental activity in this area. Although it began with the assertion that "our drug problem is getting worse" (Office of National Drug Control Policy, 1989, p. 1), it contained no reference to, or analysis of the reasons for, the failure of previous presidential initiatives. It did not explain why the conquest of drug abuse promised by President Nixon in 1971, and again by President Reagan in 1982, had not been fullfilled. On the contrary, America had been experiencing "the worst epidemic of illegal drug use in its history . . . far more severe, in fact, than any ever experienced by an industrialized nation" and in 1989 was facing "intensifying drug-related chaos" and an "appalling and deepening crisis" (Office of National Drug Control Policy, 1989, pp. 3, 5). One thing, however, was clear. Hegel's dictum that "governments have never learned anything from history, or acted on principles deduced from it" (Hegel, 1956, p. 6) was in no danger of being refuted.

The amnesia that seems to affect political leaders in regard to drug control is also evident in the executive branch of government generally and in a wide variety of policymaking commissions and committees. Most often, the reports of task forces and commissions are sufficiently arcane and bureaucratic in tone to assume that they will be of interest only to successor task forces and commissions dealing with the same topic. What is striking in regard to drug control is that previous governmental analyses of the problem seem not even to be of interest to those in charge of formulating and rationalizing subsequent government policy.

The *National Drug Control Strategy* document provides a good example of executive branch amnesia. It displays no evidence that any lesson of history – of even most recent history – has been learned. We noted that the federal drug policy in the Nixon and Reagan years was stated in terms so similar as to be almost identical. And for the two decades before the promulgation of the *National Drug Control Strategy*, federal offices, institutes, task forces, and strike forces drew up and implemented battle plans in the war on drugs along the lines initially announced by President Nixon. What is quite extraordinary here is the limited extent to which previous governmental efforts based on the same premises as the *National Drug Control Strategy* are acknowledged or referred to.

The text of the *National Drug Control Strategy* is bereft of any reference to any previous government document relating to drug control strategy or to any document produced before the mid-1980s. The earliest document cited is a New York City Police Department report dated 1985 (Office of National Drug Control Policy, 1989, p. 23). The *Strategy* document's restricted orientation produces two rather curious impressions in its readers. First, the document uses only two tenses: the present and the future. The only thing that we are told about the past is by implication, in that, for example, current circumstances are presented as unprecedented. As a result, a report that in all major respects supports a continuation of past policy gives precisely the opposite impression. Seventy-five years after the Harrison Act was passed, the White House issued a spirited defense of prohibition as if it were a brand-new policy proposal. Whatever the political advantages of this posture, it must have significant costs unless it is true that we have learned nothing in three-quarters of a century of federal-level drug prohibition.

This failure to use historical materials when considering or discussing drug control policy is a fault not confined to governmental actors. Academic policy analysts – indeed, even some of our more distinguished experts on drug control and law enforcement policy – are both sparing and highly selective in their use of historical materials when analyzing drug control options. Moreover, this inattention to the historical record is found on all sides of the many debates on drug control policy.

One illustration of this neglect of historical material may be found in a comparison of two thoughtful and well-regarded analyses in the debate on drug decriminalization. First, Princeton University political scientist Ethan Nadelmann, who favors "drug legalization," argued: "We know that repealing drug prohibition laws would eliminate or greatly reduce many of the ills that people commonly identify as part and parcel of the 'drug problem' " (Nadelmann, 1989, p. 946). But, James Q. Wilson, a political scientist at the University of California at Los Angeles, maintained that the result of such a change "would be a sharp increase in use, a more widespread degradation of the human personality and a greater rate of accidents and violence" (Wilson, 1990a, p. 28).

Yet an examination of the most thoroughly referenced recent publications of each of these scholars reveals a good deal less than total immersion in the relevant historical literature and evidence. Thus, Nadelmann's "Drug Prohibition in the United States: Costs, Consequences, and Alternatives," although it contains cursory references to alcohol prohibition in America earlier in this century, is devoted to the author's analysis of what "the past 20 years have demonstrated" (Nadelmann, 1989, p. 946), and the references listed deal almost exclusively with that period. Similarly, James Q. Wilson's "Drugs and Crime" – apart from a parenthetical remark about the debauch produced by the arrival of gin in eighteenth-century England – ventures no further into the past than the 1960s. In this case, the earliest work referred to is a drug abuse research monograph dealing with treatment evaluation published in 1984 (Wilson, 1990b, pp. 544–5).

Crack is different

There are a number of reasons for the low level of historical awareness in drug policy discussions. But one of the most powerful restraints on historical insight for drug prohibitionists is the belief that each new substance identified as presenting a public policy problem is chemically, physiologically, and psychologically both novel and unique. It is then assumed that no experience gained regarding the use and control of any other drug can be generalized or applied to the handling of the newly identified substance.

Over the course of the twentieth century, what may be called the metaphysical notion of the unique psychoactive drug has been applied to opium, heroin, marijuana, cocaine, and the amphetamines. In the 1980s, in one variation on the metaphysics of uniqueness, the same substance that early in the century had been a candidate for unique classification as "the greatest drug menace" (Grinspoon and Bakalar, 1976, p. 38) was, after a quiescent period during which it was viewed as relatively benign, renominated as uniquely malignant and different not only from all other substances but also from its previous incarnation as a public enemy. Thus, in the mid-1980s we were told that whatever we might have previously thought about cocaine, in its new form *crack* it was so singular – being "in fact, the most dangerous and quickly addictive drug known to man" (Office of National Drug Control Policy, 1989, p. 23) – that it should not be confused either with other varieties of cocaine or with any previously identified narcotic or stimulant.

Since the mid-1980s it also has been argued that marijuana, which has been the subject of partial decriminalization in some states, should once again be the subject of the kind of prohibition originally imposed under the Marijuana Tax Act of 1937, because the concentration of active ingredients has been higher in recent years than had been the case in previous decades (Elsberg, 1990). So once again the argument is made that marijuana is not only different from other drugs but also from marijuana as a substance with which we were familiar and in relation to which, after decades of experience, public policy had been revised.

Which of these drugs differs from other psychoactive substances in ways that should properly affect policy is a topic that we shall postpone considering. The point we want to make here is that allegations of a drug's uniqueness can be used as a rhetorical device to shield proponents of a prohibitory policy from counterarguments based on the history of earlier efforts at the state regulation of other substances or of the same substance in different forms or settings. Thus, in the course of arguing for an escalation in the criminal punishment of marijuana possession, a California advisory group sidestepped, to its own satisfaction, the need to confront the long history of marijuana prohibition and its outcome in that state by asserting that the recriminalization of marijuana is recommended "in light of the fact that the drug has a high THC content and is more dangerous than it was in the past" (Elsberg, 1990).

The metaphysics of drug uniqueness can be distinguished in a number of ways from the policy perspective that we call specifism. For the specifist, the recognition that different drugs have different costs and benefits calls, as a necessary consequence, for an exhaustive and judicious inquiry into the peculiarities of any individual substance (see Kaplan, 1970, 1983, 1989). By contrast, a proponent of drug uniqueness usually defends or proposes a criminal prohibition and highlights what are seen as the especially dangerous features of whatever substance is being considered.

When a rhetorician of uniqueness asserts that crack (or cocaine or heroin) is different, that does not, from this perspective, signal the beginning of an inquiry into the appropriate policy but, rather, represents the end point of analysis. The implicit minor premise in the use of uniqueness as a rhetorical device is that a drug's being, *sui generis*, also entails a corresponding distinctiveness in the social and law enforcement problems it generates, which makes irrelevant any reference to past experience with any other drug.

Drugs do vary widely in their chemical properties, their effects on users, and the social contexts of their use; and some of the most important and complex aspects of the study of regimes of drug control pertain to those differences. Unfortunately, however, the metaphysics of drug uniqueness is a rhetorical device that forecloses any consideration of those issues. For when its adherents speak of the uniqueness of whatever happens to be the *drug du jour*, that claim is advanced as a means of avoiding precisely the kind of analysis and comparative study that can teach us what features of different drugs in different settings generate different prospects for control.

II. Four prohibitions

One period in American history is invoked in arguments about drug control more frequently than are all other historical episodes and events combined. The subject is commonly labeled "the lessons of Prohibition," and the period in question is the thirteen years of the prohibition of the manufacture, sale, or transportation of intoxicating liquors within the United States that was federally mandated under the Volstead Act in the closing years of the first third of the twentieth century. In this section, we shall offer our own account of the lessons of Prohibition, for both substantive and methodological reasons.

The substantive reason is that the impact of governmental attempts to stop the use of particular drugs is one of the central issues in any consideration of the political control of psychoactive drugs. For methodological reasons, however, there are serious obstacles to drawing causal inferences about the effects of policies that were introduced in a particular historical period, when those effects cannot be viewed in isolation from all the other social and political changes taking place at the same time. The error of confounding *post hoc* and *propter hoc* is less likely to arise, however, if we can examine multiple instances of a particular phenomenon.

It so happens that in this instance, multiple examples of the attempted prohibition of psychoactive substances are available for study. Evidence is available in the emerging historical literature dealing with four periods of prohibition: (1) laws prohibiting the manufacture and sale of alcohol that were passed in thirteen American states in the mid-nineteenth century; (2) attempts, which were begun through federal law in 1914, to prevent the importation, sale, or possession of a whole spectrum of narcotic drugs and also cocaine, which have continued through three-quarters of a century without any major change in strategy; (3) the national experience with the prohibition of the manufacture and sale of beverage alcohol that was initiated by constitutional amendment ratified in 1920 and reversed by the repeal of the amendment in 1933; and (4) the national prohibition of marijuana under the 1937 Marijuana Tax Act.

Prohibition: The nineteenth-century experience

Possibly because such matters were in the past regarded as, in Macaulay's phrase, "below the dignity of history" (Macaulay, 1849, p. 3) it is only relatively recently – within the last two decades – that scholars, in works with titles like *The American Disease* (Musto, 1987), *The Alcoholic Republic* (Rorabaugh, 1979), and *Drinking in America* (Lender and Martin, 1987) have recognized and begun to explore the extensive history of the abuse of drugs in America, reaching back to the earliest years of the republic when "Americans were drinking more heavily than every before or since" (Larkin, 1988, p. 167). It has been estimated, for instance, that the yearly consumption of alcohol in 1790 was the equivalent of nearly 6 gallons of pure 200-proof alcohol for each person and that by 1810 it had risen to an all-time high of 7.10

gallons per capita. By contrast, the annual per capita consumption of alcoholic beverages in terms of absolute alcohol between 1916 and 1919, immediately before national Prohibition in 1920, has been estimated at 1.96 gallons (Lender and Martin, 1987, p. 205).

Yet in the colonial period, there is no record of alcohol's being viewed as posing a serious social problem. There were statutes in all the colonies regarding the sale of alcohol and alcohol-related behavior such as drunkenness. But the pattern appears to have been one of intemperate individuals and problem drinkers rather than of social disorder. With a level of alcohol consumption estimated at approximately double the current levels, "a general lack of anxiety over alcohol problems was one of the most significant features of drinking in the colonial era . . . certainly there were no pre-revolutionary equivalents of the temperance or prohibition movements" (Lender and Martin, 1987, p. 14).

It was not until well into the eighteenth century, after the American Revolution, that there is any evidence of major concern about the social consequences of alcohol. When a change in attitude came, it seems to have been largely due to an increase in the use of distilled spirits, which came to replace beer, cider, and wine as a principal means of alcohol consumption. It is notable that Dr. Benjamin Rush's classic *An Inquiry into the Effects of Ardent Spirits on the Human Body and Mind* is concerned specifically with the consumption of distilled spirits or hard liquor, as opposed to wine and beer, of which the author did not disapprove. Dr. Rush regarded intemperance as a threat to both personal health and the social order, and he advocated both abstention from "ardent spirits" or "distilled liquors" and firm sanctions against drunkenness. But he did not advocate total abstinence or prohibition (Rush, 1814).

In the nineteenth century, however, the idea of total abstinence, as distinct from abstention from distilled spirits, gained significant support. Early in the century, the first temperance groups were born, and the drive for prohibition had begun. "Although it remained a powerful force in many parts of the United States, the American way of drunkenness began to lose ground as early as the mid-1820s" (Larkin, 1988, p. 295). The egalitarian individualism of the Jackson era was challenged by a different ideology, which stressed the dangers of unrestrained individualism, the necessity of governmental intervention, and the imposition of legal controls in order to preserve the social and moral order. Before this time, many Americans had taken the view that "as long as their conduct hurt no one else, it was nobody's business what they did. Accordingly as long as drinking harmed no one but the drinker why worry, or more to the point, why make the behavior a national issue?" (Lender and Martin, 1987, p. 53).

Crucial to the acceptance of the need for prohibition – and a key to the

understanding of all prohibition movements – was a thesis zealously propagated by the celebrated preacher Lyman Beecher in his *Six Sermons on the Nature, Occasions, Signs, Evils and Remedy of Intemperance*. Originally published in 1827, one year after the American temperance movement was formally embodied in a national organization – the American Society of the Promotion of Temperance – Beecher's thesis can be stated in the form of two related propositions.

The first was simply that alcohol in any form was addictive and that even its moderate use led inevitably to inebriety and alcoholism. The second proposition is a corollary of the first: Because alcohol was itself inevitably addictive, it was useless to rely on "self-government and voluntary abstinence," and rather than leaving the matter to personal decision only, the abolition of the liquor traffic could save individuals and society from the multiple evils attendant on alcohol consumption (Beecher, 1843, pp. 38, 62, 73).

"The wandering missionaries of the West echoed his words everywhere. By 1834, some million Americans were enrolled in temperance societies" (Sinclair, 1964, p. 37). In addition to the evangelical Protestants, a number of secular organizations joined the crusade against alcohol. "The Washingtonians, self-styled ex-drunkards who recruited other drunkards, the Independent Order of the Rechabites of North America, the Sons of Temperance (which had 230,000 members in 1850), and the Independent Order of Good Templars all developed outside traditional ecclesiastical control" (Aaron and Musto, 1981, p. 142). Although these secular orders were primarily concerned with "personal deliverance from drinking problems . . . they also stressed prohibition," and by the late 1840s the "prohibition sentiment had reached critical mass" (Lender and Martin, 1987, p. 79). By 1851 the American Tract Society reported the distribution of "nearly five million temperance pamphlets" (Rorabaugh, 1979, p. 196).

All this enthusiasm and agitation was paralleled by a dramatic decline in alcohol consumption. In the decade between 1830 and 1840 it more than halved, falling from 7.10 gallons of absolute alcohol per capita in 1830 to 3.10 gallons in 1840. By 1850 it had declined even further, to 2.10 gallons per capita. Then, as a result of "one of the most comprehensive political efforts the nation had ever seen" (Lender and Martin, 1987, p. 84), America's first experiment with prohibition began. Starting with Maine in 1851, statewide prohibition statutes were enacted in thirteen states: Massachusetts, Vermont, Minnesota Territory, and Rhode Island (1852); Michigan (1853); Connecticut (1854); and Indiana, New Hampshire, Delaware, Iowa, New York, and Nebraska Territory (1855). In addition, in Wisconsin, prohibition passed the legislature but was vetoed by the governor; and in two other states, Pennsylvania and New Jersey, prohibition measures were only narrowly defeated.

Table 3.1. *Consumption of alcoholic beverages and absolute alcohol in each class of beverage in U.S. gallons per capita of the drinking-age population (fifteen years and over), United States, 1830–1860*

	Spirits		Wine		Beer		Total
	Beverage	Absolute alcohol	Beverage	Absolute alcohol	Beverage	Absolute alcohol	Absolute alcohol
1830	9.50	4.30	0.50	0.10	27.00	2.70	7.10
1840	5.50	2.50	0.50	0.10	6.30	0.50	3.10
1850	4.17	1.88	0.46	0.08	2.70	0.14	2.10
1860	4.79	2.16	0.57	0.10	5.39	0.27	2.53

Source: Lender & Martin, 1987, p. 205.

Moreover, by 1855 a majority of states had introduced some measures of control.

"Politicized morality," say Lender and Martin, "seemed well on its way to rolling back the tide of over two hundred years of American drinking habits" (Lender and Martin, 1987, p. 84). In fact, however, political prohibition broke down almost as quickly as it had come into operation. According to one authority, all the prohibition statutes "were repealed before the end of the 1850s" (Kyvig, 1979, p. 6). According to another, "of the 13 states that had prohibition in 1855, only 5 remained dry in 1863" (Aaron and Musto, 1981, p. 141). Lender and Martin summarized the events as follows: "Prohibition fell apart at a speed that astonished even its enemies. . . . [Prohibition statutes] crumbled to dust. Legislatures either repealed them outright, or modified them to permit liquor sales with minimal interference, or allowed them to languish virtually unenforced" (Lender and Martin, 1987, p. 85). For the time being, it seemed to have been "demonstrated that those who believed in abstinence could not succeed in imposing their own view of morality upon that portion of the population that did not share their vision" (Rorabaugh, 1979, p. 217).

It has been claimed that "despite the persistent difficulties in enforcement, and varying degrees of control imposed by the states," the efforts of the prohibitionists "did accomplish dramatic reductions in the level of consumption of hard liquor" (Aaron and Musto, 1981, p. 141). But even though there is no doubt that the consumption of hard liquor fell dramatically over the years 1830 to 1850, in the decade between 1850 and 1860 when the prohibition statutes were enforced, it appears to have increased, as Table 3.1 shows.

Moreover, although to a lesser degree, the consumption of wine and beer

also increased during that decade. Commenting on this first large-scale experiment with prohibition, Andrew Sinclair pointed out: "After using moral
suasion and emotional appeal, the prohibitionists found their most effective
method of influence in legal coercion" (Sinclair, 1964, p. 38). But although
there is little doubt that the temperance campaign had something to do with
the lower consumption of hard liquor between 1830 and 1850, it is difficult
to discern any evidence of the unique effectiveness of "legal coercion" in the
decade when it was at its peak. This first crusade for prohibition seems to
have enjoyed less-than-majority support. "Millions of Americans still prized
their right to drink. Nationally, they probably still outnumbered their dry
countrymen" (Lender and Martin, 1987, p. 80). Sooner or later it becomes
evident that the standards set by such crusades for absolute morality are impossible ones, and even supporters become disenchanted. In this case, the
passage of prohibitionist legislation seems to have "marked the high tide of
temperance influence in the antebellum years – a tide that ebbed quickly with
the approach of the Civil War" (Lender and Martin, 1987, p. 85).

The Harrison Act

Narcotics. There are many instructive parallels between American efforts to
control the use of alcohol and those to control the use of other drugs, especially the narcotics and cocaine. The narcotics referred to here are opium and
its derivatives morphine and heroin. Many writers have noted the way in
which "the antinarcotic campaign paralleled the drive for national liquor prohibition" (Musto, 1987, p. xii) and "the apparent congruence of the Antinar-
cotics Movement and the Antidrink Movement" (Clark, 1976, p. 220).

This parallelism or congruence, however, was a twentieth-century phenomenon. In the nineteenth century, there was no campaign for narcotic
prohibition, although the level of narcotic consumption was high. Indeed,
"both proportionately and absolutely the consumption of opium and morphine in American society during the nineteenth century was higher than in
any other Western nation" (Clark, 1976, p. 219). In the 1820s, American
merchants were "the principal buyers of the Turkish opium crop" (Rorabaugh, 1979, p. 176). The per capita importation of crude opium rose from
less than twelve grains annually in the 1840s to more than fifty-two grains in
the 1890s when domestic consumption reached about a half-million pounds
each year, and excessive opiate use came to be considered "peculiarly American" (Musto, 1987, pp. 5, 279–80). With opiates as freely accessible as as-
pirin is today, Edward Brecher observed that "the United States of America
during the nineteenth century could quite properly be described as a 'dope
fiend's paradise' " (Brecher, 1972, p. 3).

The one exception to the general tolerance of the opiates and the first

American legislation in the narcotics field seems to have been a reflection of anti-Chinese feeling. Beginning with a San Francisco ordinance of 1875 prohibiting the smoking of opium in smoking houses or "dens," a variety of prohibitions on opium smoking were adopted in other western states. Congress also acted, by raising the tariff on opium prepared for smoking in 1883, prohibiting the importation of such opium by the Chinese (although not by Americans) in 1887, and finally prohibiting its importation altogether in 1909. Throughout the period, "states and cities continued to pass laws against opium smoking; by 1914 there were twenty seven such laws in effect" (Brecher 1972, p. 44).

But for most of the nineteenth century there was no campaign – as there was in the case of alcohol – to prohibit opiates. So the fact that narcotic prohibition in 1914 preceded the prohibition of alcohol by five years requires some explanation, especially because the domestic demand for opium, which began to rise in the 1840s and continued to do so until it reached a peak in 1896, had thereafter declined and "the consumption curve leveled off" (Musto, 1987, p. 5).

Two main reasons have been advanced for the somewhat precipitate introduction of opiate prohibition by the Harrison Act of 1914, which made illegal the importation, sale, or possession of opiates except within medical channels. The first is that the consumption of patent medicines, which reached its peak in the late nineteenth century, at the time when the opiate content of these medicines was also at its highest point, represented a threat to the medical profession. "Patent medicines were a major competitor of professional medical treatment. . . . As a result, the American Medical Association campaigned vigorously for the prohibition of opiates outside medical channels" (Kaplan, 1983, pp. 62–63).

The second reason was also unrelated to any worries about the harmful effects of domestic consumption or the evils of narcotic addiction in the United States. Even Secretary of State William Jennings Bryan, who was a fervent prohibitionist, urged the passage of the Harrison narcotic bill principally on the ground that the United States should fulfill its obligations under the Hague Convention of 1912, which outlawed international nonmedical opium traffic (Brecher, 1972, pp. 48–49). The enactment of the domestic law "became necessary in order to avoid international embarrassment" (Musto, 1987, p. 51). "Passage of the Harrison Act in 1914 was not a question of primary national interest [but] a routine slap at moral evil [which] was approved in a few minutes, a fact not even noted that week in the *New York Times* summary of that session's work" (Musto, 1987, pp. 65–66).

In March 1918, three years after the act's passage, Secretary of the Treasury William McAdoo set up a Special Committee to study the narcotic drug problem. This was the first in a long line of government committees and commissions established to study drug abuse down the years since then, and it set a pattern that has been followed by all its successors. As Morris and Hawkins commented, over half a century later, on the 1975 *White Paper on Drug Abuse*, "There is a longstanding tradition that reports published by federal departments and agencies dealing with drug abuse should include a *tour d'horizon* of 'the drug problem in America' in which somber warnings are reinforced by the adjectival use of large numbers" (Morris and Hawkins, 1977, p. 34). That tradition began in 1919.

Thus McAdoo's Special Committee estimated that "the total number of addicts in this country probably exceeds 1,000,000 at the present time." It also reported that the use of narcotic drugs had risen since the passage of the Harrison Act and that the "consensus of opinion of those interested in the subject appears to be to the effect that the number of addicts will increase" (Special Committee, 1919, pp. 19–22). The committee's estimate of the nation's addict population was based on a fanciful exercise in the analysis of, and extrapolation from, responses to a survey of a sample of physicians to which less than one-third responded. David Musto's verdict that "the committee's report grossly exaggerated the number of addicts in the United States" (Musto, 1987, p. 138) is probably correct, although then, as now, what John Kaplan called a "morass of conflicting statistics" (Kaplan, 1983, p. 65) was conjured up by both opponents and proponents of prohibition.

Congress responded to the Special Committee's report by tightening up the legislation, enacting a law in 1924, for instance, that prohibited the importation of heroin even for medicinal use. But what effect the Harrison Act has had on the extent of drug abuse in America is not known. Edward Brecher asserted that "the per capita addiction rate, it is true, has declined since 1914 – that is, addiction has not increased as rapidly as the population" (Brecher, 1972, pp. 62–63). And it seems likely that the availability of the opiates has been substantially reduced. But as the estimates of the number of addicts before 1914 clearly belong in the category of what Max Singer called "mythical numbers" (Singer, 1971, p. 3), it is not impossible that the percentage of addicts in the population today is about the same or even higher than it was in 1914.

In regard to the benefits of prohibition for reducing the availability of heroin, although there is no doubt that significant amounts have been seized both at the borders of the country and within the United States, it is by no means clear how far, if at all, this has lowered drug consumption. The truth is that no one really knew the extent of opiate addiction before the passage of the Harrison Act in 1914, although there is little doubt that as a result of the Harrison Act, the patterns of addiction did change.

Cocaine. The opiates – opium, morphine, and heroin – which are derived from the dried juice of the unripe capsule of the opium poppy, belong to the class of drugs called *narcotics*. Cocaine, which is derived from the leaves and young twigs of the coca plant, is not a member of the opiate family and not a narcotic. The Harrison Narcotic Act of 1914, however, mistakenly classed coca products as narcotics, and "since 1914, the possession, sale, and giving away of cocaine have been subject to the same dire federal penalties as those governing morphine and heroin" (Brecher, 1972, p. 276). It is still classed as a Schedule II drug, along with opium, under the provisions of the Comprehensive Drug Abuse Prevention and Control Act of 1970, which repealed all existing federal drug laws.

Richard Ashley argued that cocaine was "wilfully misclassified" as a narcotic by "the anti-drug people" because this had "propaganda advantages." Thus "the vast majority of drug horror tales carried in the newspapers and magazines referred only to narcotics. . . by calling cocaine a narcotic the government anti-cocaine propagandists reaped the advantage of having all the drug-innocent citizens associate these frightening stories of narcotic addiction with cocaine" (Ashley, 1975, pp. 78–79). But the propagandists' confusion may not have been deliberate or disingenuous, because such confusion was widespread. Indeed, Ashley himself acknowledges that writers of crime fiction, from Conan Doyle, who was medically qualified, to Sax Rohmer and even Dashiell Hammett, did not manage to get straight the distinction between cocaine and the opiates (Ashley, 1975, pp. 37–38).

Whatever the case may be, before its prohibition in America, cocaine

was immensely popular. It was pure, cheap, and widely distributed . . . the exhilarating properties of cocaine made it a favorite ingredient of medicine, soda pop, wines, and so on. The Parke Davis Company, an exceptionally enthusiastic producer of cocaine, even sold coca-leaf cigarettes and coca cheroots to accompany their other products, which provided cocaine in a variety of media and routes such as a liquorlike alcohol mixture called Coca Cordial, tablets, hypodermic injections, ointments and sprays. (Musto, 1987, pp. 6–8)

Moreover, "bars began putting a pinch of cocaine in a shot of whiskey and cocaine was peddled door to door" (Musto, 1987, p. 8). America, says Ashley, "imported far more coca leaves, made much more cocaine and was the world's pre-eminent user from the late nineteenth to well into the twentieth century" (Ashley, 1975, p. 97).

It was not the damage done to those who abused cocaine that led to demands for its prohibition but, rather, what Musto calls the "fear of its overstimulating powers among social subgroups" (Musto, 1987, p. 8). Although at the turn of the century, overseers in the South used to add cocaine to the rations of their black laborers in order to get more work out of them (Brecher, 1972, pp. 275–76), it was also believed in the South that cocaine could be a spur to violence against whites.

Analysis of early state cocaine laws reflects the widespread fear of cocaine as an "especially dangerous drug," which is evident from the fact that more states regulated cocaine than they did the opiates and that harsher penalties were provided for cocaine violations (McLaughlin, 1973, p. 568). Further evidence of this special fear of cocaine may be found in the Harrison Act, which exempted from its coverage any preparations containing minimal amounts of opium. On the other hand, no preparation containing cocaine, no matter how small the quantity, was exempted.

As with all drug prohibitions, the prohibition of cocaine increased its price and made it more difficult to obtain. "By the 1920s illicit cocaine had risen to $30 an ounce, or three times what it had been a decade earlier," says Ashley. He adds that nevertheless, although "there is no accurate way of estimating either how many people used cocaine or how much of it was used . . . we do know that in one way or another considerably more cocaine was available to Americans *after* the Harrison Act was passed than before" (Ashley, 1975, pp. 90, 92; emphasis in original). But the evidence to support that assertion is slender. There is some proof, however, that the higher black market prices for illicit cocaine caused cocaine users to switch to heroin. As Courtwright put it, cocaine users "were forced to consider alternatives. Heroin was doubly attractive: it was cheap and it was taken in the accustomed fashion, sniffing" (Courtwright, 1982, p. 98).

By the 1930s cocaine use does appear to have diminished substantially. "Virtually every source I have consulted agrees that cocaine use was insignificant during the 1930s" (Ashley, 1975, p. 105). Two factors seem to have been responsible. First, the Great Depression meant that fewer people could afford it. Second,

cocaine was replaced by a new group of synthetic drugs, the amphetamines which were available far more cheaply than cocaine after 1932. So that during the 1940s, 1950s, and most of the 1960s, the smuggling of cocaine into the United States was curtailed and the black market in cocaine was relatively small. (Brecher, 1972, pp. 276–77)

Cocaine use, however, enjoyed a renaissance in the 1960s when the U.S. Food and Drug Administration launched a campaign against the nonmedical use of amphetamines. In 1965, amendments to the federal food and drug laws were passed to curb the black market in amphetamines. Federal, state, and local law enforcement agencies also moved against both the diversion of legal amphetamines to the black market and illicit "speed labs." In 1970 the Federal Bureau of Dangerous Drugs noted that the traffic in cocaine, which a few years previously had been insignificant, had started to expand rapidly. The bureau failed, however, "to link the revival of cocaine smuggling with the efforts [the] bureau was making to curtail the availability of speed" (Brecher, 1972, p. 302). Since then, National Institute on Drug Abuse (NIDA) epidemiological surveys and surveillance systems have "documented dramatic increases in the use of cocaine in the general adult and high school populations of the United States." According to the acting director of NIDA, Jerome Jaffe, in the decade from 1975 to 1985, cocaine "evolved from a relatively minor problem into a major public health threat" (Kozel and Adams, 1985, p. v).

Did the prohibition fail with respect to cocaine? Richard Ashley stated categorically that "the prohibition against cocaine didn't work. Those who liked it didn't stop using it any more than did the typical drinker after the passage of the Volstead Act." But evidently many of those who liked it did stop using it. Indeed, Ashley went on to say that "prohibition made cocaine more expensive . . . and eventually the poorest users had to forego it altogether." And as we noted earlier, he acknowledged that "cocaine use was insignificant during the 1930s" (Ashley, 1975, pp. 93, 105).

If we take into account all the changes in behavior attributable to the interdiction of cocaine, it is clear that prohibition was not completely ineffective. Thus, insofar as "many provisions of federal law seemed to treat cocaine as an 'especially dangerous drug' " (McLaughlin, 1973, p. 568) and some drug users switched to other drugs – presumably regarded as less dangerous – partial deterrence at least was achieved. And there appears to be no dispute about the diminished use of cocaine from the 1930s to the late 1960s. But because "there seems to be general agreement that an 'epidemic' of cocaine use . . . occurred . . . in the United States" in the 1980s (Clayton, 1985, p. 12), it would be unrealistic to claim that prohibition has been notably successful. Little is known about the impact of the law on cocaine use patterns, but at the present time, according to the National Institute on Drug Abuse, cocaine abuse "in a few short years, has reached epidemic proportions," and cocaine "threatens to become the most destructive drug in recent history" (Kozel and Adams, 1985, p. 221).

National alcohol prohibition

With the passage of the National Prohibition Act (the Volstead Act) on October 18, 1919, there began what John Kaplan described as "the nation's most ambitious effort at drug control" (Kaplan, 1970, p. 1). When the Volstead Act was passed, the evangelist and noted prohibitionist Billy Sunday, who was the twentieth-century counterpart of the nineteenth-century prohibitionist Lyman Brecher, hailed its passage in terms that suggested not that a significant reform had been achieved but, rather, that a new era was dawning. "The reign of tears is over," he cried. "The slums will soon be a memory. We will turn our prisons into factories and our jails into storehouses and corncribs. Men will walk upright now, women will smile and children will laugh. Hell will be forever for rent" (Englemann, 1979, p. xi). There is no doubt that many saw Prohibition not only as a definitive solution to all the problems associated with alcohol but also as "a millennial moral triumph" (Aaron and Musto, 1981, p. 162).

Such sanguine expectations were shared by John F. Kramer, the first national Prohibition commissioner, who declared on taking office that the law would "be obeyed in cities, large and small" and that liquor would not be sold "nor given away, nor hauled in anything on the surface of the earth, or in the air" (Clark, 1976, p. 162). There is no doubt, however, that a large amount of liquor continued to be sold, given away, and hauled on the surface of the earth and in the air. Indeed, it has even been alleged that "Prohibition, by distorting the role of alcohol in civilized life, . . . caused Americans to drink more rather than less, and to do so with increasing morbidity" (Clark, 1976, p. 144). On the other hand, it has been no less confidently asserted that "the annual per-capita consumption level [of alcohol] declined as the result of Prohibition" (Aaron and Musto, 1981, p. 164).

In a review of the evidence Joseph Gusfield stated somewhat more guardedly that although there is much to suggest that the number of drinkers and the frequency of drinking greatly declined,

we have found no convincing data which could give any accurate estimate of the amount of drinking during the Prohibition years . . . it would seem most accurate to say that during the Prohibition era less alcohol was consumed by the nation than was consumed in the 14 years before or after. This provides no statement about quantitative drop nor does it answer questions about drinking in those areas where Prohibition was most strongly resisted. (Gusfield, 1976, p. 118)

The best evidence of what actually happened is shown in Table 3.2, which gives the available figures for the consumption of alcohol between 1906 and 1946. We should, however, emphasize that the figures for the Prohibition years are conjectural, as consumption figures based on tax receipts are lacking. Moreover, no figures are available regarding the production of the "illegal stills, home breweries and bathtub gin mills by the hundreds of thousands" said to have been in operation (Clark, 1976, p. 159). In regard to that, there is, of course, a good deal of anecdotal evidence, like H. L. Mencken's reminiscence that he was able to remember only two occasions between 1920 and 1933 when he was unable to obtain alcohol (Mencken, 1943, pp. 200–13). But such assertions probably tell us more about the social circles in which their authors moved than about the general availability of alcohol.

Nevertheless, there are some other data that tend to confirm the view that at least in the early years of Prohibition there was a noticeable decline in the consumption of alcohol. Aaron and Musto summarized the evidence as follows:

Death rates from cirrhosis were 29.5 per 100,000 in 1911 for men, and 10.7 in 1929; admissions to state mental hospitals for disease classified as alcoholic psychosis fell from 10.1 in 1919, to 3.7 in 1922, rising to 4.7 by 1928. In two predominately wet

Table 3.2. *Consumption of alcoholic beverages and absolute alcohol in each class of beverage in U.S. gallons per capita of the drinking-age population (fifteen years and over), United States, 1906–1946*

	Spirits		Wine		Beer		Total
	Beverage	Absolute alcohol	Beverage	Absolute alcohol	Beverage	Absolute alcohol	Absolute alcohol
1906–10	2.14	0.96	0.92	0.17	29.27	1.47	2.60
1911–15	2.09	0.94	0.79	0.14	29.53	1.48	2.56
1916–19	1.68	0.76	0.69	0.12	21.63	1.08	1.96
1920–30[a]	—	—	—	—	—	—	0.90
1934	0.64	0.29	0.36	0.07	13.58	0.61	0.97
1935	0.96	0.43	0.50	0.09	15.13	0.68	1.20
1936–41	1.40	0.63	0.80	0.14	17.22	0.77	1.54
1942–46	1.84	0.83	1.11	0.18	23.44	1.05	2.06

[a] Between 1930 and 1933 it is estimated that alcohol consumption rose slightly.
Source: Lender and Martin, 1987, pp. 205–6.

states, the decline in alcoholic psychosis was even more dramatic. In New York, it fell from 11.5 in 1910, to 3.0 in 1920, rising to 6.5 in 1931, and in Massachusetts, from 14.6 in 1910, to 6.4 in 1922, to 7.7 in 1929. National records of arrest for drunkenness and disorderly conduct declined 50 percent between 1916 and 1922. Reports of welfare agencies from around the country overwhelmingly indicated a dramatic decrease among client population of alcohol-related family problems. (Aaron and Musto, 1981, p. 165; see also Gusfield, 1968, p. 271; Jellinek, 1947, pp. 1–43; Warburton, 1932, pp. 26, 104–6)

What is most striking about these figures, however, is that they illustrate a considerable diminution in alcohol-related pathology before the advent of Prohibition. This parallels the trend in alcohol consumption figures shown in Table 3.2 that indicate that Americans had been drinking less and less during the decades leading up to Prohibition, as also had been the case in the nineteenth century before the first prohibition experiment.

Disagreement among historians about the effects of Prohibition on the extent of alcohol consumption is matched by dispute about two other matters: the extent of crime generated by attempts to enforce it and the amount of profits made by those engaged in bootlegging. In regard to the first, the widely accepted view that Prohibition caused "the greatest crime wave in the country's history" (Vidal, 1972, p. 374) has been challenged in a frequently cited article by social historian J. C. Burnham.

Burnham argued that "there is no firm evidence of this supposed upsurge in lawlessness. . . . Apparently what happened was that in the 1920s the long existent 'underworld' first became publicized and romanticized. The crime wave, in other words, was the invention of enterprising journalists." This argument is somewhat weakened by the fact that on the same page on which he asserted that "there was no crime wave," he also maintained that "no statistics from this period are of any value whatsoever in generalizing about crime rates" (Burnham, 1968–9, p. 61). Yet his statement that "there was no crime wave" is no less a generalization than, for example, Mark Haller's statement that "all the statistics of the period suggested a crime wave of major proportions" (Haller, 1968, p. vii). And on the specific question of whether Prohibition resulted in an increase in criminal activity, it requires more than a bald assertion to refute the detailed documentation provided in such works as John Landesco's *Organized Crime in Chicago* (1968), Andrew Sinclair's history of the Prohibition movement *Era of Excess* (1964), and the Wickersham Commission report *Enforcement of the Prohibition Laws of the United States* (1931).

On this question, Andrew Sinclair wrote:

During the five years after 1924, the big-city gang wars flourished and the remnants of the respectable brewers and distillers, who were still in the illegal trade fled for their lives. In the time of the consolidation of [Al] Capone's power in Chicago, there were between 350 and 400 murders annually in Cook County, Illinois, and an average of 100 bombings each year. (Sinclair, 1964, p. 222)

Although Burnham did make frequent references to Sinclair's work, he nonetheless ignored all this and wrote instead about "hysterical journalism" and "the ballyhoo that lay behind the fiction of a crime wave" (Burnham, 1968–9, p. 62).

On the related question of the profits made from bootlegging, Sinclair wrote: "In its practical effects, national prohibition transferred two billion dollars a year from the hands of brewers, distillers, and shareholders to the hands of murderers, crooks, and illiterates. . . . Capone was making between $60,000,000 and $100,000,000 a year from the sale of beer alone" (Sinclair, 1964, pp. 222, 229). But another historian, Norman Clark, who acknowledged that Capone "exercised a virtual monopoly" over the running of beer around Chicago, observed that "in the mechanics of bootlegging beer or booze, however, there is reason to suppose that the costs were nearly equal to the profits, for Capone himself estimated that his payoffs to policemen and to other public officials ran to thirty million dollars a year." Clark left unexplained why someone he described as "an extraordinarily shrewd business man" (Clark, 1976, p. 150) should have become involved in this extremely dangerous business, in return for only minimal profits.

In fact, there is no reason to doubt that the Wickersham Commission was correct when it spoke of "the huge profits involved" in the illicit stilling of whiskey and "the enormous sums of money . . . derived from the business of illicit beer." "The margin of profit in smuggling liquor, in diversion of industrial alcohol, in illicit distilling and brewing, in bootlegging and in the manufacture and sale of products of which the bulk goes into illicit and doubtfully lawful making of liquor," the commission's report asserted,

makes possible systematic and organized violation of the National Prohibition Act on a large scale and offers rewards *on a par with the most important legitimate industries*. It makes lavish expenditure in corruption possible. It puts heavy temptation in the way of everyone engaged in enforcement or administration of the law. It affords a financial basis for organized crime. (National Commission, 1931, pp. 30, 31, 51–52; emphasis added)

Norman Clark's assertion that "Prohibition did not make it any easier than it had been before to bribe a policeman" (Clark, 1976, p. 149) ignores the fact that the extent of corruption is largely a function of the funds available for that purpose.

The commission was a cautious body, and despite what one commissioner called "the appalling conditions which this Commission has found to exist, and to be steadily growing worse" (National Commission 1931, p. 108), it reported that it was "opposed to repeal of the Eighteenth Amendment" (National Commission 1931, p. 83). In the separate statements by the commissioners appended to the report, however, a number favored either complete repeal or revision of the amendment. One of them, Frank J. Loesch of Chicago, speaking on the basis of personal observation, experience as a prosecuting officer, and the evidence before the commission, was somewhat more explicit than his colleagues were about what Prohibition meant. In his statement, he wrote of

the power of the murderous, criminal organizations flourishing all over the country upon the enormous profits made in bootleg liquor traffic. Those profits are the main source of the corruption funds which cement the alliance between crime and politics and the corrupt law enforcing agencies in every populous city. Those criminal octopus organizations have now grown so audacious owing to their long immunity from prosecutions for their crimes that they seek to make bargains with law enforcing officers and even with judges of our courts to be allowed for a price to continue their criminal activities unmolested by the law. (National Commission, 1931, p. 149)

But if the commission itself was cautious, it was also aware that Prohibition was rapidly losing popular support. It found that "adverse public opinion in some states and lukewarm public opinion with strong hostile elements in other states [presented] a serious obstacle to the observance and enforcement of the national prohibition laws" (National Commission, 1931, p. 49). Probably the truth is that there has always been in America a degree of popular ambivalence toward alcohol use. The temperance movement, says Gusfield, was "the offspring of religious revivalism" (Gusfield, 1976, p. 57). But the fact that the demand for sacramental wines increased by 800,000 gallons during the first two years of Prohibition (Clark, 1976, p. 159) suggests that even among the religious there was some degree of ambivalence. Certainly by 1930 it seems clear that ambivalent acceptance of Prohibition had been superseded by hostility to it.

What seems to have turned the tide was a piece of legislation that the administration approved while the Wickersham Commission was still gathering evidence. "At least symbolically," wrote Lender and Martin, "it is possible to date the temperance movement's final break with the majority of Americans with the passage of the Jones Act in March 1929" (Lender and Martin, 1987, p. 163). Named after its chief legislative sponsor, Senator Wesley L. Jones of Washington, the new law amended the penalties for violating the Volstead Act, providing for first-offense jailings of five years *and* a fine of $10,000; thus it was popularly referred to as the "Jones 5 and 10 law." But even though the implementation of the act quickly clogged courts and jails, principally with small-scale violators, it was extremely unpopular. "The protest which followed was immediate, national, bitter and abusive. Senator Jones found himself attacked without mercy in newspapers, in state legislatures, in Congress, even in the federal courts" (Clark, 1976, p. 195). The crucial question that therefore arose was "whether the nation would tolerate a gigantic police operation to support dry policies that growing numbers of Americans saw as out of step with the times" (Lender and Martin, 1987, p. 164).

The idea of repeal, which had until then been regarded as "an absolute impossibility" – for no amendment to the Constitution had ever before been repealed – became "irresistibly popular" (Burnham, 1968–9, p. 65). Andrew Sinclair documented the way in which "the popular press both led and reflected the change of the American people in their attitude toward Prohibition" (Sinclair, 1964, pp. 309–10). But possibly the most reliable index of the popularity of Prohibition in 1930 is the fact that in that year, three years before repeal, the Pabst (Beer) Company invested almost $1 million in the modernization of its brewery in Milwaukee, which had been closed for ten years (Lender and Martin, 1987, p. 165).

Andrew Sinclair pointed out that many of the supporters of repeal "were as fanatic as the drys." And it is true that although the supporters of Prohibition had attributed almost every ill in the United States to alcohol, some of those who campaigned for repeal suggested that Prohibition was a "major cause of all the sins of society" (Sinclair, 1964, pp. 369, 398). For many citizens, however, it must have seemed simply a matter of the costs of Prohibition being out of proportion to any benefits it produced. In any event, the Pabst Company's decision proved to have been a wise one. In the 1932 presidential election campaign, Franklin D. Roosevelt, who called openly for repeal, easily triumphed over Herbert Hoover, who had approached the issue "with massive discretion" (Sinclair, 1964, p. 374). In 1933 "Prohibition was decisively and deliberately repealed" (Burnham, 1968–9, p. 51).

Historians recorded the verdict on America's second experiment with the prohibition of alcohol as equivocal. It is commonly given in the form of answers to two questions. The first is usually phrased as "Was Prohibition a failure?" and the answers to it are nicely polarized. On one hand are those who accept Andrew Sinclair's description of "the total failure of national prohibition, its passing into limbo as though it had never been" (Sinclair, 1964, p. 414) as an adequate summation. On the other hand, K. Austin Kerr found that "the conventional wisdom overlooks one simple yet highly significant fact: Prohibition worked" (Kerr, 1985, p. 276). And according to J. C. Burnham, "the prohibition experiment, as the evidence stands today, can more easily be considered a success than a failure." Further than that, Burnham wrote explicitly of "the myth that the American experiment in prohibition was a failure" (Burnham, 1968–9, pp. 52, 67).

Somewhat less categorical is Norman Clark's conclusion that "Prohibition was at least partially effective" but also that "Prohibition was a partial failure" (Clark, 1976, pp. 158, 165). This brings us to the second question pondered in the historical literature: "Could Prohibition have been more effective?" Here, too, there are sharp divisions of opinion. On one hand, there are those who maintain that if adequate resources had been made available, effective enforcement would have been possible; on the other, there are those who regard what the Wickersham Commission referred to as "the attempt to force an extreme measure of universal total abstinence in communities where public opinion is strongly opposed thereto" (National Commission, 1931, p. 81) as ineluctably doomed to failure.

The commission spoke of the need for "more men, more money, and more and better equipment for the enforcing agencies." It reported that Prohibition administrators agreed that "a very large number of additional agents and investigators" were required to make the federal Prohibition force reasonably effective. One chief of state police incidentally estimated that "to bring about reasonable enforcement in his state, there should be 1,000 federal Prohibition agents and 200 more state police in that jurisdiction alone" (National Commission, 1931, pp. 64, 80). In 1929 the Prohibition commissioner, Dr. James M. Doran, had asked for $300 million a year to enforce the Volstead Act. But even "a modest proposal by Senator Harris of Georgia to double the appropriation of the Prohibition Bureau to $25 million was turned down, since Secretary [of the Treasury Andrew] Mellon opposed the increase" (Sinclair, 1964, pp. 356–7).

J. C. Burnham described the way in which "successive Congresses refused to appropriate enough money to enforce the laws" and refused "to admit the necessity of large appropriations for enforcement" (Burnham, 1968–9, pp. 56–57). He claimed that

after World War I and until sometime in the early 1920s, say, 1922 or 1923, when enforcement was clearly breaking down, Prohibition was generally a success. Certainly there is no basis for the conclusion that Prohibition was inherently doomed to failure, *the emasculation of enforcement* grew out of specific factors that were not organically related to the Eighteenth Amendment. (Burnham, 1968–9, pp. 60–1; emphasis added)

Burnham provides no estimate of how large the appropriations would need to have been to ensure effective enforcement of the Prohibition laws. But critics of Prohibition suggest that they would have been beyond the bounds of political possibility. One of the sources of illicit liquor was that manufactured by bootleggers, who, wrote Andrew Sinclair, "had more than a hundred times the appropriation of the Bureau [of Prohibition] at their disposal" (Sinclair, 1964, p. 184). But even this assertion seems to have been based on an underestimate. Elsewhere he mentioned "the loot of Prohibition" as being "sufficient to buy judges, state attorneys, and whole police forces" and gave a figure of "two billion dollars a year" as the bootleggers' income from illicit brewing and distilling (Sinclair, 1964, pp. 222, 230). By contrast, the average annual appropriation of the Bureau of Prohibition was approximately $10.3 million for the years 1920 to 1930 (National Commission, 1931, p. 13).

There was also the problem of the illicit importation of liquor, or smuggling. As Norman Clark put it, "smuggling along the open borders of the country was a violation which would have required a huge standing army to police in any effective way; and even a modest degree of interference with smuggling along the coasts would have required a two-ocean naval blockade." Regarding the magnitude of this problem, he commented that it seems "to raise doubts concerning the sanity or intelligence of the dry leaders" (Clark, 1976, p. 159). In fact, it seems doubtful that even if Commissioner Doran had been granted his $300 million, and a standing army along the country's borders and a two-ocean naval blockade around the coasts had also been approved, Prohibition could have been made really effective. For, as Andrew Sinclair noted, "alcohol is easy to make and simple to sell and pleasant to consume, and few men will refuse so facile a method of escaping from the miseries of living" (Sinclair, 1964, p. 415). If, as Burnham asserted, there is no basis for the claim that Prohibition was inherently doomed to failure, the claim that it was successful does not seem to be much more firmly grounded. To say that the emasculation of enforcement grew out of factors not organically related to the Eighteenth Amendment is rather beside the point. Success of this nature, as Andrew Sinclair argued, "is illusory, a mere string of words on a document. Enforcement is all" (Sinclair, 1964, p. 416).

Wartime legislation had restricted the production and sale of alcoholic beverages in 1917. The Volstead Act in October 1919 closed the gap between that legislation and the start of national prohibition under the Eighteenth Amendment on January 16, 1920. Within two or three years it broke down for lack of enforcement. Thereafter it remained fixed in the Constitution for another decade, not only as "the butt of jokes, a perennial source of irritation" (Hofstadter, 1955, p. 290), but also as the source of "widespread corruption and lawlessness" (National Commission, 1931, p. 81). It is difficult to argue with John Kaplan's verdict that "our experience from 1920 to 1933 . . . demonstrated that as bad as a drug might be, there could be laws that were worse" or with his further point that the repeal of Prohibition is "a social decision that very few seriously question today" (Kaplan, 1970, pp. 1, 303).

Marijuana

The Eighteenth Amendment was ratified and proclaimed in effect on January 16, 1920, and repealed on December 5, 1933. Four years later, in 1937 under the Marijuana Tax Act, Congress outlawed the sale, possession, and use of marijuana.

The term *marijuana* covers any of the preparations of *Cannabis sativa*, or the Indian hemp plant. But as the term is commonly used in the United States, it refers to the chopped-up leaves, stems, and flowers of this plant.

The resin produced by the flowering tops of the plant is called *hashish* and contains a much higher proportion of the active ingredient transtetrahydro-cannabinol, or THC. Like cocaine, marijuana has been improperly classified with the opiates as a narcotic drug.

The use of cannabis as an intoxicant can be traced "to the earliest beginnings of history" (Walton, 1938, p. 6). Marijuana was cultivated "throughout Asia and the Near East from the earliest known times to the present." In America, it was first cultivated for its fiber, and from the beginning of the seventeenth century until after the Civil War, "the marijuana plant was a major crop in North America and played a major part in both colonial and national economic policy" (Brecher, 1972, pp. 398, 403). From the mid-nineteenth century until 1937 it was used in medical practice for a wide range of conditions and was listed in the United States Pharmacopeia as a recognized medicine in 1850, remaining on the list until 1942. It was sold "over the counter by drug stores at modest prices" in the form of fluid extracts. Ready-made marijuana cigarettes were also marketed as a remedy for asthma. Its use for recreational purposes, however, seems to have been limited. Edward Brecher summed up as follows:

In short, marijuana was readily available in the United States through much of the nineteenth and early twentieth centuries, its effects were known and it was occasionally used for recreational purposes. But use was at best limited, local and temporary. Not until after 1920 did marijuana come into general use – and not until the 1960s did it become a popular drug. (Brecher, 1972, pp. 405, 406, 409)

The National Commission on Marijuana and Drug Abuse reported in 1972 that until the beginning of this century, the recreational smoking of marijuana was generally limited to groups of Mexican itinerant workers in the border states of the Southwest. However,

by 1910, marijuana use began to emerge in other southern states and cities, particularly New Orleans, and in the port cities along the Mississippi River. In time, these cities became distribution centers for enterprising sailors. From there, marijuana use spread cross-country to other urban centers, mining camps, railroad construction sites, farm labor camps, "bohemian" communities of artists and jazz musicians, and various other groups outside the mainstream of American Society. (National Commission, 1972, p. 32)

According to Brecher, "It was a change in the laws rather than a change in the drug or in human nature that stimulated the large-scale marketing of marijuana for recreational use in the United States" (Brecher, 1972, p. 55). The change in the law he was referring to is that embodied in the Volstead Act and the Eighteenth Amendment. Its effect was to raise the price of alcoholic beverages and to make them more difficult to secure and frequently inferior in quality. Marijuana "tea pads" were established that resembled opium dens or speakeasies, except that prices were very low. A report by the

New York Mayor's Committee on Marijuana states that there were, by the 1930s five hundred tea pads in New York City alone (Mayor's Committee, 1944/1966, p. 246).

But marijuana use does not appear to have been regarded as a problem in America until the mid-1920s. According to John Kaplan, it first began to receive public attention in 1926, apparently as the result of a New Orleans newspaper exposé in a series of articles, under banner headlines, about the grip of marijuana on blacks and schoolchildren, which included reports of violent crimes committed by drug-crazed marijuana users (Kaplan, 1970, pp. 88–89). Eventually – and mainly as a result of a campaign waged by the Federal Bureau of Narcotics and its director Harry J. Anslinger – all but two states west of the Mississippi and several more in the East had by 1931 enacted prohibitory legislation naming it a criminal offense to possess or use the drug. Then in 1932 the National Conference of Commissioners on Uniform State Laws included an optional marijuana provision in the Uniform Narcotic Drug Act. By 1937 every state, either by adoption of the Uniform Act or by separate legislation, had prohibited the use of marijuana. Late in 1937 the Congress adopted the Marijuana Tax Act, thus superimposing a federal prohibitory scheme on the state schemes (National Commission, 1972, p. 14).

"Historically," John Kaplan reported, "the most significant argument for the prohibition of marijuana use has been that the drug causes its users to commit violent crime" (Kaplan, 1970, p. 134). This certainly was the argument that the Federal Bureau of Narcotics relied on in advocating antimarijuana laws. In 1937, before the passage of the Marijuana Tax Act, Commissioner Harry J. Anslinger stated, "How many murders, suicides, robberies, criminal assaults, hold-ups, burglaries, and deeds of maniacal insanity it [marijuana] causes each year especially among the young, can only be conjectured" (Kaplan, 1970, p. 89); the implication, of course, being that the missing number was very large indeed. In fact, as Kaplan concluded a careful review of all the evidence, "the total evidence on the issue supports the view that marijuana inhibits rather than increases aggression" (Kaplan, 1970, p. 136). The British Home Advisory Committee on Drug Dependence was dismissive of the "main charge against cannabis overseas, but not in this country, that its use makes people commit crimes of violence." It went on to point out that "in the United Kingdom, the taking of cannabis has not so far been regarded even by the severest critics, as a direct cause of serious crime" (Great Britain, Home Office, 1968, pp. 13–14).

But if the argument that marijuana use led to aggression, insanity, and sex crimes provided the initial justification for criminalization, it was later superseded by a different rationale known as the *stepping-stone theory*. As John Kaplan put it in 1970, "Probably the most widely believed reason today for the criminalization of marijuana is the idea that experience with marijuana causes one to progress to the use of more harmful drugs" (Kaplan, 1970, p. 199). This theory had been expressly repudiated by Federal Narcotics Commissioner Anslinger in 1937 when, before the congressional committee considering the Marijuana Tax Act, he was asked "whether the marijuana addict graduates into a heroin . . . user." "No, sir," said Anslinger, "I have not heard of a case of that kind. I think, it is an entirely different class. The marijuana addict does not go in that direction" (U.S. Congress, 1937, p. 24).

By 1951, however, Commissioner Anslinger had changed his mind. In an interview published in *U.S. News & World Report,* in reply to a question whether marijuana was habit forming, he responded, "It is habit forming, but not addiction forming. *It is dangerous because it leads to a desire for a greater kick from narcotics that do make addicts*" (*U.S. News & World Report,* 1951, June, p. 18; emphasis added). According to Kaplan, "it is hard to determine just what caused the commissioner's change of mind" (Kaplan, 1970, p. 234). But it is clear that in 1937, having characterized marijuana use as leading to murders, suicides, robberies, criminal assaults, holdups, and deeds of maniacal insanity, it would have been both anticlimactic and somewhat perplexing to an audience to add that it was a stepping-stone to a worse drug. By the late 1940s, however, what was widely reported as a major epidemic of heroin use had broken out, and heroin had come to be seen as the paramount drug menace.

The stepping-stone theory has a history going back to the beginning of the century when it was used as an argument for prohibiting both alcohol and cigarettes. "Morphine," it was said, "is the legitimate consequence of alcohol, and alcohol is the legitimate consequence of tobacco. Cigarettes, drink, opium is the logical and regular series" (Towns, 1912, p. 770). In fact, as Kaplan pointed out, "there is a positive correlation between the use of any given drug and use of all other drugs" (Kaplan, 1970, p. 228), which may mean no more than that some people have personalities that predispose them to drug use. Kaplan concluded, in relation to the association between the use of marijuana and the use of more dangerous drugs, that an important element may be that the criminalization of marijuana precipitates the use of other drugs by bringing the marijuana user into contact with the drug culture (Kaplan, 1970, p. 230).

None of this, however, explains what Brecher called the "burgeoning of marijuana smoking" in the 1960s. For in that decade, as he put it, "the United States . . . at long last discovered marijuana." Information about the extent of this burgeoning, however, is exiguous. For despite the passage of antimarijuana laws by both state legislatures and Congress, with the exception of California, "the number of people arrested under those laws, the number

Table 3.3. *California marijuana arrests,*
1954–1968

Year	Number of marijuana arrests
1954	1,156
1960	5,155
1962	3,793
1964	7,560
1966	18,243
1968	50,327

Source: Brecher, 1972, p. 422.

found guilty, the number serving prison terms, [and] the length of terms served . . . have never been determined' (Brecher, 1972, pp. 422–3, 430).

In California, however, where marijuana smoking seems to have been most prevalent, it is evident that the number of marijuana arrests increased dramatically at this time, as Table 3.3 shows. Moreover, whereas marijuana arrests accounted for 27 percent of all California drug arrests in 1960, by 1968 they accounted for 58 percent.

Some evidence of the increase in marijuana smoking in the nation at large may be found in survey data. In September 1969 Dr. Stanley F. Yolles, then director of the National Institute of Mental Health, told a Senate Judiciary Subcommittee, on the basis of a wide range of surveys, that somewhere between eight million and twelve million Americans had smoked marijuana at least once. Of these, about 65 percent were experimenting; 25 percent were "social users"; 10 percent were "chronic users" (U.S. Senate Subcommittee, 1969, pp. 267, 277). In 1970 on the basis of further survey data, Dr. Yolles reported that the number of individuals who had smoked marijuana "may be closer to 20 million" (Yolles, 1970, p. 181).

Kaplan cited a report in the *San Francisco Chronicle* in September 1969 headed "Reagan Attacks Youth's Drug Abuse," which began: "Rebellion, contempt for their elders and even subversive elements are behind a 'near epidemic' use of drugs by California youth, according to the Reagan administration." It is evident that in the late 1960s, marijuana use had come to be seen as representing a challenge to authority and as a symbol of many emotion-laden issues. As Kaplan put it, the issues were

the proper place of pleasure in our lives; the threat of radicalism, not only to our society but also to our values; the questions of permissiveness and the proper degree of subordination of personal desires necessary to ensure survival of civilized society;

the necessity of obedience to authority . . . the issue of law and order . . . the generation gap. (Kaplan, 1970, p. 19)

It is noteworthy that what was seen as a crisis came late in the history of
marijuana prohibition. "After a third of a century," said Brecher in 1972,
"marijuana has reached an unprecedented peak to popularity" (Brecher, 1972,
p. 521). It was the last drug to be added to the list of prohibited substances.
Yet it was not until just on three decades after its criminalization that the
extension of use provoked what has been called not only a "moral panic"
(Cohen, 1972, pp. 9–12) but also a challenge to the legitimacy of the legislation.

We are dealing here with an episode in the history of drug use in America
that has not yet been thoroughly documented and is much in need of further
investigation. The most recent development, what is referred to as marijuana
law reform, has taken the form of de facto decriminalization in several states
over the last two decades. Typically, this has been the reduction of possession
felony charges to misdemeanors, the lowering of maximum and average penalties, and the creation of diversions from the criminal courts. Many of these
changes have been in place since the mid-1970s, and it seems unlikely that
they can be easily dislodged even in the context of an intensified "war on
drugs."

III. Some implications

In this section, we shall explore historical patterns of drug use and drug
control that are relevant to current drug policy debates. Our own short list
of the lessons of prohibition includes two points concerning patterns of drug
use and five concerning prohibitions and their impacts.

Drug use

Two policy-relevant conclusions about American drug use stand out. First,
levels of drug and alcohol use in America have varied widely over time and
have been subject to rather large fluctuations that cannot be attributed to
official control measures. Second, there is no basis in most of American history for the distinction commonly drawn between beverage alcohol and other
psychoactive substances described as drugs. Throughout American history,
ethyl alcohol has been the most popular and widely used drug.

Variation in drug consumption. The data on the shifts in American drug use
are compelling. With respect to alcohol, per capita ethyl alcohol consumption
varied by a factor of three and one-half over the nineteenth century and by a

factor of two over the twentieth century. The use of other drugs has probably fluctuated more than has been the case with alcohol, for which a settled institutional base has probably produced less volatility in use patterns.

One of the lessons from the first prohibition period is that wide fluctuations in alcohol use can occur independently of any legislative or law enforcement action. The sharp reductions in alcohol consumption in the nineteenth century occurred before the first prohibition legislation was passed. Nationally, per capita consumption of alcohol is reported to have dropped by 70 percent in the twenty years before the first state-level prohibition statute, a larger decrease than has occurred at any other twenty-year period in history (Rorabaugh, 1979). Although the estimates on which this twenty-year drop is based are quite imprecise, it seems clear that the per capita consumption of alcohol dropped by at least half in the United States during the first half of the nineteenth century. It is unwise, therefore, to assume when major fluctuations in use are observed that any change in the folkways of drug use must be attributed to some prior shift in stateways. Sometimes, we shall presently argue, the sequence can be reversed, with the social conditions that enable legislative reform having an independent effect on patterns of consumption before the laws change.

We are only beginning to use multiple measures to assess shifts in the consumption of a wide variety of drugs, including marijuana, cocaine, and the amphetamines. What we have learned to date about the consumption patterns of those drugs is consistent with the historical data on alcohol consumption. But many policy actors fail to realize that major fluctuations in drug use may not be related to governmental initiatives. Fluctuations in the proportion of persons arrested for felonies whose urine tests positive for the prior use of drugs are scrutinized for trends, as if upward or downward movement in percentages must reflect the response of this population to changes in law enforcement policy. Upturns that may simply be part of cyclical movements are viewed with alarm and treated as if they might continue indefinitely. Downward movements that may also be cyclical become the occasion for press conferences to claim success for government antidrug programs. Yet to have a sense of history in this area is to expect wide fluctuations in patterns of substance use and to recognize it as unexceptional and normal.

Two models can be used to interpret data on fluctuations in the use of particular drugs. One of them assumes constancy in the proportion of the population regularly using psychoactive drugs and rough parity in the extent of their use over time. According to this interpretation, the number of Americans getting "high" and the frequency and intensity of their "highs" will not vary much over time, and it is only the mix of substances they use that can be expected to change. This could be called an "equilibrium" hypothesis. A second way of looking at the historical data argues that the proportion of the population using psychoactive drugs and the extent of their use also vary widely over time. This could be called a "cycles of use" hypothesis. The historical evidence supports the second interpretation rather than the first.

There are three reasons for believing that the total volume of recreational drug use has changed dramatically over the course of American history. First, the variations in alcohol consumption in the United States have been so great as to make it highly unlikely that fluctuations in the use of other drugs could substantially flatten the sharp differences between the periods of high and low alcohol consumption. Second, the overlap between the population that used alcohol recreationally in the nineteenth-century America and those who were using the patent medicines and opiate elixirs that achieved prominence in the middle and late nineteenth century was incomplete, so that earlier declines in alcohol consumption were not closely related to increased patent medicine consumption.

Third, the temporal pattern of ebb and flow in drug usage in the twentieth century does not support a complete equilibrium hypothesis as an explanation of fluctuations in drug use. Alcohol use did not rise in the years between the passage of the Harrison Act in 1914 and the passage of the Volstead Act in 1920, as an equilibrium hypothesis would suggest. Nor was there an abrupt increase in alcohol consumption noted among the population that was taking patent medicines before the Harrison Act was passed.

The substitution of one psychoactive drug for another is a reasonable expectation when drug controls are introduced, and so this should be a major focus of drug control evaluations efforts. But the wide variations in the volume of drug taking apparent in the historical record cannot be satisfactorily explained merely as changes in the component parts of a general equilibrium.

Alcohol as a drug. The preceding discussion assumes the validity of our second major conclusion: that there is no historical basis for distinguishing between alcohol and other drugs, as though alcohol cannot properly be classified as a drug. This point is worth making in the 1990s when a government document entitled *National Drug Control Strategy* totally disregards alcohol while at the same time acknowledges that it is "the most widely abused substance in America," because "it is not a controlled substance under the law" (Office of National Drug Control Policy 1989, p. 48). This dichotomy between alcohol and other drugs, which is based on the prohibited status of most narcotic drugs and the licit if regulated status of alcohol in American society, is of relatively recent vintage.

For all the nineteenth century, neither narcotic drugs nor cocaine was prohibited in the United States, and the use of those drugs was on a common jurisprudential footing with alcohol except when alcohol was prohibited. For the first third of the twentieth century, alcohol and the narcotic drugs had parallel careers, being initially not prohibited and then subject to federal government prohibition. For the greater part of American history, then, alcohol was not only recognized as a drug but was also identified as constituting the most serious drug problem facing the country. It is only the legislative pattern of the last half of this century that can be used to attribute some kind of exclusive status to beverage alcohol.

Patterns of drug control

Our five conclusions from the history of drug control policy concern (1) the contrasting aims of prohibition policies, (2) the political nature of success for prohibitions, (3) the variability of prohibition policies, (4) the changing use patterns as a precursor to prohibition, and (5) the pattern of early crisis for behavior-changing prohibition initiatives.

The contrasting aims of prohibition. All drug prohibitions have two objectives: symbolic approval of the behavior of citizens who do not use the substance in question and effecting a change in the behavior of those who do. Both attempts at alcohol prohibition came at times when drinking alcoholic beverages was widely accepted and even aproved in the United States. This meant that the behavior-changing aims of the prohibitionists constituted their major objective.

By contrast, the extent of opiate use at the time that the Harrison Act was passed was much more limited. Thus, the salience of the prohibition in the minds of citizens and its impact on their habits were considerably lessened. It is to be expected that there will be less public resistance to laws that do not attempt to effect changes in long-established and widespread patterns of behavior. On the other hand, the less extensive the use of a drug is, the easier its prohibition will be to enforce.

The political nature of success. In one important respect, the prohibition of narcotic drugs and cocaine by the Harrison Act has been a success in that the law has not been repealed. By the same token, the two experiments with alcohol prohibition failed because the respective laws were repealed. But this says nothing about the costs and benefits of those legal regimes. There is little in the way of empirical evidence to suggest that the pattern of effects attributable to the Harrison Act differed greatly from those of the nineteenth- or twentieth-century alcohol prohibitions. One would be hard put to describe the current impact of cocaine prohibition in terms that would diverge from those used to assess the impact of alcohol prohibition in the mid-1920s.

Whether or not a prohibition has been successful is, as a political matter, simply a question of whether the legal regime of prohibition remains in place over time. And this basic political criterion of success or failure probably also has a strong influence on the morale of combatants in debates about prohibition and on retrospective historical judgment regarding the wisdom of a particular prohibition. To the extent that prohibition laws are the product of a status conflict, the persistence of a prohibition regime is a vindication of the prohibitionist's symbolic position. If the law is repealed, the vision of government and society that goes with it will also have been rejected in a way that spells failure, no matter how great a reduction in the number of cases of cirrhosis of the liver was produced by the regime. This aura of vindication or repudiation also carries over, to a surprising degree, into the judgments of history. Thus, even though many accounts seem to suggest that twentieth-century alcohol prohibitions in America were found to be mistaken and then legislatively repealed, it is at least as likely that the critical discrediting of the alcohol prohibition experiments was a function of their rejection. In this sense, it is a nontrivial point that the prohibition of narcotic drugs continues to be a political success as long as it continues to be the official state policy. It is in this sense also that the supporters of drug prohibitions view any measure of decriminalization as a victory for the enemy.

The variability of prohibition policies. The criminal law prohibition of the sale, transfer, or possession of a substance is only one element in the many strands of governmental decision that in practice make up a specific drug policy. Are sale and transfer only to be prohibited, or should possession also be banned? What should the penalties be for violation? What resources should be invested in enforcing the law against sale, as opposed to the law against possession? Should there be programs of drug testing? And if so, what should the sanctions be against test refusal or failure?

The point to note is that a wide range of criminal justice policies can exist under the umbrella of a formal prohibition posture. A corollary proposition is that policy changes can be made without affecting the fundamental character of *de jure* prohibition. Thus, the decriminalization of the possession of marijuana in many American states during the 1970s did not affect the formal character of marijuana as a prohibited substance. Instead, state and local authorities reduced the penalty terms for possessory crime, in ways that removed both the threat and the stigma of possession arrest, to a degree that also diminishes police incentives to make such arrests. Even when marijuana is widely available and freely consumed, however, the proscription of the substance remains in force. It seems likely that any moves in the near future in the direction of decriminalization will be along those lines rather than taking the form of outright repeal of the criminal law classification.

Prohibition as a consequence of changing use patterns. Changes in the law may result in changing patterns of drug use. One of the clear lessons of our historical case studies, however, is that changing patterns of drug use may create a climate that is favorable to the passage of prohibition laws. Both episodes of alcohol prohibition occurred after periods of decline in the per capita consumption of absolute alcohol in the United States. We know less about the extent of opiate and cocaine consumption on the eve of World War I. But it appears to have been neither particularly widespread nor sharply on the increase. It is noteworthy that in American history, the sharply increased use of a psychoactive drug has never been an immediate precursor to its prohibition.

The sequence of events in the recent public policy career of tobacco is typical of the general pattern. The official antismoking campaign was confined to exhortation and information for over a decade before strong pressures to eliminate cigarette smoke from work areas, public places, and airplanes produced negative zoning legislation in the late 1970s and 1980s. Measured as a percentage of the total adult population, the share of smokers had fallen for at least a decade by the time the zoned prohibitions became popular, and the social status of smokers had also dropped.

The pattern of early crisis. For prohibition initiatives that attempt to change the behavior of large segments of the population, the social friction and political turmoil associated with the beginning of a regime represent a critical test of the strength of the prohibition movement. The early years of programs of compulsory change are the period when the social costs of the new law are highest. This is a point we made earlier in relation to the radical restriction of handgun ownership (Zimring and Hawkins, 1987, p. 194), and it is equally applicable to alcohol prohibition. The brief career of state-level prohibition in the nineteenth century is consistent with the tendency of behavior-changing crusades to encounter early crisis. The fourteen years between the enactment and repeal of the Eighteenth Amendment to the Constitution in this century was also an extremely short time to achieve a structural change of that magnitude.

The lack of significant front-end friction associated with the Harrison Act and the Marijuana Tax Act of 1937 suggests that only narrow sections of the population were using the substances prohibited by the legislation just before its enactment. The crisis for the marijuana legislation did not come until about three decades into a prohibition regime, with a dramatic expansion of marijuana use despite its prohibition. In this sense, the record in regard to marijuana is more discouraging for supporters of prohibition than is the record in regard to alcohol. In the case of alcohol, the acrimonious and costly experience with alcohol prohibition in the twentieth century – and we may in this context disregard the nineteenth-century precursor, which survived only briefly – came at the beginning of the regime. So it could be argued that efforts to reduce alcohol consumption might have grown both less costly and more successful over a longer period of time.

IV. Conclusion: Some future tasks

The available historical materials can be of use in policy discussions. But it is also the case that critical issues in current policy discussions should, to some extent, shape the historical work toward addressing policy issues. What we present here, as a conclusion to this chapter, is a set of questions that we feel are directly relevant to contemporary policy choices in the drug control field. The three issues we propose here are (1) the impact of variations in prohibition enforcement, (2) the recent reforms of marijuana prohibitions, and (3) the effects of nonprohibitory antitobacco measures.

Varieties of prohibition

One such issue concerns the variable character of prohibition attempts over time, and in different areas, with special attention to the impact of different types of enforcement on the use of a prohibited substance and the social costs associated with that use. With respect to the Harrison Act and twentieth-century alcohol prohibition, it has been noted that more and less stringent varieties of law enforcement and criminal justice policy can coexist under a prohibition umbrella both over time and in different areas. In terms of the social costs of law enforcement, there may be more of a contrast between relatively passive forms of prohibition and a full-scale "drug war" than there is between passive prohibition and decriminalization. Yet little if any attention has been paid to the marginal costs and marginal benefits of additional enforcement resources or of special crackdowns, either in the early history of the Harrison Act or in the annals of alcohol prohibition. We can think of no more policy-relevant data set in this field than one that addresses the effects of increases or decreases in enforcement resources.

Marijuana reform

A second set of policy research topics concerns the dynamics and behavioral effects of the partial decriminalization of marijuana that occurred widely in the 1970s in the United States. There has been a strategic withdrawal of criminal law enforcement, on the wide front, relating to the possession of marijuana. Nowhere has this taken the form of absolute decriminalization of the possession or transfer of marijuana. Instead, diversions from felony prosecution have been created; the maximum penalties for personal possession have been reduced to trivial financial penalties; and disincentives to arrest and prosecution have been designed and implemented. All of this has taken place in the shadow of the continued prohibition of marijuana and at a time of maximum public concern about drugs and drug law enforcement.

At present, even the earliest chapters of the history of this set of legal and law enforcement changes have not been written. Yet the data are waiting to be collected. With the use of tools such as survey research, much could be learned about marijuana and other drug possession and use patterns, about the effects of the changing shape of governmental activity, and about changing patterns of citizen behavior. The political career of these marijuana reforms is also worthy of study. What is the political and public opinion climate in which these changes occur? What pressures are generated by public anxiety about drugs and increased government antidrug enforcement programs in relation to these reforms? Both sociologists of law and drug policy analysts should have much to learn from recent American history in this field.

The impact of nonprohibitory government policies

For most of the first two centuries of American independence, tobacco was not regarded as a drug or subjected to regimes of drug control. When governmental attention was drawn to tobacco as a public health problem in the late 1950s, there was no serious discussion of prohibition as a policy option in an anticigarette campaign. However, beginning in 1964 the American federal government has conducted a multifront campaign against cigarette smoking, using persuasion, medical research findings, incentives, and disincentives in a campaign relating to public transport, compulsory warning labels, and taxation. The anticigarette campaign has apparently had an effect. The apparent contrast between attitudes toward cigarette smoking in most of Western Europe and the current situation in the United States is evidence that some aspects of America's antitobacco campaign have been successful.

But if the official campaign against tobacco is the drug war we are winning, it is also a development that has not been documented or analyzed by contemporary historians. This chapter in American history is both fascinating and important in its own right, and it also provides a window into the prospects for drug policies short of prohibition. What are the handicaps in a campaign against nonprohibited substances? How does a government attempt to stigmatize behavior that it does not proscribe in its criminal law? Does the universal prohibition of the sale of tobacco to children have any preventive impact despite its nonenforcement? Can governmental communication actually affect the social status of a substance among young persons at risk? The relevance of such questions to contemporary narcotic drug control debates seems obvious. In much the same way as the British parliamentary opposition has a shadow cabinet, we have been conducting, in regard to tobacco, a shadow drug control strategy. Although no country that produces half a trillion cigarettes a year can claim victory in a war on tobacco, both the successes and the failure of the cigarette war merit the close attention of drug policy analysts.

4

The wrong question: Critical notes on the decriminalization debate

This chapter is both a summary and a critique of the current debate about decriminalization of drugs in the United States. Section I begins by rehearsing the arguments in favor of decriminalization advanced in the mid-nineteenth century by John Stuart Mill in *On Liberty* and the late nineteenth-century critique of that argument advanced by James Fitzjames Stephen, "the most powerful and penetrating of the contemporary critics of John Stuart Mill" (Quinton, 1978, p. 87). The Mill–Stephen exchange seems to us to exhaust most of the arguments currently employed in what we call the "polar debate" about drug decriminalization in the United States, a debate in which both sides believe that the only significant question is whether drugs should be prohibited by the criminal law.

Section II adds the two important new wrinkles present in the late twentieth-century continuation of the Mill–Stephen exchange as it related to drugs. These new points of emphasis, both prominent in the work of John Kaplan, are the significant role of the costs of maintaining a criminal prohibition in the calculus of policy and the likelihood that separate cost–benefit analyses for each of a wide variety of drugs will produce differing conclusions for different drugs.

Section III restates the decriminalization debate as a clash of presumptions in which those who favor decriminalization argue that when the facts are uncertain, government should presume that a policy that enhances liberty will best serve the public good, and those who support continuation of the criminal sanction contend that in uncertainty it is safest to presume that a continuation of current policy will maximize the public welfare. This conservative presumption explains why those who favor continuing prohibition do not also support extending prohibition to current licit substances. Preferring known to unknown evils is a legitimate technique of policy analysis in the drug area, and there is value in seeing the decriminalization debate as a competition of two presumptions, each with significant support in the American political tradition.

Section IV outlines our critique of the polar debate, which we find unfortunate in two respects. First, it emphasizes the question of whether the criminal law should be used in drug control when almost always the more important questions concern how, rather than whether, the criminal law will be used to control drugs. Second, the polar debate involves what we shall call "trickle-down" methods of policy determination. Both sides in the decriminalization debate think that the details of correct policy can work themselves out once the broad strokes of criminal justice policy are in place. It is assumed that the details of effective drug control can be inferred once the right answers to broad policy questions have been determined. But it is more plausible, we believe, to invest in a process of "trickle-up" policy analysis in which priority problems are identified and resources are allocated in real-world settings to particular problems.

I. John Stuart Mill and James Fitzjames Stephen

"In discussing drug control and freedom," Bakalar and Grinspoon observed, "it still makes sense to start with John Stuart Mill's essay *On Liberty*" (Bakalar and Grinspoon, 1984, p. 1). It does indeed make sense because Mill was particularly concerned about drug control laws, and his statement of the way in which they infringed on human liberty is a model of forceful argument. Writing in the 1850s at the time of America's first experiment with prohibition, he wrote:

Under the name of preventing intemperance the people of . . . nearly half of the United States, have been interdicted by law from making any use whatever of fermented drinks, except for medical purposes: for prohibition of their sale is in fact, as it is intended to be, prohibition of their use.

Mill described this development as a "gross usurpation upon the liberty of private life" and an "important example of illegitimate interference with the rightful liberty of the individual" (Mill, 1859/1910, pp. 143–5).

"No person," Mill wrote, "ought to be punished simply for being drunk" (Mill, 1859/1910, p. 138). He also objected to taxes designed to limit consumption: "To tax stimulants for the sole purpose of making them more difficult to be obtained is a measure differing only in degree from their entire prohibition" (Mill, 1859/1910, p. 156). He was opposed to laws requiring the certificate of a medical practitioner for the purchase of dangerous drugs, for this, he asserted, "would make it sometimes impossible, always expensive" to obtain them. Although he did allow that "such a precaution, for example, as that of labelling a drug with some word expressive of its dangerous character, may be enforced without violation of liberty," because "the buyer cannot wish not to know that the thing he possesses has poisonous qualities" (Mill, 1859/1910, p. 152).

The basic principle underlying Mill's attitude toward drug control was stated in an often-quoted passage:

That the sole end for which mankind are warranted, individually or collectively, in interfering with the liberty of action of any of their members is self-protection. That the only purpose for which power can be rightfully exercised over any member of a civilized community against his will, is to prevent harm to others. His own good, either physical or moral, is not a sufficient warrant, he cannot rightfully be compelled to do or forbear because it would be better for him to do so, because it will make him happier, because, in the opinion of others, to do so would be wise or even right. (Mill, 1859/1910, pp. 72–3)

Less often cited are four qualifications that Mill placed on this principle that may be regarded as significant in relation to drug control. The first concerns children and young persons, a topic we shall cover in a later chapter. "It is, perhaps, hardly necessary to say," Mill added, "that this doctrine is meant to apply only to human beings in the maturity of their faculties" (Mill, 1859/1910, p. 73). Indeed, he thought that an important reason that society should not have "the power to issue commands and enforce obedience in the personal concerns of [adult] individuals" was that it "has had absolute power over them during all the early portion of their existence; it has had the whole period of childhood and nonage in which to try whether it could make them capable of rational conduct in life" (Mill, 1859/1910, p. 139).

With regard to this exception, one of Mill's more cogent critics, John Kaplan, argued that "Mill's exception for the young is unpersuasive," in that making a drug "available to adults would render completely unenforceable any effort to prevent the young from having access to the drug." "The median age for first heroin use is currently less than nineteen," Kaplan pointed out,

and it is quite likely that giving adults freer access to the drug would considerably increase the number of users younger than this. That at least would be the natural conclusion we might derive from our experience with alcohol and tobacco, where our laws attempting to keep these drugs from the young have been rendered notoriously ineffective by their complete availability to adults.

And he suggested that Mill might have "countenanced a law making the drug unavailable to all on the ground that this was the only way of protecting youth" (Kaplan, 1983, p. 104).

This suggestion itself is unpersuasive, however, for two reasons. First, Mill, who was adamantly opposed to the prohibition of alcohol and other drugs, cannot have been unaware that giving adults free access to them raised some problems for anyone attempting to keep them from the young. Second, acceptance of the principle that the protection of children justified restrictions of this nature on adults would, in large measure, reduce adults to the status of children, and, to use Mill's own words, "there is no violation of liberty which it would not justify" (Mill, 1859/1910, p. 146). As a matter of fact, Mill did not think that prohibition was a feasible policy even for adults, and he noted that in America "the impracticality of executing the law has caused its repeal in several of the States which had adopted it" (Mill, 1859/ 1910, p. 145). But his objection to it was based on the more fundamental ground that the prohibition movement represented acceptance of a "doctrine [that] ascribes to all mankind a vested interest in each other's moral, intellectual, and even physical perfection, to be defined by each claimant according to his own standard." He viewed this as "monstrous," particularly because "there are many who consider as an injury to themselves any conduct which they have a distaste for, and resent it as an outrage to their feelings" (Mill, 1859/1910, pp. 140, 146).

The second exception to his principle related to "backward states of society in which the race itself may be considered as in its nonage." Despotism, Mill contended, "is a legitimate mode of government in dealing with barbarians" (Mill, 1859/1910, p. 73). As we shall see, Mill's most notable contemporary critic, James Fitzjames Stephen, regarded this exception as constituting a fatal flaw in Mill's argument, for in Stephen's view even in advanced, civilized communities there was "an enormous mass" of people who in relevant respects were effectively barbarians (Stephen, 1873/1967, p. 72).

The third exception to Mill's principle that is relevant to drug control relates to what he called "the right inherent in society, to ward off crimes against itself by antecedent precautions." This, he said, implied "obvious limitations to the maxim, that purely self-regarding misconduct cannot properly be meddled with in the way of prevention or punishment." In particular, he stated that although

drunkenness, for example, in ordinary cases, is not a fit subject for legislative interference; . . . I should deem it perfectly legitimate that a person, who had once been convicted of any act of violence to others under the influence of drink, should be placed under a special legal restriction, personal to himself; that if he were afterwards found drunk, he should be liable to a penalty, and that if when in that state he committed another offence, the punishment to which he would be liable for that other offence, should be increased in severity. The making himself drunk, in a person whom drunkenness excites to do harm to others, is a crime against others. (Mill, 1859/ 1910, p. 153)

We should note parenthetically here that over a century later, the British Committee on Mentally Abnormal Offenders proposed that an offense of "dangerous intoxication" should be punished by one year's imprisonment for a first offense and three years for a second or subsequent offense. The committee, however, did not go so far as Mill, who thought that intoxication alone should incur a penalty in the case of those previously convicted of violence while drunk. Rather, the commission's recommendation was intended to apply to people who, having become violent while intoxicated, might otherwise avoid conviction on the ground that they had lacked the intent necessary for the alleged offense (Great Britain, Home Office, 1975, pp. 235–7).

This third exception to Mill's principle might at first glance seem to be contrary to both his general commitment to individual liberty and his particular concern with the preventive function of government as "liable to be abused to the prejudice of liberty." For in that connection he observed that "there is hardly any part of the legitimate freedom of action of a human being which would not admit of being represented, and fairly too, as increasing the facilities for some form or other of delinquency" (Mill, 1859/1910, p. 151). In fact, however, there is no contradiction, for approval of using the criminal law to deal coercively or punitively with persons who under the influence of a drug commit crimes that harm others in no way conflicts with the principle that it should not be used against those whose conduct does no direct harm to others.

The fourth and final exception to Mill's principle pertains to the possibility of an individual selling himself into slavery, which, according to Mill, the state had a right to prevent:

The ground for thus limiting [an individual's] power of voluntarily disposing of his own lot in life is apparent, and is very clearly seen in this extreme case. The reason for not interfering unless for the sake of others, with a person's voluntary acts, is consideration for his liberty. But by selling himself for a slave, he abdicates his liberty; he forgoes any future use of it, beyond that single act. He therefore defeats, in his own case, the very purpose which is the justification of allowing him to dispose of himself. He is no longer free; but is thenceforth in a position which has no longer the presumption in its favor, that would be afforded by his voluntarily remaining in it. The principle of freedom cannot require that he should be free not to be free. It is not freedom, to be allowed to alienate his freedom. These reasons, the force of which is so conspicuous in this peculiar case, are evidently of far wider application. (Mill, 1859/1910, pp. 157–8)

John Kaplan raised the question whether this "far wider application" might permit the government to prohibit heroin on the ground that heroin addiction is a species of slavery to which the user is at risk (Kaplan, 1983, p. 106). But it seems unlikely that Mill would have accepted this. First, Mill had nothing to say about acts that might involve only *some risk* of slavery, and the use of heroin involves merely some risk of addiction. Second, Mill cannot have been unaware of both alcohol and opiate addiction, and yet he made no mention of them in this context. Incidentally, Thomas De Quincey's widely acclaimed *Confessions of an English Opium Eater* first appeared in 1821, thirty-eight years before the publication of Mill's *On Liberty*.

However one may interpret the various limits on the application of his central principle, there is no doubt about either Mill's essential position or the relevance of his ideas to America today. In fact, in contemporary America, as in nineteenth-century England, "there are many who consider as an injury to themselves any conduct which they have a distaste for, and resent it as an outrage to their feelings" (Mill, 1859/1910, p. 140). Nor is this peculiar to America. Indeed, Mill himself stated that "it is not difficult to show, by abundant instances, that to extend the bounds of what may be called moral police, until it encroaches on the most unquestionably legitimate liberty of the individual, is *one of the most universal of all human propensities*" (Mill, 1859/1910, pp. 140–1; emphasis added). Mill went on to give numerous instances of the way in which the public in his own and other countries "improperly invests its own preferences with the character of moral laws," prohibition in America being only one such example.

But Mill did regard America as providing a singularly striking example of a country in which the government and the public upheld "the pretension that no person shall enjoy any pleasure which they think wrong." There was, he noted, "in the modern world" a strong tendency toward a democratic constitution of society accompanied by popular political institutions. Moreover, he pointed out that "in the country where this tendency is most completely realised – where both society and the government are most democratic – the United States – the feeling of the majority, . . . operates as a tolerably effectual sumptuary law." And when public opinion did not provide a sufficient sanction, it was accepted that there was "an unlimited right in the public . . . to prohibit by law everything which it thinks wrong" (Mill, 1859/1910, pp. 143–4).

What Mill saw as characteristic of America in the early nineteenth century remains true in the late twentieth century. Mill's statement that "the individual is not accountable to society for his actions, in so far as these concern the interests of no person but himself" (Mill, 1859/1910, p. 149) is no more generally accepted as a fundamental principle today than it was in 1859. Gore Vidal may have exaggerated when he said that the American people are "devoted to the idea of sin and its punishment" (Vidal, 1972, p. 375). But it is certainly true that "in this country we have a highly moralistic criminal law and a long tradition of using it as an instrument for coercing men toward virtue" (Morris and Hawkins, 1970, p. 5). Now, as then, it is probable that a great many Americans would echo Thomas Carlyle's angry reaction to Mill's essay: "As if," he said, "it were a sin to control, or coerce into better methods, human swine in any way; . . . Ach Gott im Himmel!" (Packe, 1954, p. 405).

If it makes sense when discussing drug control and freedom to start with John Stuart Mill's essay *On Liberty*, it makes equally good sense to follow that with his most formidable contemporary critic's *Liberty, Equality and Fraternity*. One of the things that makes Stephen's critique formidable is that he shared Mill's basic assumptions. As Anthony Quinton put it, Stephen's assumptions "were simply a more firmly held version of Mill's own first principles. He criticized Mill's deduction from utilitarian principles from the inside." Like Mill, Stephen did not regard the ideals of the French revolutionary formula, which he took for his title, as natural rights. Rather, he saw them as "valuable only to the extent that they contribute to the overriding end of the general happiness and, in Stephen's view, they did so only in a very qualified fashion" (Quinton, 1978, pp. 87–8).

When Stephen's book appeared, Mill had only a few more months to live, but he is on record as having said that Stephen "does not know what he is arguing against" (White, 1967, p. 1). Stephen, however, was quite clear that he was arguing against what he called Mill's "religious dogma of liberty" (Stephen, 1873/1967, p. 54). In what has been called "the finest exposition of conservative thought in the latter half of the nineteenth century" (Barker, 1915, p. 172), displaying that "certain brutal directness of mind" (Quinton, 1978, p. 87) that characterized all his polemical writings, Stephen subjected that "dogma" to vigorous criticism.

In particular, Stephen was sharply critical of Mill's statement that

as soon as mankind have attained the capacity for being guided to their own improvement by conviction or persuasion (a period long since reached in all nations with whom we need here concern ourselves), compulsion either in the direct form, or in that of pains and penalties for noncompliance, is no longer admissible as a means to their own good, and is justifiable only for the security of others. (Mill, 1859/1910, pp. 73–4)

This, said Stephen, represented an exception or qualification to Mill's libertarian principle that reduced his doctrine either to an empty commonplace that no one would dispute or to an unproved and incredible assertion about the state of human society.

Either then the exception means only that superior wisdom is not in every case a reason why one man should control another – which is a mere commonplace – or else it means that in all the countries which we are accustomed to call civilised the mass of adults are so well acquainted with their own interests and so much disposed to pursue them that no compulsion or restraint put upon any of them by any others for the purpose of promoting their interests can really promote them. No one can doubt the importance of this assertion, but where is the proof of it? (Stephen, 1873/1967, pp. 67–8)

Stephen noted that Mill had allowed that compulsion was justified as a means of dealing with barbarians, "provided the end be their improvement, and the means justified by actually effecting that end," because "liberty as a principle has no application to any state of things anterior to the time when mankind have become capable of being improved by free and equal discussion" (Mill, 1859/1910, p. 73). But he interpreted Mill as believing that "there is a period now generally reached all over Europe and America, at which discussion takes the place of compulsion, and in which people when they know what is good for them generally do it. When this period is reached, compulsion may be laid aside" (Stephen, 1873/1967, p. 69).

To this, I should say that no such period has as yet been reached anywhere, and that there is no prospect of its being reached anywhere within any assignable time. Where, in the very most advanced and civilised communities, will you find any class of persons whose views or whose conduct on subjects on which they are interested are regulated even in the main by the results of free discussion . . . of ten thousand people who get drunk is there one who could say with truth that he did so because he had been brought to think in full deliberation and after free discussion that it was wise to get drunk? (Stephen, 1873/1967, p. 69)

In Stephen's view, the idea that "in all nations with whom we need here concern ourselves" the period had long since been reached in which mankind had "attained the capacity of being guided to their own improvement by conviction or persuasion" was nonsensical.

Stephen not only saw no objection to people's being coerced for their own good but also regarded it as necessary. "Men are so constructed," he asserted,

that whatever theory as to goodness and badness we choose to adopt, there are and always will be in the world an enormous mass of bad and indifferent people – people who deliberately do all sorts of things which they ought not to do, and leave undone all sorts of things which they ought to do. Estimate the proportion of men and women who are selfish, sensual, frivolous, idle, absolutely commonplace and wrapped up in the smallest of petty routines, and consider how far the freest of free discussion is likely to improve them. The only way by which it is practically possible to act upon them at all is by compulsion or restraint . . . the utmost conceivable liberty which could be bestowed upon them would not in the least degree tend to improve them. (Stephen, 1878/1967, pp. 72–3)

It is somewhat ironic that Mill, who had attacked English judges for their "extraordinary want of knowledge of human nature and life, which continually astonishes us in English lawyers" (Mill, 1859/1910, p. 126), was here in effect being told by an English judge that his own knowledge of human nature and life was defective. And Stephen took the view of human nature being what it was, it was necessary for society to use the criminal law to enforce society's moral code, whether or not breaches of it caused harm to others. "Criminal law in this country," he said, "is actually applied to the suppression of vice and so to the promotion of virtue to a very considerable extent; and I say this is right." In his view, the criminal law was "in the nature of a persecution of the grosser forms of vice," and he saw nothing wrong with that, because "the object of promoting virtue and preventing vice must be admitted to be a good one." It was therefore necessary "to put a restraint upon vice, not to such an extent merely as is necessary for definite self-protection, but generally on the ground that vice is a bad thing from which men ought by appropriate means to restrain each other" (Stephen, 1873/1967, pp. 143, 150, 152), and among those appropriate means he included the criminal law.

Stephen complained that in Mill's essay "there is hardly anything . . . which can properly be called proof as distinguished from enunciation or assertion" (Stephen, 1873/1967, p. 56; see also pp. 67, 74). And it is true that the principles enunciated by Mill are not supported by any proof; in fact they are not amenable to proof or logical demonstration. When they have read all the arguments in the debate on law and morals initiated by Mill, some readers may feel, with Herbert Packer, that "there is, perhaps, not much further to be said about it" (Packer, 1968, p. 251). But Stephen's case against Mill was not directed at Mill's principles so much as at their application in the real world, and in this connection some modern commentators have, tacitly at least, supported Stephen.

Thus in our own time, the notion that Mill's knowledge of human nature was deficient was echoed by H. L. A. Hart, who stated:

Underlying Mill's extreme fear of paternalism there perhaps is a conception of what a normal human being is like which now seems not to correspond to the facts. Mill, in fact, endows him with too much of the psychology of a middle-aged man whose desires are relatively fixed, not liable to be artificially stimulated by external influences; who knows what he wants and what gives him satisfaction or happiness; and who pursues these things when he can. (Hart, 1963, p. 33)

Hart maintains that Mill carried his protests against paternalism "to lengths that may now appear to us fantastic."

In particular, Hart cited Mill's criticism of restrictions on the sale on drugs as interfering with the liberty of the would-be purchaser:

No doubt if we no longer sympathise with this criticism this is due, in part, to a general decline in the belief that individuals know their own interests best, and to an increased awareness of a great range of factors which diminish the significance to be attached to an apparently free choice or to consent.

In this connection, Hart took the view that "a modification in Mill's principles is required." Such a modification, he argued, need not abandon Mill's objection to the use of the criminal law to enforce morality. It would "only have to provide that harming others is something we may still seek to prevent by the use of the criminal law, even when the victims consent to or assist in the acts which are harmful to them" (Hart, 1963, pp. 32–33). But it is clear that acceptance of this modification of Mill's principle provides a rationale for a drug prohibition policy directed at traffickers and purveyors, if not consumers.

John Kaplan was another critic of Mill who appeared to disagree with Mill's "conception of what a normal human being is like." He observed: "It almost seems to be the nature of man to regard some types of predominantly self-harming conduct as, for one reason or another, the proper subject of official prohibition." He asserted that "the great majority of us do not agree with Mill's principle to begin with. Indeed, no modern state (or, so far as is known, any premodern state) has ever followed Mill's principle with respect to all activities." Kaplan then cited, as an example of "confrontation between Mill's principle and our nation's actions," the laws in about half of the American states requiring that motorcyclists wear protective helmets, although a helmetless cyclist does not pose any threat or cause any harm to others. In this case, the justification for the law is that helmetless cyclists expose all of us to the risk that we as taxpayers may, in the case of an accident, have to pay for expensive hospital treatment and, if they have families, to provide public assistance for them (Kaplan, 1983, pp. 106–7).

As with Stephen, it is the application of Mill's doctrine to the real world that Kaplan questioned. Thus he prefaced his discussion of the likely costs of legalizing cocaine by noting that the question is one that cannot be decided by reference to John Stuart Mill's "simple principle." Mill's rule regarding self-harming conduct, Kaplan believed, is "probably unworkable in a complex, industrial society – particularly one that is a welfare state," and moreover it "seems singularly inappropriate when it is applied to a habit-forming, psychoactive drug that alters the user's perspective as to postponement of gratification and his desire for the drug itself" (Kaplan, 1988, p. 36).

II. Contemporary polarity

A survey of current opinion shows that the general terms of the decriminalization debate have not changed much at all. Most of the commentary we observe at the end of the twentieth century owes a great debt (most often unacknowledged) to the Mill–Stephen exchange. But sampling the current arguments of a wide variety of contemporary writers has value beyond making this basic point. Our canvas reveals a split among political conservatives between the Stephen-style prohibitionism of the *National Drug Control Strategy* and the laissez-faire sentiments regarding Mill's principles expressed by Milton Friedman and William Buckley. The texture and style of these general sentiments can be contrasted with the cost–benefit rhetoric of specific policy analyses as practiced by John Kaplan.

For legalization

Although many critics have said that "we will never return to the social and intellectual conditions that made possible Mill's opposition to all drug laws" (Bakalar and Grinspoon, 1984, p. 69), there are today a number of intellectual descendants of Mill who have reaffirmed his basic principle that adults should be free to live their lives in their own way as long as their conduct is not directly hurtful to others (though others may think it foolish, perverse, or wrong). Some of them also reinforce Mill's concern with the "mischief of the legal penalties" (Mill, 1859/1910, p. 92) by enumerating the excessive collateral social costs of endeavoring to preserve various prohibitions. These writers are arguing, in effect, that the changing social conditions since Mill's day have not made irrelevant his opposition to drug laws but, instead, have provided powerful, prudent reasons for supporting his principled objection to them.

Many of these critics, however, see the crucial question as being not so much a matter of the collateral disadvantage costs or harmful side effects of prohibitions but, rather, a question, in Mill's words, of "the proper limits of what may be called the functions of the police; how far liberty may be legitimately invaded" (Mill, 1859/1910, p. 152). Thomas Szasz, for example, like Mill himself, is primarily concerned with the moral or ethical aspects of drug control in a free society dedicated to individual liberty. But unlike Mill, who declared "I forego any advantage which could be derived to my argument from the idea of abstract right" (Mill, 1859/1910, p. 74), Szasz maintains that we should regard "the freedom of choosing our diets and drugs as fundamental rights" (Szasz, 1987, p. 342).

Economist Milton Friedman is another authority who believes that we have no right in respect of adults

to use the machinery of government to prevent an individual from becoming an alcoholic or a drug addict. . . . Reason with the potential addict, yes. Tell him the consequences, yes. Pray for and with him, yes. But I believe that we have no right to use force, directly or indirectly to prevent a fellow man from committing suicide, let alone from drinking alcohol or taking drugs. (Friedman, 1987, p. 135)

The correspondence with Mill's words is so close as to be almost paraphrastic. In such cases, wrote Mill, there may be "good reasons for remonstrating with him, or reasoning with him, or persuading him, or entreating him, but not for compelling him, or visiting him with any evil in case he do otherwise" (Mill, 1859/1910, p. 73).

Another opponent of drug prohibition laws, Gore Vidal, sees Mill's admission that a precaution such as "labeling the drug with some word expressive of its dangerous character may be enforced without violation of liberty" (Mill, 1859/1910, p. 152) as providing a solution to all the problems of drug addiction:

It is possible to stop most drug addiction in the United States within a very short time. Simply make all drugs available and sell them at cost. Label each drug with a precise description of what effect – good and bad – the drug will have on the taker

. . . it seems most unlikely that any reasonably sane person will become a drug addict if he knows in advance what addiction is going to be like. (Vidal, 1972, pp. 373–4).

Not all the opponents of drug prohibition laws, however, have emphasized questions of liberty. Ronald Hamowy summarized some of the arguments offered in recent years "by a host of writers calling for repeal of our drug laws" as follows:

Complete abandonment of all prohibitory laws . . . the decriminalization of marijuana, cocaine, and the opiates would halt the current massive drain of public funds and the substantial suffering brought about through attempts to enforce these unenforceable laws. Evidence indicates that legalization would do much to reduce the current crime-rate and thus contribute to restoring the safety of our city streets. It would reduce the amount of government corruption, which is partly a function of the immense fortunes that are constantly made in the drug trade, and it would play a large part in decreasing the profits that flow to organized crime. (Hamowy, 1987, p. 32)

Herbert Packer – who thought that "a clearer case of misapplication of the criminal sanction" than its use to enforce a policy of suppressing drug abuse "could not be imagined" – noted a number of other socially harmful effects of this misapplication:

A disturbingly large number of undesirable police practices – unconstitutional searches and seizures, entrapment, electronic surveillance – have become habitual because of the great difficulty that attends the detection of narcotics offences. . . . The burden of enforcement has fallen primarily on the urban poor, especially Negroes and Mexican-Americans. . . . Research on the causes, effects and cures of drug use has been stultified. . . . A large and well entrenched enforcement bureaucracy has developed a vested interest in the status quo, and has effectively thwarted all but the most marginal reforms. (Packer, 1968, pp. 332–3)

Ernest van den Haag argued that from the history of the prohibition of alcohol in America "one may infer a general principle. In a democracy one can regulate, but one cannot effectively prohibit, sumptuary activities desired by a substantial segment of the population. Unenforceable attempts to prohibit certain substances will cause more harm than good." Van den Haag, who describes himself as not a "libertarian ideologue" but, rather, as "a strong political conservative," stated that his "argument for the legalization of marijuana, cocaine and heroin rests on the fact that their prohibition can be no more effective than the prohibition of alcohol." Those drugs, he asserted, "must be made as legal as alcohol is" (van den Haag, 1985).

William Buckley is another conservative who, although a one-time opponent of legalization in regard to heroin, now believes that "the accumulated evidence draws me away from my own opposition on the purely empirical grounds that what we now have is a drug problem plus a crime problem plus a problem of a huge export of capital to the dope-producing countries." Buckley also derides the possibility of making prohibition more effective: "Maybe we should breed 50 million drug-trained dogs to sniff at everyone getting off a boat or an airplane; what a great idea!" He advocates "legalization followed by a dramatic educational effort in which the services of all civic-minded, and some less than civic minded, resources are mobilized" (Buckley, 1985; p. A11).

Milton Friedman, whose opposition to drug prohibition we noted earlier, also supplemented his libertarian case against it by reference to the social costs of prohibition. He argued that even if it were ethically justified, "considerations of expediency make that policy most unwise." Prohibition, he observed, is "an attempted cure that makes matters worse – for both the addict and the rest of us." Not only are addicts driven to crime to finance their addiction, but also "the harm to us from the addiction of others arises almost wholly from the fact that drugs are illegal" (Friedman, 1987, pp. 135–6).

Those who advocate legalization tend to emphasize the social and fiscal costs of prohibition and the benefits of legalization as though legalization were, if not a wholly costless policy at least, unlikely to involve any serious costs. Friedman, for example, pointed out that "legalizing drugs might increase the number of addicts, but it is not clear that it would." And he went on to say that if controls were removed and drugs were made legally available, not only would they lose the attractiveness that "forbidden fruit" has, but also the drug pushers would be put out of business because "any possible profit from such inhumane activity would disappear" (Friedman, 1987, p. 136). The latter point was also made by another economist, Thomas Schelling, when serving as a consultant to the 1967 President's Commission on Law Enforcement and Administration of Justice: "If narcotics were not illegal, there could be no black market and no monopoly profits, and the interest in 'pushing' them would probably be not much greater than the pharmaceutical interest in pills to reduce the symptoms of common colds" (Schelling, 1967, p. 124).

One advocate of legalization who has paid more than parenthetic attention to the probable costs of that policy is Ethan Nadelmann, who acknowledged that "all the benefits of legalization would be for naught, however, if millions more Americans were to become drug abusers" (Nadelmann, 1988, p. 24). But he maintains that there are "reasons to believe that none of the current illicit substances would become as popular as alcohol or tobacco, even if they were legalized." In particular, he asserted that "none of the illicit substances can compete with alcohol's special place in American culture and history."

There is good reason to doubt that many Americans would inject cocaine or heroin into their veins even if given the chance to do so legally . . . the drugs and methods of consumption that are most risky are unlikely to prove appealing to many people, precisely because they are so obviously dangerous.

Nadelmann does not deny that legalization might lead to an increased consumption of the illicit drugs in their more benign forms. In his view, however, because in those forms they are less damaging to the human body than alcohol or tobacco and less strongly linked with violent behavior than alcohol, this does not invalidate "the logic of legalization" (Nadelmann, 1988, pp. 28–29).

For John Stuart Mill, drug prohibition represented an intolerable infringement of the moral and political principles of a free society. In our time, much greater emphasis is placed by opponents of prohibition on the social costs that such a policy is thought to entail. "Essentially," said Thomas Schelling, "the question is whether the goal of somewhat reducing the consumption of narcotics . . . or anything else that is forced by law into the black market, is or is not outweighed by the costs to society of creating a criminal industry" (Schelling, 1967, p. 125). Those who favor legalization are doubtful about the extent to which consumption of the proscribed substances would be lessened by prohibition, and they even contend that consumption of them in their more harmful forms is frequently increased. They argue also that such reduction as may be achieved is always outweighed by its social costs, including the criminalization of consumers, the corruption of law enforcement, and the increase in organized crime.

For prohibition

Section 6201 of the Anti-Drug Abuse Act of 1988 states categorically that "(1) proposals to combat sale and use of illicit drugs by legalization should be rejected; and (2) consideration should be given *only* to proposals to attack directly the supply of, and demand for, illicit drugs" (*Criminal Law Reporter*, 1988, p. 3011; emphasis added). This legislative interdiction of considering the repeal of drug prohibition laws has had little effect on either those who favor legalization or those who oppose it. In regard to those who oppose it, it is probably because those who favor the status quo – and prohibition in regard to drugs has been the status quo in America since 1914 – rarely feel the need to defend it unless it happens to be threatened, and it has never been seriously threatened.

This is certainly true at the present time when the policy of prohibition is largely unquestioned and the "war on drugs" appears to enjoy wide public support. As Ethan Nadelmann put it:

No "war" proclaimed by an American leader during the past forty years has garnered such sweeping bipartisan support; on this issue, liberals and conservatives are often indistinguishable. The fiercest disputes are not over objectives or even broad strategies, but over turf and tactics . . . on the fundamental issues of what this war is about, and what strategies are most likely to prove successful in the long run, no real debate – much less vocal dissent – can be heard.

As for legalization: "Politicians and public officials remain hesitant even to mention the word, except to dismiss it contemptuously as a capitulation to drug traffickers. Most Americans perceive drug legalization as an invitation to drug-infested anarchy. Even the civil liberties groups shy away from this issue" (Nadelmann, 1988, pp. 3–4). It may be true, as Nadelmann asserted, that there is "a significant silent constituency in favour of repeal, found especially among criminal justice officials, intelligence analysts, military interdictors, and criminal justice scholars who have spent a considerable amount of time thinking about the problem." It may also be true that for many individuals in those categories, "job-security considerations, combined with an awareness that they can do little to change official policies, ensure that their views remain discreet and off the record" (Nadelmann, 1988, pp. 4–5). Insofar as those assertions are correct, they may explain why drug prohibition laws are not seen as needing justification. Silent constituencies do not require audible responses, and off-the-record views call for no on-the-record rebuttals.

An important exception to what might otherwise almost seem to be a conspiracy of silence can be found in the writings of James Q. Wilson, who in 1972 was appointed chairman of the National Advisory Council for Drug Abuse Prevention by President Nixon, with "marching orders . . . to figure out how to win the war on heroin" (Wilson, 1990a, p. 21). Wilson specifically takes issue with advocates of legalization like Milton Friedman and Ethan Nadelmann and provides a rationale for drug prohibition and a defense of its political legitimacy. Just as those who advocate legalization emphasize the costs of prohibition, those who favor prohibition tend to stress the costs of legalization. Thus, Wilson summarized his views as follows: "I believe that the moral and welfare costs of heavy drug use are so large that society should bear the heavy burden of law enforcement, and its associated corruption and criminality, for the sake of keeping the number of people regularly using heroin and crack as small as possible" (Wilson, 1990b, p. 527).

The distinction between moral and welfare costs reflects the distinction between those libertarians who are concerned primarily with the moral costs and those who are more concerned with the economic, social, and fiscal costs of prohibition. Wilson pointed out that the costs of legalizing drugs are "difficult to measure, in part because they are to a large degree moral." His account of this aspect of drug use as a problem is in total accord with James Fitzjames Stephen's view of the proper role of the criminal law in ensuring "the suppression of vice" and "the promotion of virtue" (Stephen, 1873/ 1967, pp. 143, 150, 152). According to Wilson,

The moral reason for attempting to discourage drug use is that the heavy consumption of certain drugs is destructive of human character. These drugs – principally heroin, cocaine, and crack – are, for many people, powerfully reinforcing. The pleasure or oblivion they produce leads many users to devote their lives to seeking pleasure or oblivion and to do so almost regardless of the cost in ordinary human virtues, such as temperance, fidelity, duty, and sympathy. (Wilson, 1990b, p. 523)

Society, Wilson believes, has an "obligation to form and sustain the character of its citizenry." In regard to "libertarians [who] would leave all adults free to choose their own habits and seek their own destiny so long as their behavior did not cause any direct or palpable harm to others," Wilson maintains that "government, as the agent for society, is responsible for helping instill certain qualities in its citizens" (Wilson, 1990b, p. 524). The use of drugs can "destroy the user's essential humanity" and "corrodes those natural sentiments of sympathy and duty that constitute our human nature and make possible our social life." In short, "dependency on certain mind-altering drugs is a moral issue and their illegality rests in part on their immorality . . . legalizing them undercuts, if it does not eliminate altogether, the moral message" (Wilson, 1990a, p. 26).

One of the principal advantages "of making certain drugs illegal and enforcing the laws against their possession," according to Wilson, "is that these actions reinforce the social condemnation of drug use and the social praise accorded temperate behavior." They help "alter the moral climate so that drug use is regarded as loathsome" and help also "in shaping the ethos within which standards of personal conduct are defined" (Wilson, 1990b, pp. 542–3).

But Wilson is concerned not only with what he called "the tangible but real moral costs" (Wilson, 1990b, p. 527) of legalization but also with the social costs that he believes are underrated by those he referred to as "academic essayists and cocktail-party pundits." If the legalizers prevail,

then we will have consigned millions of people, hundreds of thousands of infants, and hundreds of neighborhoods to a life of oblivion and disease. To the lives and families destroyed by alcohol we will have added countless more destroyed by cocaine, heroin, PCP, and whatever else a basement scientist can invent. (Wilson, 1990a, p. 28)

Even if we decided that government

should only regulate behavior that hurt other people, we would still have to decide what to do about drug-dependent people because such dependency does in fact hurt other people . . . these users are not likely to be healthy people, productive workers, good parents, reliable neighbors, attentive students, or safe drivers. Moreover, some people are directly harmed by drugs that they have not freely chosen to use. The babies of drug-dependent women suffer because of their mothers' habits. We all pay for drug abuse in lowered productivity, more accidents, higher insurance premiums, bigger welfare costs, and less effective classrooms. (Wilson, 1990b, p. 524)

Apart from Wilson's essay on the subject, the strongest defense of current drug prohibition policies may be found in the Office of National Drug Control Policy's *National Drug Control Strategy*. Although possibly somewhat more strident in tone than Wilson's writing is, the rationale for prohibition provided in the latter document is essentially the same as his, and most of the differences are matters of emphasis.

The only apparent substantial disagreement relates to the effectiveness of drug prohibition as presently administered. According to Wilson, "Though drugs are sold openly on the streets of some communities, for most people they are hard to find" (Wilson, 1990b, p. 525). Whereas in the *National Drug Control Strategy* it is said that "here in the United States, in every State – in our cities, in our suburbs, in our rural communities . . . drugs are available to almost anyone who wants them" (Office of National Drug Control Policy, 1989, p. 2). But despite the disagreement about the availability of drugs and, by implication, about the current effectiveness of drug law enforcement activities, there is no dispute about the need for drug prohibition or about the nature of its justification.

Like Wilson, the authors of the *National Drug Control Strategy* see drug use as primarily "a moral problem." Although "people take drugs for many complicated reasons that we do not yet fully understand," for "most drug users" it is the result of "a human flaw" that leads them to pursue what is "a hollow, degrading and deceptive pleasure." It is necessary to take "a firm moral stand that using drugs is wrong and should be resisted." A person's "first line of defense against drugs is his own moral compass" (Office of National Drug Control Policy, 1989, pp. 9, 48, 50, 53).

Unfortunately, too many citizens appear to have defective moral compasses, and so America faces "a crisis of national character." Although "this crisis is the product of individual choices," it is not a matter that can be left to individuals, for "a purposeful, self-governing society ignores its people's character at great peril." It is necessary, therefore, for the state, by such means as "tough and coherently punitive anti-drug measures," a "significantly expanded . . . criminal justice system," and "the creation of more prison space," to ensure that "the number of Americans who still use cocaine and other illegal drugs, to the entire nation's horrible disadvantage, is . . . dramatically reduced" (Office of National Drug Control Policy, 1989, pp. 2, 7, 9, 26).

It cannot be said that the current debate about drug decriminalization has produced any particularly novel or illuminating insights into the issues of political principle or practice at stake. On the one hand, there is the libertarian's almost ritual invocation of Mill's assertion of the individual's right to do what he likes with his own body, providing that he does no harm to others. On the other hand, Stephen's assertion of the legitimacy of using the criminal law to regulate individual conduct, whether or not breaches of it cause harm to others, is re-echoed. On the conceptual level, the solution to "the drug problem" is viewed, for the most part, as a matter of choosing between diametrically opposed alternative expedients.

Specifism

A notable exception to such oversimplification may be found in the writings of John Kaplan, who recognized that whether or not John Stuart Mill's understanding of human nature was more or less accurate than that of Fitzjames Stephen or H. L. A. Hart, the fact is that the world he lived in – early nineteenth-century England – was very different from late twentieth-century America. Moreover, America in the 1990s bears little resemblance to America in the 1890s when today's illicit drugs were freely available. Thus, Kaplan made the point, in relation to the possibility of making heroin freely available, that we should hesitate "to extrapolate from our past experience in a predominantly rural, relatively crime-free, free-enterprise society to our present urban, crime-ridden, partially-welfare state." There was

no turning back the clock. If we made heroin available today, it would be made available under very different conditions, with social variables such as the purpose and meaning of use and the availability of group support all very much changed. Even the drug would be different. Before the Harrison Act, the problem was opium or morphine drunk in tonics and medicines. Today it is injectable heroin. (Kaplan, 1983, p. 112)

Kaplan regarded the rehearsal of past pieties as largely irrelevant to present problems. Mills's principle regarding self-harming conduct might have been "correct for early Victorian England," but today it was best viewed "as a very wise admonition to restraint in an exceedingly complex and emotion-laden area" (Kaplan, 1983, p. 106).

Two features distinguish Kaplan's approach to problems in the drug area from that of most other scholars. The first is his emphasis on what Herbert Packer called "the practical or 'social cost-accounting' aspects of the criminal process" (Packer, 1968, p. 266). The Kaplan analysis places special emphasis on the costs of administering a criminal prohibition. The premise of this kind of cost-accounting approach is that

every law that seeks to control human behavior entails social costs, as well as social benefits and that laws should be chosen to maximise the excess of benefits over costs. The clear implication is that, at the least, we should choose controls that entail more benefits than costs – or we should have no controls at all. (Bartels, 1973, p. 441)

Kaplan – in his first book on drug policy, in the first chapter on marijuana, which he then saw as "the key problem in the drug area" – put it as follows: "The wisdom of a law should be determined in pragmatic terms by weighing the costs it imposes upon society against the benefits it brings. The purpose of this book is to apply this principle to the laws criminalizing marijuana" (Kaplan, 1970, pp. x, 18).

This emphasis on cost–benefit analysis rather than the ideological or political aspects of drug policy is a feature of all Kaplan's writing on drugs. His book on heroin was, in his own description of it, "devoted to examination of the costs and benefits of different policies toward heroin" (Kaplan, 1983, p. 237). In his last contribution to the debate on drug policy in regard to cocaine, he stated once again that "the issue boils down to a careful weighing of the costs of criminalization of each drug against the public-health costs we could expect if that drug were to become legally available" (Kaplan, 1988, p. 37).

The reference to "the criminalization of each drug" in that passage reflects the other feature of Kaplan's analysis of the problems in a criminal justice policy toward drugs: his rejection of the idea that psychoactive drugs represented a unitary social problem to which the solution must be either prohibition or decriminalization. "Criminalization and legalization," he maintained, "are not the only possibilities." More importantly, he added that "if the choice for each of the 'recreational' drugs is between criminalization and some kind of legalization, then *it must be made on a drug-by-drug basis*" (Kaplan, 1988, pp. 35, 36; emphasis added).

Kaplan's emphasis on the specificity of the problems presented by each of the psychoactive drugs and his close attention to such variables as the singular pharmacological makeup of each of them and the costs of attempting to suppress them contrasts sharply with the approach of James Q. Wilson. Wilson sees all illicit drugs as representing an equal threat to "the moral climate" and as indistinguishable items in the total of "tangible but real moral costs" of drug use (Wilson, 1990b, pp. 527, 542).

In regard to that kind of generalization, Kaplan, in his book on marijuana, demonstrated that objective analysis led to a very different conclusion. Before becoming a professor of criminal law, he had, as an assistant U.S. attorney, prosecuted many violators of the federal drug laws. He commented that "like many Americans of my generation, I cannot escape the feeling that drug use, aside from any harm it does, is somehow wrong." He found it "easy to understand how, under the historical and social conditions present in this country at the time, the emergence of a strange intoxicant such as marijuana might have been felt to justify the official and popular apprehension it received" (Kaplan, 1970, pp. x, xi). However, in 1966 as one of the reporters to the Joint Legislative Committee to Revise the Penal Code of the State of California, Kaplan was assigned the drug laws as his first major item of concern. After reading everything available on the drug laws and the drugs themselves and discussing the relevant issues with law enforcement officials and the natural and social scientists most concerned, he decided that the only way to achieve a rational solution to the problems of drug control was to subject each drug and the relevant legislation to a separate analysis.

Alcohol prohibition, he maintained, had taught us that "a law is in essence society's purchase of a package of social effects." Whether or not the law was a wise one depended on the answers to two crucial questions: "(1) What are the total social and financial costs attributable to the law, and (2) what are the benefits that flow from this outlay?" "The important thing to note is that all laws have their costs" (Kaplan, 1970, pp. 1–2). After a detailed analysis of all the factors entering into the costs and benefits of the marijuana laws, Kaplan concluded that in this case there was "an enormous disparity between the costs and benefits of the marijuana laws" and that "the social and financial costs directly and indirectly attributable to the criminalization of marijuana far outweigh the benefits of this policy." In the circumstances, he said, "the only responsible course of action . . . is a liberalization of the marijuana law so extensive as to constitute an abandonment of primary reliance on the criminal law in this area" (Kaplan, 1970, pp. xi, 311, 374).

There are, of course, many difficulties in this kind of analysis. It is impossible to quantify with any precision the costs of criminalization, and it is no easier to predict the consequences of removing prohibitory laws in regard to illicit drugs. As Robert J. Michaels pointed out, "Anyone wishing to predict the consequences of legalized opiates must first invest in some facts . . . we clearly need numerical data about the present situation, summarized into relevant conceptual categories." But he went on to say that although all statistics are imperfect, "those related to drug use are egregiously bad." In particular,

while they are frequently circulated and quoted with alarm, figures on the number of users and the volume of crime for which they are responsible are meaningless political constructs. They are highly sensitive to the use of arbitrary assumptions and are dependent on surveys or registers whose methodology is questionable and whose coverage is poor. (Michaels, 1987, pp. 289, 290, 324–5)

In short, it seems as though none of the conditions for plausible prediction can be met, for to offer quantitative forecasts regarding the future in the absence of reliable data about the present is to infer from the unknown to the unknown. Kaplan acknowledged that "it is hard to measure with precision the costs of laws, especially the human costs" and that "aside from more or less intelligent guesses, we are usually uncertain of the benefits of laws" (Kaplan, 1970, pp. 1–2). But he did not agree that because existing estimates are unable to provide reliable quantitative predictions of the consequences of legalization, therefore nothing could be said or all conjecture must be futile. Moreover, it is significant that when Kaplan applied the same mode of analysis that he had used for marijuana to heroin and cocaine, he reached very different conclusions regarding the probable consequences of decriminalization. In regard to both heroin and cocaine he demonstrated that it is possible to show some of the likely features of a world in which those drugs were legal and freely available and, in particular, what costs such a policy might entail.

Kaplan acknowledged that as far as the free availability of heroin is concerned, "the predictions are quite uncertain and difficult." But he stated that if we are to decide the wisdom of a free availability policy, we have to "attempt to predict what our society would look like if such a policy were adopted." Accordingly, he considered "the two most relevant social variables." These, he said, were "how many people would use the drug in various use patterns, and how harmful would their use be for them and for society?" (Kaplan, 1983, pp. 111, 112).

In regard to the first of these variables, he argued that the "statement that opiate availability is a major determinant of use . . . means that within wide limits, the more available opiates are, the higher the rate of use – and of addiction." As examples of this, he cited our experience with American ground troops in Vietnam, where heroin was cheaply and easily available, and some 14 percent became addicted to the drug, with considerably more being non-addicted users. He also brought up the fact that the medical profession, which has greater access to opiates than the rest of us do, had an addiction rate estimated at about twenty times that of the general population. Moreover, he gave reasons for thinking that neither the Vietnam experience nor the extent of use among members of the medical profession "provide[s] a ceiling on the use to be expected under free availability" (Kaplan, 1983, pp. 113–14).

Kaplan agreed with Ethan Nadelmann that there seemed to be a psychological barrier against using a hypodermic needle. But he pointed out that heroin could be either smoked in cigarettes or snorted and that of the users in Vietnam, who began by smoking or sniffing the drug, a good percentage went on to intravenous use. Kaplan then quoted from a study that suggested that many young people, "sustained apparently by peer encouragement and the promise of euphoria," took their first heroin intravenously, and so the psychological barrier might not be so formidable after all. In addition, he contended that the act of making heroin legally accessible might change the message we convey about the dangers of the drug and, indeed, could be taken to indicate that it was safe enough to try. In addition to this disadvantage inherent in the repeal of any drug prohibition, he noted another consequence of free availability, that it would accustom the population to moderate users and thus weaken the incorrect but "perhaps functional" belief that heroin use leads inevitably to addiction and serious social and health consequences.

As to the likelihood of increased addiction, Kaplan maintained that there was no reason for confidence that the availability of pure, cheap heroin would not lead to sizable increases in addiction. Certainly the little evidence that existed on the use of opiates under conditions of free availability (e.g., the medical profession and the American soldiers in Vietnam) provided no support for any hope of low addiction rates. Moreover, apart from its effect of increasing addiction, free availability would be likely to make addiction longer lasting and more difficult to cure, for the most important reasons that addicts give up heroin – the trouble and expense of maintaining a "habit," the fear of legal sanctions, and the inability to obtain good heroin – would be removed (Kaplan, 1983, pp. 112–26).

With regard to the second variable, the harmfulness of the increased use of heroin both for the users and for society, little is known about the consequences of addiction under conditions of easy access and, in particular, about the long-term health consequences of heroin use. In this connection, Kaplan noted that although tobacco use is recognized today as an important cause of sickness and death, this was not recognized until investigations were carried out "far more probing than those to which chronic use of heroin has been subjected." The long-term health consequences of heroin use may well constitute a major public health problem.

In addition, there is the possibility that the free availability of heroin might produce a widespread unwillingness or inability to work. If this were the case, it is possible that the lowering of productivity and increased welfare payments resulting from the use of heroin could impose even greater social costs than do our present efforts at its suppression. There are, Kaplan contended, reasons to believe that for many people addiction would be incompatible with productive work, and "one would have to be an incurable optimist to believe that heroin could be made freely available without a considerable degree of social dislocation" (Kaplan, 1983, pp. 126–46).

Kaplan's analysis of the anticipated costs of legalizing cocaine followed the same lines as did his calculation of the costs of legalizing heroin. In the case of cocaine, however, he noted that it was "far more prevalent than heroin [and] imposes greater social costs upon us – from the amount of money flowing into criminal syndicates to the number of users arrested for predatory crimes." In addition, he noted the widely held view at that time, that cocaine was the more benign of the two drugs, which, he said, was "probably mistaken."

Kaplan offered no estimate of how many more people would use cocaine after it was legalized but pointed out that it was an extremely attractive drug with the highest "pleasure score" and greatest "reinforcing power" of any drug known to us. Although most of those who used the drug had not become dependent, this was mainly because it was both expensive and difficult to procure. But if the drug were made easily available and cheap, and the inconvenience and criminal danger to the user was removed, we should anticipate a considerable increase in the damage – psychiatric symptoms and general debilitation – brought by heavy cocaine use.

There was, moreover, a considerable problem in regard to preventing teenagers from gaining access to cocaine, for legalization would make it, de facto, available to the young, as are alcohol and tobacco. And being less bulky and more easily concealable than alcohol is and creating no aroma of smoke, cocaine would be even more difficult to keep from minors. In addition, even if it were taxed as heavily as possible, the financial costs of cocaine would be greatly curtailed by legalization. Kaplan calculated that because the cost including tax would have to be sufficiently low to make bootlegging unprofitable, the cost of one "hit" would be lowered to "only forty cents – a figure well within the budget of almost all grade-school children" (Kaplan, 1988; p. 41).

As for adults, Kaplan argued that the serious negative effects of heavy cocaine use on its users would render it extremely damaging in a complex, mechanized, and interdependent society such as ours. And there was no guarantee that legalization would not produce a fiftyfold increase in the number of those dependent on cocaine. In such circumstances, he reminded his readers that "it is the height of irresponsibility to advocate risking the future of the nation." In an ideal world it might be that the best way to mitigate the damage done by illegal drugs would be to persuade everyone not to use them, but in the real world we have to use coercion (Kaplan, 1988, pp. 36–44).

However one evaluates John Kaplan's drug-by-drug analysis and projections, the method he employed was quite different from the rhetoric on both sides of the decriminalization debate. First, the unit of analysis in Kaplan's policy universe is the single psychoactive substance. By contrast, the principal protagonists in the decriminalization debate seem to agree that the appropriate unit of analysis is the fortuitous assortment of drugs that happen to be currently prohibited. The second distinction between the specifist approach and the main part of the decriminalization debate concerns the basis for choice between policies. Kaplan's criteria for policy choice are exclusively pragmatic and can thus render those choices disconfirmable by subsequent experience. In arguing as a strict pragmatist that the prohibition of a particular drug generates more benefits than costs, whereas the prohibition of another drug does not, the specifist holds to a standard that makes predictions about cost and benefit, in principle at least, testable against historical events.

Both sides of the decriminalization debate – and the tradition extends from Mill and Stephen on through to Nadelmann and Wilson – support their preferred policies for a mixture of moral and prudent reasons that make their proposals impossible to assess objectively and virtually incontestable. If the operative costs of either policy seem too steep, its proponents can always retreat to the moral high ground. At that level the claim that "adult Americans have the right to choose what substances they will consume and what risks they will take" (Nadelmann, 1988, p. 11) is countered by the claim "that society has [an] obligation to form and sustain the character of its citizenry" (Wilson, 1990b, p. 524). And there is nothing that can count decisively against either claim.

Whether the imponderable element is the responsibility of the government for character formation or the freedom of adults to choose their own habits and seek their own destiny, the admixture of those elements with others that are at least in principle measurable renders the claims of both parties logically unassailable. In this respect the prohibitionist and the libertarian are closer to common ground with each other than either of them is to the specifist. So it is possible to read the specifist analysis of drug policy as an implicit critique of both sides in the decriminalization debate, a critique that we shall seek to extend in the next two sections.

III.   The clash of presumptions

Although the contending parties in the decriminalization debate disagree on a number of factual issues, the debate itself is not centered on factual matters. What fundamentally divides the disputants is the contrast between them in regard to assumptions about what kind of policy should be preferred when only incomplete information is available.

Those on John Stuart Mill's side in the debate hold to a presumption of liberty. They claim that in regard to drugs and drug control – about which knowledge is limited and the outcomes of policy options cannot be predicted with any certainty – it is prudent to choose the course of conduct that maximizes individual liberty and freedom of choice. They assume that adults are capable of making up their own minds rationally and that rates of drug addiction are unlikely to soar if decriminalization is put into effect. They assume also that the interests of children are unlikely to be irredeemably compromised by the abandonment of drug prohibitions.

The contrary presumption associated with those who support drug prohibition is not so much a presumption in favor of authority or social control but more a presumption in favor of social continuity and adherence to established customs and institutions. As Edmund Burke put it, "It is a presumption in favour of any settled scheme of government against any untried project" (Burke, 1803/1890, p. 146). We know of no one who has argued that in the absence of perfect knowledge, all psychoactive substances should be proscribed. Instead, the prohibitionists discuss the risks of decriminalization in ways that suggest that in the absence of any definitive proof to the contrary, it is prudent to preserve and maintain the governmental policies that have been developed and not to subject them to innovative change and thereby disturb a settled traditional scheme of things.

Adherence to the presumption of continuity means opposition to the decriminalization of any currently prohibited substance. But it does not afford support for initiatives directed at restricting the availability of drugs that are currently not prohibited. In the absence of complete information, it is considered prudent to maintain, for instance, the prohibition of marijuana. But the presumption in favor of social continuity provides no reason for imposing restrictions on substances like alcohol and tobacco, the sale and consumption of which are currently permitted. Those who accuse prohibitionists of being inconsistent in their attitudes toward alcohol and other psychoactive drugs fail to recognize the underlying consistency implicit in a preference for the status quo that is the fundamental basis of the prohibitionist position.

Recognition that the prohibitionist side of the decriminalization debate is grounded in a presumption in favor of continuity renders intelligible the limited scope of the prohibitionist case in regard to psychoactive drugs. Even as they recognize the damage done by alcohol, none of the prohibitionist spokespersons in the modern era see this as an argument for prohibiting alcohol. Instead, they contend that things would get even worse if yet more substances were added to the list of currently available psychoactive drugs; this point was made in James Q. Wilson's earlier cited admonition that legalization would mean that "to the lives and families destroyed by alcohol we will have added countless more destroyed by cocaine, heroin, PCP, and whatever else a basement scientist can invent" (Wilson, 1990a, p. 28).

Both the presumption in favor of liberty and the presumption in favor of continuity have deep roots in American culture. The sentimental enshrinement of personal liberty is reflected in all facets of American life, from the Declaration of Independence to much popular music. And the preference for preserving the status quo, and for known evils over those unknown, is reflected in such popular slogans as "if it ain't broke don't fix it" and "why trade a headache for an upset stomach."

The debate on drug decriminalization is a tug-of-war between these two powerful sentimental forces, with the presumption in favor of liberty invoked in support of removing criminal sanctions on drugs and the preference for continuity providing support for the current categorization of licit and illicit substances. This clash of presumptions in regard to drug decriminalization differs from arguments concerning alcohol prohibition because in the case of that "noble experiment" (Fisher, 1930), the prohibition involved never achieved the tenure and consequent venerability that could have led people to see it as a stable and continuous feature of an historically evolved, established tradition.

The need to choose between the presumptions of liberty and continuity creates some strange crosscuts in customary political alignments in the United States. Both William Buckley and William Bennett are identified as staunch political conservatives. Yet in the current decriminalization debate they are diametrically opposed to each other. This contraposition, however, is readily intelligible in terms of Buckley's preference for the presumption of liberty and in Bennett's preference for the presumption of continuity.

The conservative political tradition in the United States is unique in that it combines both libertarian and continuative principles or presumptions. But these presumptions are not invariably consonant, and so a potential for divisiveness in the conservative ranks is always present. Nor are political liberals immune to dissension in the drug decriminalization debate. The mainstream liberal tradition in American politics incorporates both a reverence for established customs and institutions and a powerful attachment to libertarian principles. In arguing that this clash of presumptions is the subtext in the decriminalization debate, we do not suggest that the combatants themselves would use this vocabulary to describe their differences or to explain what animates their disagreement. But it seems to us that an explanation in these terms is consistent with the positions adopted by both parties to the debate. At the same time it renders intelligible the somewhat incongruous assortments of political bedfellows that have emerged as public spokespersons for both decriminalization and prohibition.

IV. The wrong question

The debate about drug decriminalization is lively and educational, but it threatens to become a distraction when decriminalization becomes the focus of a discussion of drug control policy. As a policy centerpiece, the decriminalization debates are flawed because they pose the wrong central question and because they use inappropriate methods to identify and resolve priority problems in drug control policies.

From John Stuart Mill to the morning newspaper, the decriminalization debate is about whether or not the criminal law should be a major element in the government's efforts to control drugs. Yet a world in which the administration of the criminal law and governmental efforts to control drugs inhabit totally different policy spheres is not only unprecedented but also unimaginable. The key question is not whether criminal law should play a significant role in the control of drug behavior but how a criminal law of drug control should be constructed. In making this assertion, we do not take sides in the decriminalization debate: The criminal law of drug control would be substantial and multifaceted in the United States even if the decriminalization movement carried the day.

Even if the substantive goals of decriminalization could be achieved, the strong likelihood is that efforts at decriminalization would come by amending rather than repealing criminal laws and leaving the formal structure of prohibition intact. We need look no further than the more than a dozen experiments with marijuana in the American states and in Canada to discern a common pattern of reducing rather than abolishing penalties for possession of small quantities for personal use. This is the functional form of steps toward decriminalization for both symbolic and practical reasons. Retention of the criminal sanction not only pays lip service to the tradition of prohibition, but it also allows some selective enforcement of the laws against suspected traffickers, as well as a continued police enforcement presence.

Further, the administrative burden of decriminalization tends to increase the number and complexity of criminal law controls in drug markets. Reducing the criminal penalties for using drugs generally does not mean withdrawing substantial penalties for drug trafficking in the same substances. Even with formal decriminalization, the tax and administrative regulations that come with the change in the status of substances increase the criminal law controls. The most famous example of this was the aftermath of the repeal of alcohol prohibition in 1933. Within three years, the number of people in federal prisons, for violating the tax laws and other administrative regulations produced in the post-Prohibition period, was nearly equal to that serving sentences for violating the Prohibition regulations just before its repeal. In his 1934–5 report, the director of the Federal Bureau of Prisons spoke of the failure of the repeal of Prohibition to reduce the number of liquor violators, remarking that "penitentiary commitments for liquor are substantially the same as they were during Prohibition days" (U.S. Department of Justice, Bureau of Prisons, 1936, pp. 1–3).

The likelihood that criminal prohibition would remain on the books for drugs historically treated by such prohibitions would mean that these drugs would generate even more business for the criminal law even as reliance on prohibition was de-emphasized. In his statement of the case for "the repeal of drug prohibition laws," Ethan Nadelmann made it clear that it is not "a call for the elimination of the criminal justice system from drug regulation." An "effective plan for legalization" would involve not only "consumption taxes" but also "restrictions on time and place of sale, prohibition on consumption in public places, packaging requirements, mandated adjustments in insurance policies, crackdowns on driving under the influence" (Nadelmann, 1988, p. 30). In addition to taxes and administrative controls, any regime of decriminalization would include the prohibition of drug use for minors and significant criminal penalties for those who supply minors. So, no matter how far toward an emphasis on regulatory and taxing controls the law might push, the residual role for the criminal law would be substantial.

Further, if there are behavioral links between drug use and predatory criminal activity, these linkages must be addressed within the criminal law and the correctional system, no matter what the formal status of the substances themselves. Whether and to what extent the number of drug users sent to our prisons would be decreased by various regimes of decriminalization is an empirical question not yet able to be answered. If alcohol can be considered a precedent, the link between serious drug abuse and the prison system would remain strong.

But what kind of criminal law of drug control? Where should drug control rank among the many other responsibilities of the criminal justice system? Which drugs and which strategies of enforcement of the criminal law should receive priority? These are the questions that by its terms the decriminalization debate does not address, and they are also among the most important issues that policy planners must confront.

The "trickle-down" fallacy

The broad strokes of the decriminalization debate are just as troublesome to us as is the fact that the wrong central question is addressed. Both sides in that debate assume the correctness of what we shall call "trickle-down" policy determinations, a process in which people assume that details such as strategies of law enforcement and levels of resource allocation will be worked out as a matter of course once the large and general questions have been settled. The propensity to avoid questions of detail is the major intellectual vice of the decriminalization debaters.

General conclusions about whether criminal prohibitions should be maintained provide very little guidance to how drug policy should be conducted, because we live in a world where drug control competes with many other problems for public resources, where many different substances are subject to prohibition and thus compete with one another for antidrug resources, where many different methods of combating drugs are alternative candidates for funds, and where the single-umbrella term *prohibition* describes a range of public policies that vary from the passive toleration of marijuana in many states to high-intensity police activity in anticrack and antiheroin campaigns elsewhere.

What we call the trickle-down fallacy has been the particular vice in recent years of those who maintain that for many drugs, criminal prohibitions should be continued. Many prohibitionists simply ignore the detailed questions of enforcement priority and strategy. For these participants, inattention to the particulars of policy is a sin of omission, regrettable because the general propositions of the debate on decriminalization are the only topics considered. But there are also prohibitionists who seem to argue that the conclusion that drugs should be prohibited can translate into specific policy choices. For these actors, the trickle-down fallacy is a sin of commission.

Illustrations of why specific policy cannot be deduced from a prohibitionist stance are not hard to find. First, there are many claims for police, court, and prison resources, and so drug control must compete with other social problems that also have been deemed worthy of criminal prohibition. Should the marginal dollar or prison cell go to an antidrug campaign this year, to child sex abuse, or to convenience-store robbery?

Second, certain drugs must compete with other drugs for enforcement resources. Should the new task force emphasize marijuana or crack cocaine? To spread the available resources evenly across all prohibited drugs requires the agreement that all drugs are equally deserving of criminal prohibition, and this is not a popular sentiment.

There is a third reason that drug control policy cannot be deduced from a prohibitionist stance. Many different drug control strategies compete with one another as alternative means of achieving the objectives of antidrug campaigns. Simply because heroin qualifies for the use of the criminal prohibition, this does not mean that an extra police officer is the best method available for spending $50,000 in public funds to combat heroin dependence. Prohibition means that police and methadone maintenance can compete for antiheroin resources, but it does not mean that the police have a preferred position in that competition.

Those who propose decriminalization have also ignored issues of detail, but their failure is somewhat more understandable in that they are advocating a radical structural change in the status quo. Still, as the history of alcohol control has shown, decriminalization does not make drugs a less compelling subject for government attention and resources. And the history of tobacco has shown us the importance of governmental choice and the complexity of the choice process even when criminal prohibition is absent. Thus, decriminalization may be part of a drug control policy, but it cannot be the whole of drug policy.

If we are correct in arguing that the particulars of governmental drug policy cannot simply trickle down from broad generalizations about the use of the criminal sanctions, where should drug policy guidance come from? The second part of this book is an argument for (and application of) what we shall be calling a "trickle-up" policy process, in which specific readings on the problems posed by particular substances, and experience with the effectiveness of different drug control strategies, feed into a larger policy-planning process. Ours is a preference for an explicit trial-and-error method. In this process, the debate over decriminalization is something of a preliminary to the choice of specific policies. As long as the dialogue about the wisdom of prohibition complements rather than displaces the policy-planning process, the public interest can be served.

PART TWO

The drug control policy process

Introduction

What we call trickle-down processes of determining drug policy are unsatisfactory, for two reasons. First, any policy position that can be deduced from sweeping principles is probably itself too broad to serve the public interest efficiently. Second, policy choices usually cannot be inferred at all from broad attitudes toward illicit drugs. Policy choice in drug control is a matter of providing answers to questions like: How many government resources should we devote to drug control rather than other pressing societal problems? Which drugs should be the priority focus of government programs? What specific deleterious consequences of drug use should treatment and prevention programs regard as special priorities for prevention and treatment? What mechanisms should we choose to reduce the supply of illicit drugs? These are questions of means as well as ends, specific choices that force us to identify those aspects of drug use that we regard as particularly problematic.

The right kind of drug policies should be built from the ground up, based on a determination of priority problems. The materials presented in this part of the book have been organized in accordance with this view of the policy process. Chapters 5 and 6 address what are regarded as the two most important problems associated with illicit drug taking: child endangerment and predatory crime. Each chapter assesses what is known about the nature of the problem and the implications of current knowledge for specific patterns of drug policy.

The analysis in Chapter 7 of the governmental organization of drug control continues our preference for discussing specific aspects of policy analysis. We explore the connection between the choice of a particular branch and level of government to put in charge of making drug policy and the sort of policy that is likely to emerge. Often we find that the influence of the particular office on the substance of policy can be so strong that it appears that the medium is the message.

The first three chapters in this section attempt to disaggregate drug policies into their separate strands: concerns about child welfare, crime prevention,

and government organization. Chapter 8 seeks to weave some of these separate strands into a more coherent national drug control strategy for the 1990s.
Framed as a memorandum to a new drug czar, this chapter suggests five
shifts in organization and orientation that will facilitate rational choice in
drug control policy.

5

The universal proposition: Children and drug control policy

If there is a universal proposition that is accepted by all parties to the debate on drugs, it is that children and youth should not have unregulated access to potentially harmful psychoactive substances. Even the most ardent libertarians assent to this. There is agreement not only on the direction of drug policy toward the young but also on the priority among all other goals of drug policy that should be accorded to the protection of children and youth. No commentator questions the high, if not dominant, status of child protection. This unanimity extends far beyond the speeches of politicians, being apparent as well in the most substantial works currently available dealing with the drug problem.

There are three reasons that child protection is an especially important aspect of drug control policy: the significance of children as a social resource, many children's lack of capacity for mature decision making, and the difficulty of reversing drug dependencies and habits acquired by children and youth.

Across all areas of public policy, child development is important because children represent the generation that will succeed contemporary adults. The young are also regarded as both immature and vulnerable. As we shall see in the next section, if the lack of capacity for decision making is used to justify paternalistic state drug policies, this absence also calls for a larger investment of resources. Because the young are judged incapable of mature and well-considered decision making, larger amounts of resources should be invested in treatment and prevention programs for this especially vulnerable group.

Drug habits acquired in youth have a tendency to bedevil both the habitués and their society for many years thereafter. With respect to licit drugs, it is noteworthy that most adult cigarette smokers acquired the habit as adolescents and that most of them later regret it (Zimring, 1982, p. 137). With respect to illicit drugs, an early-age onset of an illicit drug habit is associated with longer and more serious problems of abuse and higher rates of criminal behavior (Greenwood, 1982, p. 105). The long and costly half-life of drug habits acquired in youth thus provides yet another justification for giving the protection of the young a high priority in drug control policy.

But how should we protect children and youth? In the first section of this chapter we shall first examine the jurisprudential basis for treating separately the access of young persons to psychoactive substances. Section II then discusses the variety of possible legal approaches to restricting young persons' access to drugs. Section III addresses the problems encountered when determining penalties for young drug offenders. Section IV contrasts the basic strategies of prevention and treatment for reducing the costs of drug abuse among the young, and also the ways in which the two strategies may provide conflicting guides to youth drug policy choices.

I. The rationale for child protection

In one sense the prohibition of mood-altering substances to children and youth is not only universal across jurisdictions but also consistent across substances, as almost all mood-altering substances are covered by prohibition. Unlike the crazy-quilt pattern that applies to adults in Western industrial countries, any substance recognized as a recreational drug in a culture is likely to be prohibited to children and youth. The justification for imposing a total prohibition on the young derives from concern about immaturity and its effects on the capacity to make intelligent decisions about drug use.

Recognition of the necessity for protecting the young from the consequences of their own decisions is a relatively recent development. When John Ruskin asserted in 1851 that it was "indisputable" that the first duty of a state was to ensure the well-being of every child born therein "till it attain years of discretion" (Ruskin, 1851/1874, p. 815), it was in fact neither indisputable nor widely accepted. But the way in which children in the nineteenth century, "a powerless minority, exploited and then cast aside, came to enjoy schooling and the protection of effective, enforced legislation by the end of the century" has been well documented (Jordan, 1987, p. xiii; see also Zelizer, 1985).

Less well documented is how children's protection from neglect, injury, and exploitation by others was extended to include protection from potential harms arising from their own choices and actions, although it is evidently related to what has been called "the discovery of childhood," with "incompetence" as its "distinguishing feature" (Skolnick, 1975, pp. 38, 64–67). When at the end of the nineteenth century a law was passed in England "prohibiting the sale of liquor to children for consumption on the premises," according to Sydney and Beatrice Webb, it represented "an entirely new departure" (Webb and Webb, 1903, p. 144). In America, too, "youthful drinking during most of the nineteenth century was not selected as a special problem in need of special legal attention." And when at the end of the century, as in England, restrictions were introduced, "this state intrusion on childhood decisions was a major break with the past" (Mosher, 1980, pp. 16, 19).

But the classic statement of justification for this form of child protection may be found in John Stuart Mill's essay *On Liberty*, in which he qualifies his doctrine that "over himself, over his own body and mind, the individual is sovereign" by adding that

it is perhaps, hardly necessary to say that this doctrine is meant to apply only to human beings in the maturity of their faculties. We are not speaking of children, or of young persons below the age which the law may fix as that of manhood or womanhood. Those who are still in a state to require being taken care of by others, must be protected against their own actions as well as external injury. (Mill, 1859/1910, p. 11)

More recently, the first report for the National Commission on Marijuana and Drug Abuse stated: "We think *all* drug use should continue to be discouraged among the young, because of possible adverse effects on psychological development and because of *the lesser ability of this part of the population to discriminate between limited and excessive use*" (National Commission, 1972, p. 136; emphasis added).The special status of children and youth in drug policy is not only uncontested in the literature on drug policy; it is also unexamined. Little has been written on the topic by either academics or policy analysts, yet there is much to be explored on this topic beyond noting the limited capacities of children and youth.

Although some general reservations about the judgment of young people can justify the prohibition of all drug use, there is a significant difference, for example, between the rationale for prohibiting to children what is also prohibited to adults and the attempt to limit the access of the young to mood-altering substances that are recreationally available to adults. To deny children's access to drugs that are also prohibited to adults does not require any special judgment about childhood incapacity. A criminal law against drug use reflects a social judgment that all potential users are at risk of making unsound decisions about drug use. A social judgment requiring general prohibition may also express a social judgment that the use of a particular substance is morally wrong (Office of National Drug Control Policy, 1989, p. 53).

When, on the other hand, access to a substance is prohibited for the young but permitted for adults, it is only a special judgment about the incapacity of the young that can justify the partial prohibition. The restricted access of the young to substances such as tobacco and alcohol gives rise to what are defined in law as "status offenses": conduct that is contrary to law only because of the age of the person committing it (Zimring, 1982, pp. 69–76). By contrast, prohibiting a child from using drugs not available to adults is analogous to special policies regarding a wide variety of crimes committed by young of- fenders, in that moral condemnation of the offense may be outweighed by our need to protect the young offender. But the wrongfulness of the conduct may nonetheless be the basis for punishing the young offender.

The distinction between status offenses and general prohibitions has both moral and social dimensions. Drinking and tobacco smoking by the young are much easier to regard as inappropriate behavior than as morally wrong, because the same behavior is permitted for adults. Even though the use of such substances by the young may be more dangerous than parallel drug use by adults, it is difficult to condemn such acts as intrinsically immoral or to attach punishments to them that convey high levels of stigma. With respect to generally prohibited substances, it is easier to portray what would be wrongful drug use by adults as also morally wrong when performed by mi- nors. Yet the very conception of immaturity that justifies special age-specific prohibition for some drugs should also mitigate the moral turpitude of those young people using generally prohibited drugs. The same concept of imma- turity that justifies special age-specific prohibitions also can provide a defense against full responsibility, and it supports lower levels of condemnation and punishment for those young persons using generally prohibited substances (Zimring, 1978, pp. 80–1).

There is also a social distinction between the use of drugs only selectively prohibited to the young and the violation of general drug prohibitions. That is, we might regard a young person smoking or using alcohol before the age of majority as trying to assume adult privileges prematurely, but it would be difficult to interpret such behavior as an act of rebellion against the estab- lished social order. The recreational use of tobacco and alcohol is usually an imitation or rehearsal of adult roles in society rather than a rejection of social behavioral norms, and acts that children perform in this imitative manner are frequently viewed as such by their elders. Johnny is seen as merely demon- strating that he is "a chip off the old block" when drinking with high school friends. The fact that he is doing so before entitlement may merely reinforce the view that his behavior is "just like his father's."

By contrast, when young people use drugs that are prohibited to their elders, such behavior can more easily be seen by them and their parents as acts of rebelliousness and rejection. To the extent that rejecting adult norms is part of the appeal of some generally prohibited drugs, decriminalization may diminish that appeal. Thus, the general availability of a substance like marijuana under a regime of partial decriminalization may deprive that drug of one aspect of its attractiveness to some young user groups (Morris and Hawkins, 1970, p. 10).

The moral distinction between general and age-specific prohibitions operates principally as a restraint on the penal measures that should be seen as justified in responding to drug use by the young. The difference in the social significance of generally prohibited drug use by the young, as opposed to the imitative use of drugs permitted to adults, is considerable. And it predicts very different climates of social acceptance and generational conflict with respect to use by young persons of drugs classified as illegal for all age groups.

After reviewing the mechanisms available to restrict drug use by the young in the next section, we shall return to this distinction in Section III when discussing appropriate social controls for young drug users.

II. Some strategies of child protection

Prohibition

Although all drugs are prohibited to children, the techniques used to enforce this prohibition vary. One significant distinction is that between child protection policies in which substances are available for adult consumption and policies for child protection in regard to substances that are prohibited to adults. The range of child protection policies available for segregating children from patterns of adult use is much wider than that of special policies invoked for generally prohibited substances. But the prospects for enforcing child protection are probably better when general prohibition is in force.

Most special regimes of child protection and regulation are not available when a substance is the subject of general prohibition, because the fine-tuning of regulation is not available as an overlay to criminal prohibition. Thus there are special structures available in Western countries to deny access to alcohol and drugs for children, and bureaus have been dedicated to enforcing that restriction in the case of alcohol. Yet there is no special enforcement bureau dedicated to denying children access to heroin, crack cocaine, or marijuana. That is not to say that the government has been more successful in denying access to children of those substances available to adults. Indeed, the reverse is usually the case. One of the most powerful arguments for general prohibition is that it is a more effective way of denying access to children and the immature than are any special child protection policies in the context of general availability (Kaplan, 1988, p. 39; Wilson, 1990a, pp. 22, 26). This argument that the best way to protect children is to deny everyone access to substances – which we shall call the "bootstrap" argument for prohibition – is frequently made to justify the continued prohibition of some substances currently not generally available (e.g., marijuana). The bootstrap argument is less frequently and less forcefully advanced as a ground for the criminalization of currently generally available substances, although it would seem to apply with equal force.

Spillover enforcement. But whatever the aggregate effect of general prohibition is on children's access to prohibited substances, the basic strategy of child protection is one – which we shall call "spillover" – in which the basic mechanisms that restrict availability to children and youth are the same as those put in place to enforce general prohibition. There is far less specialization possible in a regime based on criminal law prohibition, and frequently there is less special emphasis on child and youth protection even in the wake of partial decriminalization.

To the extent that prohibition policies make drugs more difficult or more expensive for adults to acquire, the same policies will mean that young persons will encounter a prohibited drug less often and will often be unable to afford to purchase it even when a source is located. This is a "spillover" tactic, in that child prevention is achieved as a by-product of creating a broader pattern of scarcity. Thus, not only is the basic child protection strategy of marijuana prohibition a spillover strategy, but it is usually the case when there is partial decriminalization for adults – so that the possession of small amounts of marijuana is subject only to small fines – that these partially decriminalized regimes also make no special regulatory provisions for children or youth. The alcoholic beverage control regime in the state of California employs a small army of enforcement officers whose job is to reduce minors' access to alcohol. But in the wake of California's partial decriminalization of marijuana in 1976 there has been no parallel enforcement group in the police or anywhere else.

Special rules and penalties. The only specific legal attempts to supplement the spillover strategy for children are those enhancing the penalties for narcotic sales to children or in special child protection zones, such as areas in proximity to schools (e.g., N.J. Stat. Ann. §2C: 35-7 [West Supp. 1989] New Jersey; Ill. Ann. Stat. ch. 56½, para. 1407[b][1] [Smith-Hurd Supp. 1989] Illinois; Ind. Code Ann. §35-48-4-1, 2 [Burns Supp. 1989] Indiana; Fla. Stat. Ann. §893.13[1][e] [West 1987] Florida; and Utah Code Ann. §58-37-8[1][a][ii] [Supp. 1986] Utah). Such penalty enhancement provisions, which occasionally have gone as far as the death penalty in some American states, are usually added to penal law provisions governing the most seriously regarded drugs, such as heroin and cocaine, rather than introduced for marginally penalized drugs at the shallow end of criminal prohibition or in the transition between criminal prohibition and decriminalization. Although the impact of softening criminal prohibitions on availability to children is mentioned in policy debates, usually no special provisions for child protection accompany the steps toward decriminalization.

Regulation

A larger number of devices are available for restricting the access of children to generally available substances, but the aggregate impact of the segregation mechanisms is smaller in most cases than is the force of general prohibition. Among the mechanisms that can be used to restrict the access of the young to generally available drugs are sales and distribution barriers, the zoning restriction of drug use, identification systems that reveal whether an individual has recently used drugs, and regimes designed to channel and moderate drug use through supervision rather than prohibition.

Sale and distribution barriers. By far the most frequently used mechanisms to deny generally available drugs to young persons are restrictions on their sale and distribution to minors: laws that prohibit selling or giving tobacco or alcohol to young persons and make it a criminal offense for minors to obtain or possess such substances. In extreme instances, all adults have virtually unregulated access to psychoactive substances, whereas minors are forbidden both to possess and to receive generally available substances. This pure form of age-specific prohibition is extremely limited in its effectiveness when adult access is unregulated and the substance in question is common and inexpensive. For example, about 680 billion cigarettes are consumed in the United States every year (U.S. Bureau, 1989) and are freely dispensed in machines and sold to adults in large quantities, for which the individual purchaser is not made accountable. Under such circumstances, it would be astonishing if middle and older adolescents had any difficulty at all obtaining cigarettes in large quantities. In these conditions, the legal policy toward adolescent smoking is a hostage to public policy dictating the free availability of tobacco to adults.

This case study of tobacco is not evidence that all sale and distribution restrictions are similarly futile. When a substance is more expensive, when adult access is also regulated to some degree, when adults are held accountable for possessing large supplies, and when substances are not in common use, then distribution policies that attempt to restrict selectively the access to the young may be more effective.

Expense and a slightly more onerous regulation of adult consumption make alcoholic beverages somewhat more difficult than is tobacco for children to obtain outside their own homes. Restriction and accountability provisions imposed in the United States on the sale of prescription drugs make them difficult for minors to obtain in large quantities. There is irony in the fact that prescription drugs of abuse may be less easily obtained in quantity by children in cities than are illicit drugs that have major supply channels in urban areas. Firearms, which are both costly and subject to some degree of access regulation for adults, are probably less available to adolescent offenders than to adult offenders, if the lower level of gun usage by younger violent offenders is reliable evidence of lesser availability (Zimring, 1984, pp. 308–9).

Not only do sale and distribution restrictions work better for some commodities than others, but it also is easier to restrict supplies to children and younger adolescents than it is to minors approaching the adult age boundary of drug use. Persons just over the age boundary of, for example, alcohol use, are frequently socially involved with persons somewhat younger than themselves. In this context it has been said that privileges leak downward from the age boundary of formal prohibitions – say twenty-one – to younger age groups, for which friendship and dating behavior patterns mean that what is not legally available is in fact practically available to eighteen- and nineteen-year-old friends and associates (Zimring, 1982, pp. 109–10, 129–30). However, the restriction to age twenty-one may still be effective in denying access to younger children who lack peer relationships with young adults or do not themselves look adult enough to buy commodities restricted to adults. Younger minors also rarely have enough money to buy from black or gray market sources of expensive adult-restricted commodities.

Two general policy implications of these factors deserve separate mention. First, if immaturity alone is the ground for child protection, the more substantial impact of such prohibitions on availability to younger age groups would seem consistent with greater policy priority being given to protect the most immature. On the other hand, to the extent that older children have access to other privileges that make them more dangerous (e.g., automobile drivers' licenses), the diminished effectiveness of age-specific prohibitions on older minors may make such regimes least effective when they are most necessary. On the ground of maturity of judgment alone, the law should place greater value on keeping alcohol out of the hands of eleven-year-olds rather than their seventeen-year-old siblings. But the fact that only the seventeen-year-olds are driving makes the lesser effect of age restrictions in older teenagers a matter of concern.

The second policy point that needs to be emphasized is that the age structure of the availability of substances sold to adults depends to some extent on legal standards, but the differential availability of illicit substances should not reflect any distinctions in the formal law, thus constituting a special application of the aphorism that "it is impossible to regulate behavior that is prohibited" (Morris and Hawkins, 1977, p. 21). The raising or lowering of the age boundaries decreed for nonprohibited substances can have measurable effects on the availability of substances to mid-adolescents (Williams et al., 1975). Legal distinctions do not have such impact on the availability of generally prohibited substances to adolescents. It may be that the greater mobility, independence, and economic power of older adolescents make it easier for them to obtain generally prohibited substances. But there is no reason to expect the law to be able to fine-tune availability by age.

Zoning. It would not stretch the truth about current regulation by zoning to say that although there is a considerable capacity to keep underage persons out of taverns and bars, it is still not possible to limit the capacity of youths to possess and consume liquor. This contrast in the efficacy of two forms of regulation serves to introduce the concept of zoning restrictions and to explain why such restrictions have a limited impact on contemporary American life.

Regulations that are designed to keep young persons out of taverns are a form of use zoning. Specific premises are defined, solely or principally, in terms of the consumption of beer and alcohol on the premises, and the admittance of or service to minors is prohibited. Those who manage such premises are made responsible for screening out the young, and they stand to lose an extremely valuable privilege if detected to be in noncompliance.

This system works much more effectively in keeping minors from drinking in bars than in keeping minors from drinking alcohol, as beverage alcohol in large quantities is available in package stores and can be freely purchased by age-eligible individuals for redistribution to the young. As soon as channels of distribution include large numbers of people without special economic incentives to observe regulations, the capacity of the system to restrict the availability of substances is sharply curtailed. We suspect that bar drinking is a relatively small fraction of the total amount of underage drinking in the United States. But the potential significance of use zoning as a drug control strategy is much greater in systems and cultures in which access to and the use of substances is restricted to special zones. If alcohol were available only in taverns, the restriction on underage drinking would be much easier to enforce.

For cultural as well as legal reasons, drug use in a number of societies is administered by specialized agents in restricted zones. A familiar example of this is the smoking house, or "opium den," that was a recurrent feature of Chinese and East Indian cultures and of enclaves of Chinese immigrants, as in London and San Francisco in the late nineteenth century and in other cities throughout the world (Blum, 1969a; Scott, 1969). If the only place to obtain and consume opium is an opium den, restricting access to adults (and male adults at that) is an effective means of restricting the availability of the drug, as long as all that is obtained on the premises must also be consumed there. A similar system of use zoning has been used in methadone maintenance programs and clinics in the United States and in heroin maintenance programs in Great Britain (Trebach, 1982).

If drug consumption can be concentrated in high-visibility, public use premises, the prospects for reducing their access to children and youth will be much brighter. The restriction of a particular drug to such public use opportunities will always generate some pressure for a black market to supply excluded classes of users and to provide opportunities for private use where dosage and social interaction are not subject to public scrutiny. But if a majority of the total market for drug use is allowed into use zones, and the price differential between public use zones and private sources and venues is substantial, then such a policy may pay significant dividends in return for the lesser availability of regulated substances to prohibited classes of users and for the diminished use by the young.

Two aspects of the United States' social context militate against effective regimes of use zoning. First, American society is the world capital of home entertainment: For example, music, videotapes, and psychoactive recreational drugs all are available for domestic consumption. If the shrinking black market demand for a particular drug depends on channeling a critical mass of adult demand for that drug into publicly regulated locales, America may well prove resistant to a public use monopoly of drugs.

A second obstacle to effective regimes of use zoning in America is that many drugs of principally counterculture appeal target young people, who would be prohibited from zoned use, as the majority of their market. Creating environments of approved marijuana use for persons over twenty-one years of age would leave a very large part of the total demand in the black market channels, where it now resides. Rates of illegal use would remain high, and whatever moral force might at one time have animated general prohibition would seem even more attenuated.

This is not to say that zonal restrictions would necessarily be ineffective for a new drug that now lacks established channels of use. Also, for the regulation of drug use in institutional settings, use zoning is a before-the-fact control that is usually more effective than sale and distribution restrictions are.

User identification. The evolving technology of urine, blood, and tissue sample testing has created an after-the-fact identification of drug users that can be employed to monitor patterns of drug use, to screen out young persons at risk, or to follow those previously identified as being at high risk. Table 5.1 provides data on the cost and use period that can be detected and the substance analyzed for the most widely used drug tests.

Table 5.1. *Current technologies and cost of drug testing (urine specimens)*

Substance	Duration of detectability after last use[a]	Approximate cost of least expensive test[b]
Heroin (opiates)	1–3 days	$10
Cocaine	2–5 days	$10
Alcohol	½–1 day	$10
Marijuana (cannabis)	2–21 days[c]	$10[d]

[a] Miike and Hewitt, 1988, pp. 641–82: For blood drug tests, "approximate detectable time" is usually "a matter of hours." Also, except for alcohol, correlations between blood drug levels and degrees of impairment are poor.
[b] Compare McBay, 1987, pp. 647–52: "Large numbers of [urine] specimens can be screened for a very limited number of drugs" for between $10 and $25 (each). Confirmatory tests cost two to five times more.
[c] Dubowski, 1987, p. 530.
[d] Hudner, 1987, pp. 553–62: The EMIT test, produced by Syva Corp. of Palo Alto, CA, versus $60 to $100 for "more sophisticated testing."

Although drug testing is a technique that can be used to identify and monitor drug users of all ages, the capacity to obtain chemical evidence of drug use creates a distinctive method of screening and surveillance that can be used to keep young persons from psychoactive substances available to their elders.

Aside from the cost, inconvenience, and technical limitations of testing procedures (and those limitations seem to be responding to rapid technological progress), there are two inherent limitations to drug testing as an age-segregating mechanism. First, identification and surveillance systems do not make drugs more difficult to obtain. That is, aside from the deterrent impact of the prospect of drug testing, identification systems cannot perform a preventive function. They can operate only in a preventive way by also intervening in the lives of identified users in other ways designed to make drug taking more difficult and more risky. Thus, even if testing were not costly and intrusive standing alone, a system designed to use test results for prevention would have to adopt expensive and intrusive adjunctive means in order to achieve that aim. It is only to the extent that fear of detection operates as a preventive that a testing program or regime has any independent preventive force.

The second limitation associated with the after-the-fact character of chemical tests relates to the limited conclusions that such tests can support (Dubowski, 1987, pp. 526–28). A test can provide evidence that at some time in the past a particular substance was present in an individual's system in nontrivial amounts. It thus can demonstrate the status of a person as a past drug user. It cannot necessarily show that the individual was impaired by use either at some point in the past or under the drug's influence at any time proximate to the test. Only under a control system that defines any use whatsoever of a particular drug as sufficient to justify intervention would the current available testing procedures provide the necessary justification.

In part because of these limitations, there are more proposals for intervening in the lives of young persons in the form of drug testing for generally prohibited drugs, ranging from marijuana to cocaine and heroin, than for alcohol and tobacco. But even in the case of generally prohibited drugs, punitive intervention on the basis of evidence of historical use seems uncomfortably close to precisely the kind of punishment for status that is disfavored in American criminal justice (see *Robinson v. California*, 370 U.S. 660 [1962]). It could, of course, be said that interventions based on drug testing are designed solely to protect young persons and are therefore not subject to the restrictions of criminal punishment. But both the limitations of testing programs for the detection of illicit drugs and a realistic assessment of the operation of contemporary juvenile justice render implausible such a uniformly benign characterization of the objectives of youth drug testing.

Technical advances in drug use–testing methods could ameliorate some of the problems currently encountered when such testing is used as a basis for extensive intervention. This might be the case if tests could be developed that would differentially establish repetitive prior use and historically high blood levels of a particular drug, thus providing a more convincing basis for intervening in the lives of identified subjects (Dubowski, 1987). Moreover, it is possible that techniques of drug testing may be devised that could reverse a paradoxical pattern of currently available tests: At present, residuals of marijuana remain as markers of historical use far longer than in the case of substances such as cocaine and alcohol (see Table 5.1). The impact of this differential on what sorts of users are detected and which sorts are overlooked is obvious. Less obvious is the fact that the use of such drug-testing systems – to the extent that it has any influence on the behavior and life-style of test subjects – might push them toward the use of less easily detectable but more dangerous drugs.

Channeling and training. There is a further category of state policy that attempts to use limited and controlled exposure to psychoactive substances as a training transition to the responsible use of substances whose consumption is permitted for adults. Most of the examples in current American life concern alcohol, for which parents are usually regarded as exempt in their homes from the ban on providing alcohol for children (Mosher, 1977). In addition, some jurisdictions provide for a low-alcohol beer – up to 3.2 percent – to be available for younger ages than the full range of beverage alcohol. Training and channeling rules for alcohol exist also in public institutions such as schools and military installations where there are high concentrations of young persons. Historically, there were some such rules governing the time, place, and manner of tobacco use in military and educational institutions. But this kind of channeling logic is inconsistent with the current public hostility to smoking. Indeed, in the 1990s it seems that the dominant view is that there is no such thing as responsible tobacco use to be inculcated into the emerging generation of Americans.

With regard to illicit drugs, the degree to which young persons should be informed of their differential dangers is a contentious issue in drug education. A policy of providing full information might channel those who experiment with illicit drugs away from more dangerous to less harmful drugs. But for those who consider the consumption of any and all illicit drugs as constituting an approximately equal offense against public order, such channeling is not regarded as a desirable educational goal (Office of National Drug Control Policy, 1989, pp. 47–50).

Perhaps the sharpest debate over channeling policies for illicit drug users concerns needle exchange programs designed to abate the HIV infection spread associated with needle-sharing behavior (Stryker, 1989). Public funds and permission extended to needle exchange programs are seen by some to condone the use of needles for illegal drug abuse. But the public health advantage of reducing HIV infection among drug users and thus the spread from the drug-using population to nonusers presents a strong case for state-sponsored channeling policies directed at illicit drug use.

III. The young offender

Young persons are both the subject and the object of criminal prohibition on drugs. The clash between protection and punishment is thus nowhere more apparent than in official motives for dealing with young offenders. Paternalistic instincts permeate discussion of drug policy, for if drug control strategy is not aimed at protecting the young, who should be protected? Young drug users, and more particularly young drug offenders, also alarm their elders, so that generational conflict is a major theme in this context. The forces that influence public policy toward the young drug offender are important in their own right. But discussing sentencing policy toward young drug offenders also reveals crosscurrents that operate in all aspects of drug control policy, making this topic both significant and exemplary.

Our discussion will analyze three different types of drug offense that can be committed by young persons: possession violations of status prohibitions, possession violations of general prohibitions, and sale and distribution offenses. The separate analysis of these three different classes of offense will enable us to contrast different strands of policy and also will help us explore policy toward young offenders for continuity as the contexts shift. Should policy be consistent across the three categories? If so, with what animating purposes?

Possessory violations of status prohibitions

The possession and use of substances prohibited to minors is an important category of "status offense": an act defined as forbidden only because of the youth of the subject. The more modern understanding of this category of offense suggests that state policy should be paternalistic, nonpunitive, and pragmatic with respect to those who violate status prohibitions (Zimring, 1982, pp. 69–76). A paternalistic orientation to status violations is justified because the same lack of mature judgment on which the age-specific prohibition is based suggests that the offender is not competent to decide independently whether to use the substance or whether treatment for substance dependency is necessary. If young persons lack the capacity to make decisions about substance use, compulsory treatment programs can be defended against objections based on the subject's autonomy.

But there is a broad consensus that status offenders should not be subject to punitive and stigmatic sanctions (Institute of Judicial Administration, 1982; President's Commission, 1967). The premature use of a generally allowed substance is an act of disobedience. But such disobedience alone, at least in the current understanding, is not a crime of moral turpitude. Whereas coercive intervention may be justified on paternalistic grounds, the intentional infliction of suffering and the imposition of social stigma are regarded as morally undeserved consequences in regard to status offenses.

The distinction between coercion and punishment may seem subtle, especially to those subjected to them, but the restriction of state response to the former does have practical implications. First, if the state's intervention is limited to the pursuit of paternalistic ends, then the government is obliged to provide the means to pursue such ends. Not all young persons who drink and smoke have a right to state-supported treatment programs as a result of such behavior. But if the sole justification for coercive intervention is the protection of youth, a right to treatment would extend to all those young persons who are made subject to compulsory state programs.

The nonpunitive orientation of state intervention should also mean that coercive intervention is justified only to the extent that it works. If a program cannot produce positive change in those subjected to it, public agencies cannot fall back on symbolic, admonitory, or deterrent functions to justify such programs. If the state's power is to be limited to a paternalistic interest in the well-being of its subjects, such programs can be justified either on pragmatic grounds or not at all.

In the past two decades, coercive programs for truants and runaways have often been curtailed in the United States on pragmatic grounds, particularly when the use of secure institutions has been part of the treatment programs (Zimring, 1982, pp. 69–75). That compulsory truancy and runaway programs have been found ineffective does not mean that alcohol treatment programs will necessarily meet the same fate. But it does seem clear that the same pragmatic standard should be applied when considering the justification of such programs.

Possessory violations of general prohibitions

There is one important distinction between the violation of status prohibitions and the possession and use of substances prohibited to persons of all ages, but there is disagreement about how much weight this distinguishing feature should carry in determining the appropriate punishment for young persons. The degree of immorality seen as involved in a youthful possession of alcohol is significantly limited by the fact that adults are allowed to possess it. For that reason, the offender's only error may be seen to be the disobedience in prematurely exercising a privilege.

But to the extent that the prohibition of a substance to all citizens implies a judgment that the possession and use of that substance is morally wrong, the young offender can be regarded as indulging in immoral conduct rather than merely being precocious. If it is wrong for adults to use or possess a prohibited substance, it must also be wrong for young persons to do so. There is thus a substantive harm that can be identified in the young offender's conduct that can be the basis for ascribing blame and justifying punishment.

Two features of drug control policy limit the force of this distinction in setting high levels of culpability for drug possession. First, immature minors are almost always regarded as less blameworthy than are adults who commit the same offense. The limited capacities of the young that justify different policies toward them on paternalistic grounds also mitigate judgments of blameworthiness. A second limit on the ascription of blame derives from a paternalistic regard for the young as entitled to some degree of protection. The same features of immaturity and amenability to change that justify paternalism toward the youthful population as a whole applies also to this group and must be taken into account and weighed against the impulse to condemn and the desire to punish.

With respect to possessory crime, blameworthiness is qualified further by the fact that the primary risk of harm in the possessory offense is to the offender. The more dangerous the drug is, the greater will be the offender's need for help. And the more innocuous the substance is, the less will be his or her culpability in possessing it. In either event, the juvenile in possession of a generally prohibited drug cannot be regarded as having forfeited all the entitlement to special concern that attaches to youthful status.

Sales offenses

A minor who is guilty of selling a prohibited substance inflicts direct harm on another and is thus eligible for greater condemnation than is a possessory offender. This element in the sales transaction justifies a harsher view of the minor involved, just as it aggravates culpability in an adult offender.

With respect to sales, the distinction between status prohibitions and generally prohibited substances does not seem as clear as it does in relation to possession. For the sales offense, the harm is caused to another minor in each case. Yet even with this compounded basis for condemnation, the juvenile drug seller remains a candidate for mitigated blame on grounds of diminished responsibility and paternalistic state concern. Young drug sellers are therefore regarded as less blameworthy than older sellers are and are also felt to be more entitled than adults are to treatment and rehabilitation. Further, the youthfulness of the offender may especially complicate the scope of penal liability in those cases in which the youth of the buyer is an aggravating circumstance. Earlier we mentioned special laws to provide enhanced penalties for sales to minors or in geographical zones such as schools where vulnerable youthful populations congregate. Should these enhanced penalties apply when the guilty party is himself or herself a minor?

The jurisprudence of child/child sale offenses has not, to our knowledge, been spelled out in detail. But two of the more persuasive justifications for imposing a special liability on sales to the young do not apply if both the buyer and the seller are peers. Thus, there is not the gratuitous disregard for youthful vulnerability involved when an offender chooses to cross social barriers, as an adult does to offer prohibited substances for sale to children. When children sell to one another, they are selling drugs in the same social settings in which they live their lives. They are not invading a different social milieu in order to commit the offense, nor is there anything especially predatory about the presence of the young seller in the social setting where the transaction takes place. Further, when the sellers and buyers are age peers, the element of exploitation that the law presumes when adults sell to children may also be diminished or absent. In the case of sales and transfer offenses, the eligibility of the young offender for punishment may legitimately be enhanced because a sale took place. But further aggravation on the ground of the purchaser's immaturity does not seem to be justified.

We are aware of one recent examination of this issue that reached a contrary conclusion. In the *National Drug Control Strategy* (1989) discussion of "schoolyard laws" establishing stiff minimum and mandatory sentences for anyone caught distributing drugs within one thousand feet of a school, playground, pool, youth center, or video arcade, it is said that "schoolyard laws should also apply to minors selling drugs inside these zones." The justification offered for this is that it will "prevent dealers from utilizing underage drug 'runners' to circumvent the law" (Office of National Drug Control Policy, 1989, p. 126). It is difficult to think of an appropriate comment on the deviousness of a proposal to punish children in order to discommode the adults who are exploiting them.

IV. Two strategic objectives

Sentencing policy toward young drug offenders is a narrow concern of limited impact on the totality of youth drug policy. The strategic objectives we speak of now are general goals that help define policy and animate policy choices throughout the whole range of circumstances in which state action might influence the experience of a young person with drugs. This section will contrast prevention and intervention as methods of reducing the harmful effects from psychoactive substances on the young, and it will also discuss ways that prevention and intervention strategies may both complement and compete with each other in framing youth drug policy.

The basic distinction between prevention and intervention mechanisms is clear. One effective way to reduce the problems associated with a particular form of drug use is to create policies that keep young persons from using the drug. The ultimate prevention program would be one aimed at producing a generation of drug-free young people. In practice, however, the United States is anything but a drug-free society, and the aim of prevention programs is to minimize as much as possible the exposure of young persons to illicit drugs while concentrating preventive efforts for licit drugs on lessening the abusive use of these drugs and altering the circumstances of drug use in ways that would lower their total cost. Thus, programs that attempt to keep young persons from smoking either marijuana or tobacco are pure prevention programs. The advertising campaigns put on by breweries that tell young people to "know when to say when" or that hope to eliminate driving while under the influence of alcohol also are preventive programs, but with limited-loss prevention objectives.

Intervention programs attempt to minimize the harmful consequences of drug abuse for the young by intervening when the circumstances are risky or harmful. Whereas prevention programs try to keep young people from starting careers with either marijuana or tobacco, by means of persuasion or supply interdiction, intervention programs concentrate on rescuing young people who are already involved from the harmful effects of particular kinds of drug use. Prevention programs try to make drug abuse more difficult to begin, whereas intervention efforts try to make careers in drug abuse easier to end.

These two general goals are complementary, of course. Balanced programs of youth welfare can seek both to minimize exposure to drugs and to provide effective transitions from patterns of drug abuse back to nonimpaired adolescent development, just as persons concerned with water safety can support swimming lessons and warning signs as a preventive effort and still provide life-guard rescue for the imperiled. Yet programs emphasizing prevention and intervention may compete for priority in funding, may conflict over the level of social and legal stigma that should accompany drug use, and may subscribe to differing images of the breadth and nature of the drug problems that threaten American youth.

The most obvious competition between prevention and interventional emphases concerns the competition for scarce public funds. As long as only so many millions, or indeed billions, of dollars are available for youth drug policies, those who wish to spend those funds treating youthful drug users and those who would rather emphasize programs that aim to stop potential drug users from becoming actual drug users are involved in a zero-sum competition. There are two, less obvious, aspects of such competition that are of some significance in the contemporary American drug policy debate. First, to the extent that these two approaches compete for funds, the proponents of each strategy may become invested in denigrating the claims for effectiveness associated with the other mechanism. The two ways that one successfully competes in a zero-sum competition for funding are to claim success for one's own approach and to denigrate the efficacy of that of one's opponent. To the extent that there is some incentive for prevention proponents to downgrade the success possibilities of treatment, and for treatment proponents to question the effectiveness of prevention, we can expect something very much like negative campaigning in the competition for drug program support.

A second contrast between competing models of youth welfare has to do with who the youthful audiences of prevention programs, as opposed to intervention programs, turn out to be. With respect to illicit drugs, the targets of prevention programs are nonusing children and youth. Although an effective targeting of resources might suggest a concentration of them among nonusing populations who are at a particularly high risk, the tendency in prevention programs is to seek out broad audiences from all economic and social classes as the target for the messages to be conveyed. Intervention, by contrast, concentrates its resources on children and youth already experiencing difficulties in patterns of drug abuse. This is a smaller segment of the population than the prevention targets and is usually urban, poorer, and older and contains a greater percentage of minority young persons than does the general youth population. To the extent that the targets of programs are considered their beneficiaries, the competition between prevention and intervention models is a competition between serving broad general populations and directing resources more intensively toward a smaller and more disadvantaged segment of the youth population.

Apart from the competition for resources, there are two other issue areas in which strategies of prevention and intervention seem to conflict. The first pertains to the extent to which stigma should attach to drug use and drug users, and the second concerns the breadth of behavior included in the definition of the drug problem and the continuity between licit and illicit drugs. In both cases, distinctive patterns associated with the interventionist and preventionist camps do not flow logically from emphasis on prevention or treatment, but the associations noted seem strong nonetheless.

If the job of prevention programs is the insulation of most normal young persons from a first use of a particular substance, there is an incentive to characterize the use of this substance as deviant, dangerous, and wrong. The task of running a prevention program thus is to paint a portrait of drug use as behavior well worth avoiding. Any stigma that attaches to drug use inevitably spills over and results in a negative portrayal of drug users. The drug user in this portrayal is seen as not only foolish but also blameworthy and, in some important sense, permanently damaged by his or her association with the substance. The social and legal stigmas attached to drug users therefore augment the mission of prevention programs in creating barriers to first use among the nonusing population of young persons.

When recruiting and intervening in the lives of drug users, the treatment professional is vested in an image of drug users that is contingent and variable, subject to positive change with appropriate intervention. From a treatment perspective, the best view of the drug user is of a good person in trouble, capable of rehabilitation and the continuation of a normal life. Indeed, those associated with intervention programs tend to treat drug abusers who voluntarily participate in programs as more victims than wrongdoers. In part, these different views of drug use and drug users stem from the different ideologies regarding drug use that come with the emphasis on prevention versus treatment. But there is also a process of differential association that reinforces the systemic bias. Those who administer drug prevention programs spend their time with nonusing audiences in a social environment where drug use, as they define it, is deviant behavior. Drug interventionists relate to and identify with persons who, almost without exception, have extensive histories of drug abuse. For persons in this setting, drug use is statistically normal behavior.

The tendency of each school of thought to associate with social groups that reinforce its preconceptions is, of course, a circular one, widely observed in social relations. People in prevention programs go into prevention in large part because they can deal and identify more easily with nonusing populations than with using populations. Many on the intervention side identify with and can more easily relate to those with a history of drug use. So the interveners wish to diminish the personal stigmas associated with drug abuse for personal reasons as well as to maximize the positive incentives available for drug users wishing to embark on a program of personal change.

Related to different perceptions of stigma is a tendency for the different emphasis groups to have different perceptions of the nature of the drug problem. It is in both the material and ideological interests of the preventionists to define the drug problem as involving abnormal substances that present a special danger to society quite distinct from broader behaviors like alcohol and tobacco use. That image of drug use reinforces the stigma and makes the majority of the population more suited to prevention programs (targeted at nonusers). That image also maintains a moral distinction between the tobacco and alcohol user and the user of illicit drugs.

The interventionist, by contrast, has both a material and an ideological investment in seeing a broader segment of the population needing his or her services. The interventionist is thus invested in a broader definition of drug use that is likely to include alcohol and tobacco. That such behavior can be socially construed as normal is no threat to the interventionist view of drug abuse because it conforms to the larger picture of drug abuse that such persons tend to carry in any event.

Those involved in programs that emphasize drug prevention tend to draw a bright line between illicit drug use on the one hand and alcohol or tobacco use on the other, for this facilitates the stigmatization of illicit drug use. Often such persons will talk of alcoholism as if it is a medical problem requiring a medical solution, without seeing the obvious parallel between licit and illicit drug abuse.

There is, of course, nothing inevitable about the potential conflict between intervention and prevention specialists. Still, it is noteworthy that many of those professionally involved in child-centered drug programs can find themselves in fundamental conflict with other antidrug groups that claim children as their priority. There is at least the potential for civil war on drugs in the distinctive specializations that have emerged in antidrug programming.

V. Conclusion

Worry about drugs and the young is not only an important aspect of drug policy, but it is also, for most Americans, the paramount concern to be addressed by governmental policies. This means that concern about children and youth should have a major influence on the dimensions of overall drug policy. The topics addressed in this chapter suggest what some of these general policy issues might be. Three points in particular merit mention in a conclusion.

1. *Youth welfare is a restraint on drug control policies.* Concern for the welfare of children and adolescents because it necessarily includes caring about children who use drugs restrains the range of antidrug policies that should be undertaken. We pointed out that the same lack of maturity that justifies age-specific prohibitions and worries about the special vulnerabilities of young persons to drugs should serve to reduce the moral turpitude and thus the punishment of the young drug offender. This seems to us axiomatic, but the implications of such a policy are not uniformly recognized.

If those under twenty-one lack the maturity of judgment to be given alcohol, then they probably also should not be penalized as harshly for violating alcohol or drug laws as older persons are. Thus if California bans sales of alcohol to persons under twenty-one, the punishment of nineteen- and twenty-year-olds who use or sell cocaine or heroin should be smaller than that of older sellers.

A consistent theory as to why youth is important need not produce policies in which the subject's age is the only significant variable. A nineteen-year-old drug seller and a nineteen-year-old drug taker may properly call for different governmental policy responses because of the other factors to be weighed against an individual's youth in the former case. But however the balance is struck, it must include youth as a mitigating influence, and this may to some extent limit the efficacy of antidrug policies. Yet it is only by honoring the larger purpose of youth protection that a drug policy principally concerned with children and youth can remain coherent.

2. *Concern for youth welfare necessarily leads to a broad definition of problem drugs.* Each of the special reasons for concern about drugs and children mentioned in the opening to this chapter apply also to alcohol and tobacco and to many drugs available on prescription. It is for this reason that age-specific prohibitions of otherwise generally available substances are justified. A corollary of the justification for broader prohibitions is that a concern for youth welfare demands a definition of the drug problem in relation to this constituency that includes tobacco and alcohol.

The formal distinction between legal and illegal drugs that exists in the adult world provides no justification for failing to recognize alcohol and tobacco as a major part of the problem of drug abuse for minors. The practical importance and public health costs of tobacco and alcohol use by American teenagers are high. In fact, these two substances generate a far greater number of deaths and disabilities than do any of the illicit drugs, mainly by way of alcohol-related automobile accidents and incipient conditions associated with tobacco and alcohol consumption.

We would argue a case for two complementary propositions: First, anyone concerned with the traditional concepts and measures of youth welfare must also be concerned with a broad spectrum of problematic substances. Second, anyone concerned, more narrowly, only with illicit substances must not be placing a high policy priority on adolescent and child welfare. This point may sometimes be of trivial significance. One should not expect border patrols to be composed of child welfare specialists. Yet when various different drug control strategies compete with one another for limited resources, the discord between broad conceptions of youth welfare and narrow definitions of problem drugs can be important.

3. *A broad conception of child welfare requires a substantial investment in treatment and intervention programs.* There are two reasons that a broad conception of child welfare demands a substantial investment in treatment. First, a broad conception of child welfare takes account of the life prospects of children and youth who are already using, and suffering from the ill effects of using, drugs. Second, as soon as the list of problem substances is extended to include alcohol and tobacco, we create a policy climate in which most children will be experimenting with, and many will be regularly using, problem drugs. Under such circumstances, creating safe and constructive transitions away from patterns of drug abuse must become a major element in a publicly mandated drug control program. Whatever else government may do, it must do that.

6

Drug control policy and street crime

In the United States the social world of street criminality is also a major arena for the use of alcohol and almost all illicit drugs. It is beyond dispute that drug use and crime overlap and interact in a multiplicity of ways. Moreover, the connection between drug use and predatory crime, along with the possible corruption of the young, constitute the major source of public fear and apprehension regarding drugs.

We shall not attempt in this chapter to survey the whole range of relationships between drug use and criminal behavior, which run the gamut from significant questions such as what should constitute a crime all the way to staff and visitor searches in the prison system. Instead, we shall focus on one group of criminal offenses – predatory street crime and burglary – and on the linkage between changes in drug control policy and levels and patterns of that category of criminal activity.

We shall restrict the category of crime that we consider here in this way because it reflects what appears to be at the center of public alarm and concern in relation to drug use. By concentrating on the potential impact of changes in drug control policy on the nature and extent of these crimes, we can direct our attention to the practical significance that should be attached to this topic. It is only by analyzing the effects of those changes that we can discover what is possible for government to accomplish in this field.

Confining our attention to the impact of changes in drug control policy on street crime is not as restrictive as it might seem. For in analyzing the likely impact of policy changes on such crimes, a wide spectrum of issues relating to drug use and criminality has to be considered. But although the spectrum of issues is wide, giving priority to the effects of policy change provides a focus for drugs and crime discussion that combines a degree of theoretical novelty with substantial practical implications.

The following chapter is organized under three headings. The first section briefly discusses the basic statistical relationship between drug and alcohol use and predatory street crime. In it we shall show why even the substantial overlap between these two behavior systems cannot provide a basis for estimating the impact of changes in drug supply and use on the rates and patterns of criminality.

The second section deals with several hypothesized links between the variations in drug supply and use and the patterns of crime. The phenomena that we shall consider range from the pharmacological, such as the direct impact, measured at the individual level, of drug use on the affected subject's propensity to commit crime, to the sociological, such as changes in community structure and morale brought about by patterns of drug use that may influence crime rates in indirect but significant ways.

The third section of this chapter discusses the policy choices that we endorse, notwithstanding the uncertainty that characterizes current understanding about the relationship between drug use and crime.

I.   Questioning the drug–crime connection

The starting point for analyzing the linkage between drug use and crime is documenting the degree to which drug taking and criminality overlap in the American city. Figure 6.1 shows the percentage of male arrestees who tested positive for recent drug use in nineteen American cities from July to September 1989, as reported by the National Institute of Justice, Drug Use Forecasting (DUF) Program, in March 1990.

A majority of arrestees tested positive for a drug at the time of arrest in all the test cities, in a range extending from 53 percent in San Antonio, Texas, to 84 percent in New York City. The median city, New Orleans, reported 65 percent positive for a drug at the time of arrest. In ten of the nineteen cities, a majority of those arrested tested positive for recent cocaine use. Positive drug test results of this magnitude are significant in their own right, and they contrast dramatically with survey and drug test results from broader samples of the population. Recent use of cocaine is nowhere reported in surveys by as much as 10 percent of the population. Yet more than 75 percent of all male arrestees in New York City tested positive for cocaine.

What is the significance of the high concordance of these two measures? A relationship of this differential magnitude inevitably raises the question whether drug taking may not have had a causal role in the commission of the crimes with which the arrestees were charged. If two-thirds of all arrests involved recent drug use, does not that implicate drugs as a causal factor in crime? We think that the correct answer to that question is negative. But a detailed explanation of that negative conclusion may provide a helpful introduction to the cluster of drug–crime issues that this chapter addresses.

Only a small percentage of all urban adults commit predatory crimes like robbery, burglary, and life-threatening assault. A much larger segment of the

Percent Positive

City	Percent Positive Any Drug	2+ Drugs	Cocaine	Marijuana	Amphetamines	Opiates	PCP
New York	84	41	77	24	0	20	2
San Diego	83	52	42	46	37	23	6
Philadelphia	81	33	73	25	1	8	1
Los Angeles	76	30	57	25	6	14	5
Houston	70	24	58	24	2	3	0
Cleveland	70	17	58	18	0	4	2
Fort Lauderdale	69	27	52	32	0	3	0
Washington, DC	68	24	61	13	0	8	11
Detroit	67	22	57	24	0	6	*
New Orleans	65	24	56	23	0	5	2
Dallas	65	29	55	23	4	11	*
San Jose	65	25	35	27	11	7	13
Portland	64	28	37	35	10	15	0
Birmingham	63	21	52	22	*	5	*
Indianapolis	62	23	29	48	0	5	0
St. Louis	61	24	48	24	*	6	7
Phoenix	60	32	36	38	9	14	*
Kansas City	59	20	43	24	2	2	5
San Antonio	53	22	28	27	3	15	*

* Less than one percent.

Figure 6.1. Drug use by male arrestees – positive urinalysis, July through September 1989. (From National Institute of Justice, *Research in Action*, March 1990.)

population frequently partake of illicit drugs, but this is still a small proportionate section of the population. The small segment of the population that puts itself at the risk of arrest differs from the rest of the citizenry in a number of respects. These include willingness to risk the consequences of breaking the law and a desire to obtain rewards swiftly.

Because the same personality traits and preferences put an individual at high risk of both illicit drug use and crime, the large overlap between drug use and crime could be simply a function of that sort of self-selection, independently of any contribution that drugs might be supposed to make to criminal impulses and activities (Speckart and Anglin, 1985). The smaller is the proportion of the general population engaging in illicit drug use, the more we would expect the population at risk for drug use to be composed of persons who are predisposed toward committing a crime.

It is as if we had identified two behaviors involving risks that only a small fraction of the American population were willing to take, for example, hang gliding and volunteering for extremely hazardous duty in the armed forces. If we then found that a very large proportion of the soldiers who volunteered for hazardous duty also enjoyed hang gliding, we might assume that hang gliding predisposed soldiers to volunteer for hazardous duty. In fact, however, this might simply be evidence that the taste for both types of behavior derived from a preference for, or a tolerance of, risk taking that predisposed subjects independently to indulge in these two different forms of risk taking. With respect to drugs and crime, those at high risk of arrest have displayed both a preference for, or a tolerance of, risk and a willingness to ignore the threat of moral condemnation. And these two characteristics seem to be powerfully predisposing toward illicit drug use. The same sort of covariation can be expected to occur in social settings. Conditions of social disorganization that invite high levels of predatory crime prove to be least resistant to the spread of illicit drugs.

An experimental paradigm

One way of exploring the pervasive problem of self-selection is to design an experiment that can address the drug–crime linkage without selection problems and to compare the logic of that experiment with some of the nonexperimental evidence that is commonly adduced when analyzing the drug–crime connection.

The uncontaminated experiment – which is, incidentally, an unthinkable procedure – would randomly allot thousands of individuals into two contrasting drug availability groups. If the drug to be studied were heroin, all the members of Group A would be in a setting where heroin was readily available and relatively inexpensive, whereas the members of Group B would be living in a condition of heroin scarcity (to the extent that current prohibition policy could secure that). If the rate of heroin use were much greater in Group A than in Group B, then we would expect a causal relationship to produce a higher rate of crime and arrests for Group A than that for Group B.

The reader should note the limited extent to which the problem of self-selection has been confronted in this experiment. One cannot compare crime rates among heroin users in either group with crime rates attributable to nonusers, because those who choose to use heroin will be different from non-users in other respects. It is only the total arrest and crime rate for the easy-availability group that can be compared with the total arrest and crime rate for the lesser-availability group as a basis for valid inference. In an ideal experiment, all other individual and social circumstances that are related to rates of criminality would be the same for both groups. Thus, ideally, Group A and Group B would be drawn from the same community.

Any comparison between heroin users and nonusers on the crime dimension is obviously flawed by the self-selection process that this experiment is designed to avoid. But what about analyses that compare the arrest or crime rates attributable to heroin users while they are actively using heroin, with the arrest or crime rates of those same persons during periods when they are not using the drug? If, as has been reported, heroin users have lower rates of predatory crime during periods of lower heroin use (Anglin and Speckart, 1987), does not that establish heroin use as directly contributing to the propensity to commit crimes?

The problem with this inference relates to the process that produces abstinence in heroin users and whether that process itself may not affect the propensity to commit crime. A religious conversion or the adoption of a new life-style could result in both diminished criminality and drug abstinence even if there were no direct causal link between drug taking and rates of criminality. It is only when the circumstances that produce drug abstinence or lower drug use seem independent of the choices and predilections of the drug users that nonuse approaches the terms of the experimental logic. Certainly, the act of volunteering for treatment is exactly the kind of self-selection that cautions against attributing lessened levels of criminality to changes in drug-taking behavior.

What about a comparison between City A, with a ready availability of drugs, and City B, with a restricted availability? If City A has a higher crime rate, can we not conclude that it is the higher drug involvement that produces the higher level of crime? Reasoning along these lines, one would compare New York City, with its 84 percent drug use, with Indianapolis, with its 62 percent drug use, and attribute the difference in crime rates in the two cities to their different drug use profiles.

The problem with this, however, is that the factors that condition the cities' different rates of drug use may be precisely the same factors that make them more or less vulnerable to crime. Unlike the cities in an experimental design, the cities in the DUF program were not randomly sorted into those with high and low drug availability conditions. Thus, New York City and Fargo, North Dakota, have very different levels of cocaine availability and also very different homicide rates. But it would be ludicrous to suppose that the difference in levels of cocaine availability is an independent variable that explains the different homicide rates of these two extreme values at opposite ends of the American social spectrum. It is only to the extent that the differential availability of drugs is unconnected to the culture and character of a city that third-factor or common-cause problems do not invalidate comparative exercises that seek to explain differential crime rates by referring to differential rates of drug use.

What about the "natural experiment" that occurs when drug availability apparently changes over time in the same community? Can ensuing changes in levels of crime be attributed to changes in drug use patterns? The problem here is that changing patterns of drug use may be the product of other variations in conditions that may independently affect crime rates. On the other hand, if changes in drug availability and use are unconnected to other aspects of a city's life, it may be more plausible to infer a drug–crime causation from this sort of time study. Thus, short-term changes in heroin price in Detroit in the 1970s do not appear to have been a function of some larger social process that might have had an immediate impact on crime rates. In that case, the attribution of the change in crime patterns to the alterations in heroin availability and price seems plausible (Silverman and Sprull, 1977, pp. 80–103).

To a greater or lesser extent, third-factor or common-cause and self-selection problems bedevil all nonexperimental attempts to interpret the drug use–crime relation when they co-occur and seem to be associated in frequency and severity. These constraints, however, do not necessarily render all nonexperimental studies futile. Indeed, the normal processes of social and political change do provide opportunities for nonexperimental evaluation in which selection biases may be minimal. Moreover, even though any single comparative study may be imperfect, investigations of a variety of imperfect comparisons in which the threats to the validity of one set of comparisons are different from those to a complementary piece of research can sometimes produce reliable conclusions. This may occur when each different but imperfect study may remove an element of doubt left by another imperfect exercise.

This process, which Hans Zeisel called the "triangulation of proof" (Zeisel, 1968, pp. 190–9), in which the imperfection of one study may be to a large extent canceled out by another, also imperfect, study, means that the cumulative impact of a series of imperfect approaches to the same question may be significant. It is a situation in which, as we noted in relation to deterrence research, an inversion of a familiar maxim seems appropriate: Two wrongs, if carefully combined, may sometimes come close to making a right (Zimring and Hawkins, 1973, p. 291).

II. A taxonomy of hypothetical effects

If little is known about the impact of drug use and drug policy on patterns of crime, a great deal is hypothesized. Policy discussion on drug control is rich with suggestions about the variety of ways in which drug use – and, by extension, drug control policy – may have an impact on rates and patterns of predatory crime. Some of the suggestions relate to the effects that drugs have on individuals, as when the ingestion of a drug is said to increase the propensities for, or reduce the inhibitions against, particular kinds of criminal behavior. Others relate to social or environmental effects, as when a drug economy, or the widespread use of drugs, is said to create new criminal opportunities that in turn lead to higher crime rates in a community. The effects of drugs that have been hypothesized can also be ranged on a continuum from those that are direct to those that are indirect. Moreover, different types of drugs are said to have many different types of impact.

In these circumstances, the construction of a list of major headings is no simple task, and possible subdivisions multiply rapidly. The next section will discuss six different kinds of hypothesized drug–crime relationships, a list that is illustrative rather than exhaustive. It also excludes many acts of violence that are incidental to the organization of illegal drug markets, as well as to the spillover effects of changes produced by illegal drug markets on weapon availability and other variables that may influence patterns of predatory crime.

Effects on the individual

Any facet of drug control policy that has an influence on crime rates must ultimately affect the behavior of individuals. In that sense, all drug policy impacts are individual. Accordingly, we shall restrict our definition of individual-level effects to policy impacts that can be measured by data about individual subjects. If, for instance, those individuals who wish to obtain money to purchase drugs commit more crimes when drug prices are high, this process can be studied by tracing the arrest behavior of drug users as the street price of a drug rises and falls. If, however, the existence of a large number of intoxicated persons increases the number of criminal opportunities for robbery and the robbery rate, the most appropriate measurement of this phenomenon is at the community level. Robbery thus should be higher in cities with high rates of publicly intoxicated citizens. This sort of impact we call *community-level effects*. The three individual-level effects that we shall discuss here are hypotheses about the pharmacological, economic, and psychological impacts of drugs on behavior.

Pharmacological impact. We begin with the pharmacological effect of drug ingestion on an individual's propensity to commit crime. In the taxonomy just suggested, such an effect would be classified as individual and direct, but within that broad category a number of drugs have been said to have a variety of different types of effects on affective states.

Substances such as alcohol, cocaine, and the amphetamines are said to heighten aggressive and sexual impulses and thus to be conducive to the criminal expression of such impulses. But alcohol, along with the tranquilizers and central nervous system depressants such as the barbiturates, have also been nominated as agents that can moderate and dampen impulses that could be expressed criminally.

Psychoactive substances are said to have disinhibitive effects, in that they neutralize or weaken moral or emotional restraints that ordinarily control behavior (see Fagan, 1990, pp. 260, 292–3). As a result, it is argued, people are more likely to indulge in behavior that is considered risky or immoral or deviant. And this increases the likelihood that individuals or groups of individuals will engage in criminal acts. In the literature, alcohol has featured most prominently in expositions based on the disinhibition hypothesis, but the opiates and marijuana have also been listed as setting in motion the physiological or pharmacological processes that are thought to underlie disinhibition. In addition, it has been suggested that psychoactive substances may affect cognitive capacity in such a way as to increase an individual's propensity to behave criminally. Intoxication, it has been suggested, alters psychological functions so that people become free of these cognitive restraints on behavior. Not only alcohol but also a number of other chemical agents are thought to be liable to induce neurotic or psychotic conditions that may be criminogenic.

Withdrawal, moreover, from dependency on such psychoactive substances as alcohol, heroin, and the amphetamines can occasionally be accompanied by deviant and sometimes criminal behavior. There is an extensive literature on the effects of alcohol and of alcohol withdrawal, but it stops considerably short of any consensus either on the behavioral consequences of alcohol intoxication in terms of crime or aggression or on the degree of dangerousness associated with withdrawal psychoses and other alcohol-induced affective states.

Instrumental impact. A second set of hypothetical drug–crime linkages relates to the use of criminal means to obtain money or property that can be exchanged for drugs that are desired or felt to be necessary by drug users, the drug dependent, or the drug addicted. This sort of crime, which has been called instrumental in that it is "instrumental to the attainment of some other goal" (Chambliss, 1967, p. 708), does not play an important role in the literature on alcohol, although there are numerous accounts of individuals committing property crime in order to obtain money for alcohol.

In regard to expensive illicit drugs such as heroin and cocaine, however, this kind of instrumental criminality is a significant individual effect that is thought to arise from the drug–crime relationship. Hypotheses regarding instrumental criminal behavior designed to obtain funds to purchase drugs have less obvious implications, in relation to drug availability and the drug–crime connection, than do those that rest on premises regarding the physiological or pharmacological effects of drugs. If drug use and drug-induced intoxication produce higher levels of criminality, then the greater the availability of drugs is, the higher the rate of criminality we should expect. But if the principal motive for criminality is the desire to obtain resources to buy drugs, then by contrast the scarcity and the higher prices that a prohibition policy might produce could motivate more crimes by those who are persistent in their desire or need for scarce and expensive substances.

To the extent that this contrast holds, the major concern regarding the free availability of drugs will be the physiological or pharmacological effects of high levels of drug usage on criminality. On the other hand, instrumental crimes would seem to be more significant as the scarcity and price of drugs increase. This contrast, however, depends to some extent on what economists call the *elasticity of demand*. For unless the demand for a particular drug is extremely inelastic among a population of potential customers, a high price might dissuade or deter many more potential customers than it will motivate to commit instrumental crimes in order to obtain money to pay that price. In those circumstances, the criminogenic consequences of prohibition-induced high prices would be relatively small.

The reinforcement of deviant life-styles. The third individual-level hypothesis relates not so much to the economics of drug use as to its social psychology and culture. For many individuals, the use of alcohol, as well as illicit drugs, is part of a pattern of life on the streets, detached from either regular employment or family responsibilities. In the case of illegal drugs, the social milieu and network of support and the hustling life-style associated with using, first, heroin and then crack are an often-observed feature in urban sociological studies. In our simple taxonomy, we regard such reinforcement as individual but indirect, unlike the pharmacological and instrumental hypotheses.

It is frequently argued that illicit drug use both leads to the recruitment of individuals to patterns of life that include predatory crime and also reinforces a nascent or tentative commitment to such patterns. According to this account, the pleasures of drug use and the socially supportive networks associated with it make crime much more attractive than it would be as a solitary pursuit. But the evidence regarding drug use as providing a recruiting dynamic for criminal behavior is equivocal. In a straightforward recruiting sequence, drug use would precede participation in crime, but analysis of juvenile delinquent and adult criminal careers research suggests that this sequential pattern is comparatively rare. Instead, recurrent minor criminality seems to precede regular illicit drug use, often by many years (Chaiken and Chaiken, 1990, p. 216).

With respect to more serious forms of predatory crime, however, the age of onset is much closer in most criminal careers to the stage at which substantial illicit drug usage commences (Chaiken and Chaiken, 1990, pp. 217–18). So it may be plausible to speak of drug use as a recruiting mechanism for serious or persistent patterns of criminality. Further, to the extent that a gestalt image of attractive criminal life-styles is an important element in the socialization of delinquents, widespread drug use may function from a distance as an attractive feature of such a life-style as perceived by an adolescent. Most plausibly, drug use and its supporting culture serve as a powerful reinforcement to people already involved in crime and experimenting with illicit drugs. Such reinforcement tends to lessen the rate of desistance from crime at any given age among drug users, and it would also tend to encourage longer average criminal careers than might be the case in the absence of drug use.

The individual-level data are consistent with this hypothesis but are far from providing proof of it. Those persons displaying a pattern of extensive criminality, together with a high level of drug usage, do tend to have longer criminal careers and lower rates of desistance than do non-drug-taking delinquents (Chaiken and Chaiken, 1990, pp. 219–20). But the problem is that a self-selection process may be operative. That is, the deep-end drug users may simply be more impervious to risk or more immune to the lessons of experience than are other delinquents. So their persistence in criminal behavior may simply be evidence of their particular psychological makeup rather than of reinforcement provided by drugs and a supportive drug culture.

The common-cause or third-factor problem also raises doubt about the conclusions that can properly be drawn from studies that show that criminal behavior is reduced after the subjects enter drug treatment programs, because reduced drug use may not be the cause of the lessened crime. Even if subjects have been coerced into treatment, the influence of the treatment program, rather than just reduced drug use, may cause the lower number of crimes committed after intervention.

Closer to the experimental paradigm discussed in Section I would be the finding that the epidemic use of a particular drug in an urban area was associated with lengthening criminal careers in street criminality of a type not found in less drug-impacted cities. Even this finding, however, would be subject to the objection that the same forces that single out a city for a drug epidemic might independently exert pressure on the lengthening of criminal careers. Nevertheless, a discovery of this sort derived from a geographic comparison would provide credible circumstantial support for the reinforcement hypothesis.

Effects on the community

There are a number of ways in which drug control policy can influence crime rates by altering the environment of a community rather than directly influencing the behavior of individual offenders. Such community-level effects are not often precisely defined and are formidably difficult to measure. But they are no less important to a balanced assessment of drug control policy because of these problems.

Drugs and criminal opportunities. There are several ways in which extensive drug use in a community may influence opportunities for predatory crime. A large number of publicly intoxicated persons on the streets present easy targets to robbers and thus will probably increase robbery rates. There can be no "drunk rolling" if there are no drunks; and the larger the number of such vulnerable targets is, the higher the rate of robbery is likely to be.

At the same time, the presence of a large illicit goods-for-cash economy in poor neighborhoods raises the number of attractive targets for larceny and robbery in a way that is likely to increase the number of these types of offenses. There is, however, a countervailing tendency, in that opportunities to make money by selling drugs or otherwise serving the drug economy provide alternative illegitimate income sources. So that as easy money becomes available in the illicit drug market, some persons may abandon their involvement in property crimes (Speckart and Anglin, 1985).

Not only will the size of an illicit drug use pattern affect levels of crime, but it also can influence the selection of targets by active criminals and thus the distribution of criminal victimization among various population groups. Drunk rolling may increase the aggregate amount of robbery. But to the extent that the intoxicated become a preferred target, it may reduce the level of purse snatching. Cash robberies from drug sellers may substantially raise the robbery rate but at the same time lower the rate at which convenience stores and liquor stores – potential alternative cash targets – are victimized. The shift from convenience or liquor store robbery to drug seller robbery redirects robbery events to victims who do not report them to the police. As a result, even if the gross number of robbery events climbs, this redirection will produce a decrease in the recorded robbery rates. The lower reported robbery rate in and around Washington, D.C., during the 1980s is consistent with the hypothesis of robbery target redirection. At the same time, a booming drug economy might also reduce the amount of robbery by diverting labor resources from robbery into drug commerce.

The reciprocal relationship among the different types of robbery target can be expressed in the inexact language of direct and indirect effects. Thus, the change of target from purse snatching to robbery of the intoxicated seems to us to be a direct community effect, as also does the shift of targets from convenience or liquor stores to drug sellers. The notion of drug selling's substituting for predatory crime as an income source, however, seems somewhat less direct.

Systematic studies of the way in which drug availability affects alternative criminal opportunity structures have not yet been carried out. The changes just outlined are therefore hypothetical rather than established by empirical investigation. It seems likely that greater drug availability will create tendencies in the direction of both increasing and reducing predatory crime. But a priori reasoning provides no way of estimating the exact nature, let alone the magnitude, of the criminogenic effects that may be attributable to a greater availability of illicit drugs on the streets.

Drugs and the criminal environment. Shifts in drug control policy may also have indirect effects on levels of predatory crime because they restructure the allocation of criminal justice resources. Obvious examples of this kind of indirect effect are the impact of shifts of police resources and punishment resources from a focus on street crime to a drug control agenda. If fewer targeted police resources lower the apprehension risks associated with burglary and robbery, this lowering of risk might in turn lead to higher levels of burglary and robbery associated with the lessened deterrent effects of the law or the smaller levels of incapacitation attributable to lower arrest rates. Reallocation of punishment resources from street offenders to drug offenders could diminish both deterrence and incapacitation restraints on the levels of predatory street crime. Proponents of drug decriminalization argue that diverting resources from other crime control functions to drugs can be criminogenic, but no statistical analysis has yet been presented that purports to demonstrate the crime costs of resources diverted to drug control policy.

Just as the diversion of police or punishment resources into drug control policy can make urban environments less hazardous for the predatory criminal, a special focus on drug control at the street level can also have the opposite effect. Concentrating police resources on the "cleaning up" of areas known for high drug trafficking can make a targeted area more hazardous for robbers or burglars to ply their trade in those areas. If antidrug initiatives also augment the total police presence, it is plausible to suppose that this might escalate the riskiness of nondrug predatory crime on a communitywide basis. And the incapacitation effect achieved by locking up large numbers of drug offenders might even lower the levels of robbery and burglary if the persons at risk for drug conviction are also active property offenders.

Substantial increases in drug control emphasis might thus either suppress levels of street criminality or increase nondrug crime. Which impact is the more likely outcome of a particular antidrug policy depends largely on what kind of resource shift occurs on the street and also on the particular environment where the policy change takes place. If drug control initiatives raise the general level of street policing in high-crime areas, the risks for street crime need not deteriorate. If the police presence shifts geographically away from burglary or robbery zones, or if there is a shift in emphasis at the crime detection level from street crime to drugs, the risk environment for property crime may, however, deteriorate.

A clear conflict between drug control and crime control is more likely to occur in the competition for punishment resources. As drug sellers occupy larger proportions of jail and prison cells, the displacement of property offenders is likely. Early-release programs and nonprison alternatives for burglary and other nonviolent male property offenders is one likely outcome of a drug control emphasis in state prisons. Another is the use of scarce women's prison space for female drug offenders instead of, perhaps, female property offenders. Whatever competition between drug control and street crime might occur at the federal level will be much less direct – if only because of the smaller share of federal prison space devoted to state and local street crime.

Drug control and social organization. The availability and use of illicit drugs may have substantial effects on the social organization of urban areas, and these aspects of social organization can in turn have a very important impact on levels of predatory crime. For example, a thriving illicit drug economy in a slum neighborhood may weaken the power and influence of legitimate social institutions. There is a seductive appeal to a drug economy in a community when drug dealers are driving expensive cars. And when they are virtually the only persons driving expensive cars, the credibility of teachers and police and legitimate businesspeople may be undermined in the eyes of the young, and the morale of conforming segments of the population may suffer. An atmosphere of demoralization can thus set in, making all forms of illegitimate activities seem both more attractive and less credibly stigmatized.

This potential for resentment may be becoming a special part of the social order of many black and Hispanic urban slum neighborhoods. Here the trappings of high income seem to be the exclusive province of drugs and gambling, and in this atmosphere, all types of crime proliferate. At the same time, organized criminal enterprise and particularly vice markets have provided some opportunity and upward social mobility in slum settings. Gambling and alcohol are two examples of enterprises that have served as engines of social mobility for disadvantaged minorities. There is no reason to suppose that the current markets for illicit drugs are any exception to this time-honored pattern. There is more than anecdotal evidence that the economic rewards of even sporadic street-level drug dealing exceed the legitimate labor opportunities available to most young persons in many urban environments. To some extent, therefore, illegal markets for drugs provide opportunities for social mobility that can have some positive impact on the community.

Nobody would wish to limit urban communities to a choice between additional income and social mobility at the price of extensive demoralization of a struggling middle class versus a slum setting almost completely devoid of economic opportunity. There are, however, neighborhoods where these options appear to be the field of choice.

The impact of changes in drug control

Changes in drug control policy might have several impacts that in turn would be related to levels of predatory crime. A shift in the amount or kind of enforcement could affect the availability of a particular drug, the mix of drugs in a community, the organization of drug markets, or the levels of violence associated with drug commerce. Any one of these changes might affect patterns and levels of street crime.

The current discussion has centered on the trade-off between the crime reduction that may be achieved because criminal sanctions reduce the availability of drugs and thus their criminogenic impact, and the crime-generating impact of illegality because of the higher prices for drugs and an underground and violence-prone distribution network. Yet assessing the likely impact of marginal changes in drug control policy is not necessarily the same as determining the trade-off between prohibition and decriminalized markets. The critical questions for the near term concern the effect of 50 percent price changes and 25 percent changes in supply levels on crime rates in the short and middle run. It is not obvious that any of the effects of drug prohibition are linear. But these sorts of marginal determination of impacts on crime are no less necessary because of their indeterminate complexity.

Some conclusions

These hypotheses do not exhaust the possible relationships between variations in drug control and levels of predatory street crime. We have tried to

illustrate the range of possible effects rather than to construct an encyclope-
dia of potential drug policy impacts. But our hypotheses seem sufficiently
broad to support three conclusions.

First, there are plausible hypotheses that cut both ways when discussing
the relationships between the availability of illicit drugs and the levels of
predatory crime. In some circumstances it seems likely that active illegal drug
markets will escalate street crime, but in other circumstances the increased
availability of drugs may decrease risk, at least for some potential victim
groups.

Second, the impact of particular drug countermeasures on levels of predatory crime may vary in accordance with the surrounding community environment. Lowering the availability of drugs may decrease predatory crime where
the number of dependent users is small and the elasticity of demand is extremely high. But raising the price of drugs for large numbers of dependent
users who habitually commit crimes to obtain money to buy them can have
the opposite effect. Because these impacts vary with the setting, the capacity
to generalize about the criminogenic effects of drug control policy shifts is
necessarily limited.

Third, the indirect and difficult-to-measure effects of drug control policy
may be more important than are the more direct and more easily measured
effects. The impact of drug markets on morale among conforming segments
of the population is not the sort of short-term, overt, or direct effect that can
be easily included in a statistical study of the results of drug control policy
shifts on street crime. But the impact of morale shifts may nonetheless be
substantial. Accordingly, the latent, long-term, and indirect influences of drug
control policy are essential to understand, albeit difficult to measure.

Our overall conclusion is that the impact of shifts in drug control policy
on crime is at present an empirical question, difficult to predict from the
available evidence in either its direction or magnitude. The causal role of
illicit drugs in the dynamic of predatory crime in the American city may be
substantial, but the case has not been proved. Very few measurements have
been made, and some of the greatest influences produced by variations in
drug availability may be quite difficult to measure statistically. Even episodes
of successful measurement encounter hazards of generalization because the
particular environment in which a policy is executed has such a profound
influence on its impact. It is thus best to regard the variations in drug control
policy now taking place as experimental trials. Such policy shifts should be
viewed as the basis for learning more about drug–crime links rather than as
the basis for confident assessments about the drug–crime connection. The
problem we see is that very few shifts in drug control policy are approached
as if they are meant to explore the direction and nature of the drug–crime
connection. And if not constantly challenged, the hypotheses that animate
official drug control strategies will harden into orthodoxy with amazing speed.

III. An agnostic agenda

Uncertainty about the nature and magnitude of drug policy impacts on crime
rates is no license for inaction, and so this section is a guide to the kinds of
decisions that we think should be taken under these uncertain conditions.
We shall first suggest a distinction between the priority that should be given
to drug issues in the allocation of crime control resources and the priority
that should be given to crime issues in the allocation of drug control resources. The policy implications that we shall derive from current levels of
uncertainty are quite different for these two policy spheres.

The second part of this section will then apply the general perspective by
exploring the justification of three drug measures in criminal justice policy:
drug treatment programs for once-convicted offenders, drug surveillance as
a crime control technique, and differential sanctions for drug-involved street
criminals. The final section will consider crime problems as a drug control
priority. We shall argue that a major investment of discretionary drug control
resources is entirely appropriate in those areas and groups where drug use
and predatory crime coincide.

Contrasting priorities

We shall begin with two contrasting conclusions. The state of current knowledge does not justify giving drug control countermeasures any special preference when selecting methods for controlling predatory street crime. At the
same time, it is entirely appropriate when allocating drug control resources
to give special attention to those drugs, persons, and areas where illicit drugs
are bound up with patterns of predatory criminal behavior.

If a million dollars were to be budgeted for the control of robbery and
burglary, how much of that sum should go to the apprehension and conviction of drug sellers or drug users? Based on the present evidence, not much.
There is no persuasive evidence that modest variations in the supply of particular illicit drugs have a dramatic impact on rates of street crime, and there
is no reason to believe that drug countermeasures have marginal effects on
rates of burglary and robbery that would exceed the impact achievable by
focusing the same amount of resources on measures that are specifically aimed
at burglary and robbery. Thus, it seems likely that deploying police officers
as an antiburglary squad has more promise of affecting the burglary rate than
would enlisting the same officers in a buy-and-bust operation for heroin or
crack cocaine. In a similar vein, apprehending and punishing larger numbers
of robbers, whether or not those robbers are active drug users, seems a better
bet for lowering the robbery rate than would spending the same prison resources on locking up drug sellers as a method of reducing robbery rates.

For this reason, if fear of street crime were the only reason for investing resources in antidrug campaigns, very few resources would be justified. There would simply be more promising uses for the same resources. But fear of crime is not the only reason that drugs are made criminal and that substantial resources are invested in a criminal law of drug control. In these circumstances, how substantial should be the priority given to those settings where illicit drug use and high levels of street crime coalesce?

Our answer is, very substantial. This is in no way inconsistent with our previous suggestions that anticrime resources are not most effectively spent on combating drugs. Those drugs more closely associated with high levels of predatory crime should receive larger shares of drug program funding than should illegal drugs with smaller proportionate representation in the urine tests of burglars and robbers. Those drug users who are more apt to be arrested for predatory street crime should command more attention from drug law enforcers for that reason. Other things being equal, an area with both high drug abuse and high predatory crime rates should merit the investment of many more drug countermeasures than should an area with high drug abuse but low predatory crime rates. The multiplicity of reasons that drug use and drug users are a public policy problem means that not all antidrug resources should be invested in the intersection of drugs and crime. But no one should argue against the proposition that places, persons, and drugs with higher levels of predatory crime involvement deserve higher levels of drug control resource investment.

Drug priorities in crime control

There are three aspects of crime control policy in which a special focus on drugs does seem justified. First, substantial crime control resources should support drug treatment programs in prisons and in those community settings where convicted offenders are dealt with. A substantial drop-off in predatory criminal activity follows successful drug treatment. Whether diminished involvement with drugs is a cause of this drop-off is beside the point. As long as the relationship is a predictable one, drug treatment is a good crime control investment. High-rate drug-involved criminals are a priority target not because they are a good subject for treatment but because of the great costs that will be avoided if their treatment succeeds. Even for prison programs whose effectiveness has not been established, the opportunity costs of drug treatment programs in correctional settings are minimal. Thus, drug treatment programs for serious criminal offenders should be a crime control priority.

Surveillance programs for drug use that can be directed at persons at a high risk of recidivism to street crime are a second area in which crime control resources should be invested in drug programs. Drug surveillance programs are an important tool in preventing street crime because there is evidence that high levels of criminal activity are associated with drug use among individuals with extensive histories of street crime. Again, as long as the predictive power of drug involvement is strong, a priority case for investing crime control resources has been made even if no cause-and-effect relationship between drug use and recidivism has been established.

A final justified program of drug-policy-as-crime-control is higher levels of restraining sanctions for offenders with recent drug use histories. When convicted offenders with particular patterns of drug involvement have higher risks of committing predatory crimes, criminal sanctions that are effective in reducing these risks should be differentially directed at these offenders. Considerations regarding the confinement of the extent of punishment to what is deserved by the offender may limit the extent to which such concentration should be permitted. But within desert limits, special sanctioning policies can efficiently cut crime.

The drug treatment, drug monitoring, and differential sanctioning programs we discuss here are examples of policies for which drug emphasis makes sense in the competition for crime control resources. Together, these patterns of emphasis will absorb a very minor share of a crime control budget, almost certainly less than 10 percent. By contrast, we shall argue that a majority of antidrug funding should be targeted at patterns of drug use closely associated with predatory crime.

An emphasis on crime in drug control

We announce ourselves agnostic regarding a causal relation between illicit drug use and predatory crime, yet we would concentrate a majority of control resources where the drug–crime nexus is greatest. Does this commitment of up to a majority of drug control resources not indicate a foxhole conversion to the ranks of those who believe that drugs play a major causal role in patterns of predatory crime in the United States? Not necessarily. A concentration of drug control resources at the intersection of drugs and crime in American life makes sense even to those who do not consider the causal connection of drug use and crime to have been established yet.

The strongest case can be made to focus resources on those areas in American cities with high rates of drug use and high rates of predatory crime. Concentrating drug control resources, particularly treatment resources, on these areas might reduce the level of crime even if drug use is not the original cause of criminal activity. We rely here on the data that indicate that successful drug treatment at the individual level is associated with diminished levels of criminal activity.

Further, concentrating drug control resources in high-crime zones cannot hurt if the drug–crime nexus turns out to be spurious and will turn out to be quite efficient if there is a causal relationship between drugs and crime. This strategy could be compared with Pascal's wager, in which nonbelievers were advised to act as if God existed, on the grounds that it would not do them any harm and indeed might be highly beneficial. In our view, this pattern of thinking would be a poor basis for deciding to invest substantial new resources in drug control. But as long as a particular level of resources is already committed to antidrug efforts, the possibility of substantial savings represents an argument for investing in crime-impacted areas, as opposed to nonimpacted areas.

There is also a powerful argument for concentrating drug program resources in high-crime urban areas that operates independently of any expectation of crime savings. An emphasis on high-crime zones meshes well with other priorities that should govern the allocation of discretionary resources in drug control. High-crime areas in the city are precisely where children and youth are most at risk of becoming involved in crime and delinquency, where drug traffic is most demoralizing to the middle class, and where social structure is most at risk of disorganization. Crime rates can thus serve as a proxy for a complex of factors that represent a concentration of the greatest costs associated with illicit drugs in modern America. We thus regard crime-impacted areas in American cities as high-priority candidates for any resources targeted to combat urban problems and would regard drug control funds as no exception.

The case for concentrating discretionary drug resources on those drugs frequently associated with other kinds of criminal activity is different from the case for concentrating on high-crime areas. Drugs frequently used by those arrested for nondrug felonies are more likely to be causally implicated in crime and are thus more appropriate candidates for a concentrated effort, even if the causal case has not been proved. Further, the use of these drugs in a social setting where other drug users are also committing crimes extensively is probably more dangerous to children and youth for that reason than in the case of other drugs. But if a particular drug is associated with a high overdose and death risk or other negative health indicators, these cost factors, too, can justify enforcement resources.

One approximation of the degree to which drugs lead to crime is a comparison of drug test results among those arrested with self-reported rates of drug taking from government household surveys. Table 6.1 shows such a comparison for nineteen drug use forecasting (DUF) cities and the government's household survey for marijuana and cocaine. The third column in Table 6.1 shows that cocaine use is 8.6 times as frequent among arrestees in the nineteen cities as among individuals in households nationally, whereas the parallel concentration for marijuana is only 1.6 times as frequent. Because

Table 6.1. *Positive tests for arrestees, use in last year, and concentration among offenders for marijuana and cocaine*

	1 Median % positive at arrest in DUF cities	2 % citizen reports of use in last year	3 Concentration in crime (col. 1/col. 2)
Cocaine	56	6.5	8.6
Marijuana	24	15.0	1.6

Source: U.S. Department of Justice, Office of Justice Programs, 1990; U.S. Department of Health and Human Services, 1988.

the tests for marijuana are sensitive for a much longer time than are the tests for cocaine, this probably understates the contrast between the two drugs. Obviously, giving priority to drugs with high-crime concentration favors cocaine over marijuana as a resource target.

The DUF data show substantial city-to-city variation in arrestee drug patterns that should be reflected in any policy that focuses on crime-involved drugs. Opiates, principally heroin, were found in a range from 2 to 23 percent of all arrestees, with no clear regional pattern. Three-quarters of the DUF cities found amphetamines in less than 5 percent of persons arrested, but San Diego reported a 37 percent proportion of positive tests. A consistent policy of focusing on crime-involved drugs will produce a wide variation in substance priority from city to city and probably also over time.

The case for concentrating drug enforcement resources on those persons also engaged in street crime is weaker than the argument for concentrating on high-crime communities. The advantage of concentrating incapacitating sanctions such as jail and prison on drug offenders who are also active criminal predators lies in the collateral incapacitating benefits of crime prevented when such multiple offenders are restrained. It is not generally true that those active in both street crime and drug use are more vulnerable to apprehension or conviction for their drug activities. Instead, the pattern is the reverse, with only about one-third of California prison inmates who reported selling drugs in the prior three years being in prison for drug sales, whereas 90 percent of the inmates who reported committing any robberies were in prison for robbery (see Peterson and Braiker, 1980).

If a more evenly enforced punishment threat may serve as a credible deterrent to drug sales and possession, this must be balanced against the incapacitation advantages of focusing on those drug users who frequently commit collateral crimes. And the relative ease with which we can apprehend robbers and burglars means that a special focus on street criminals in drug enforcement is not an obvious necessity.

Some of the things that drug enforcers need to learn about policy impacts can be gleaned from carefully assessing ongoing enforcement initiatives. These soundings can help us determine the effect of a policy on drug availability as well as the effect of these availability changes on crime patterns. But we also need to continue research at the individual level, on how different types of drug users who frequently commit street crime respond to changes in drug price and availability. Much more work on the impact of prison-based and other compulsory drug treatment programs, and also a rigorous assessment of drug monitoring of persons at a high risk of street crime, including random assignment experiments, is required. To the extent that drug use is an important precursor of crime, drug monitoring in the community can be viewed as a competitive method of social defense with imprisonment for incapacitation.

Knowing as little as we currently do, there can be no greater harm done to the prospects for rational drug control policy than failing to support an aggressive research program on drug control and predatory crime.

7

The federal role in a national drug strategy

This chapter will explore the role of the federal government in determining and carrying out drug control policy. The United States is a nation of myriad different governments that share responsibility for public order and crime control. There are thousands of different police forces in the United States, and many cities have police from three or four different levels of government deployed in the same domain. Fifty-one different prison systems and thousands of local jails share responsibility in the United States. Often, just as government functions overlap, some responsibilities that all would agree should belong to some form of government lie substantially unperformed, as each level of government waits for another level to take the lead in providing or paying for a service. An effective drug control policy thus cannot be designed without taking into account the distinctiveness and complexity of the governmental system in the United States.

A whole chapter on the role of the federal government? Intergovernmental relations seems like an arid, technical topic altogether lacking the elements that enliven debates about drug control. Not surprisingly, the issue of an appropriate federal role has attracted little interest as a conceptual matter, and important issues regarding federal responsibility have been decided in Congress in an offhanded manner on an ad hoc basis. Yet drug control is the important test case of federalism in criminal justice in the 1990s: the subject of the most significant experiment in enlarging the federal lead in taking responsibility for crime control in this century. Moreover, issues of federal and state relationships can have a substantial impact on the implementation and the chances of success of any drug policy.

There is another reason that we think that an extended consideration of the federal role is necessary here. The current discussion of federal aid, federal standards, and the appropriate federal function in drug control seems to be conducted in almost complete ignorance of the previous experiment with extensive federal government involvement in criminal justice: the so-called war on crime of the 1960s, 1970s, and early 1980s. This ignorance prevails even though the current war on drugs is rather obviously a replacement for the war on crime as a federal-level response to public anxiety and alarm about crime and violence. Between 1968 and 1981 the federal government spent $8 billion through the U.S. Law Enforcement Assistance Administration on a "national war on crime" (Cronin et al., 1981). Yet in the current drug control debate, the obvious parallels with that earlier episode have been ignored. One way to compel attention to our previous experience with the competence and limits of federal government action in this area is to devote sustained independent analysis to issues of the public administration of drug control.

The first part of this chapter deals with the distribution of drug control functions and authority among three different levels of government: federal, state, and local. The second section discusses the assignments of responsibility among different branches of government for drug-related programs. We shall ask whether a program dealing with crack-damaged children should be the responsibility of that branch of government responsible for drug control or of that in charge of child welfare, and what set of principles should determine this choice. The third section of the chapter considers three basic questions of organizational strategy for the federal efforts. We shall first examine whether the federal government should seek balance in the total programs of drug control at all levels of government or seek to balance it with federal efforts only. We shall look at how federal assistance can foster state and local experiments in drug control. Finally, we shall consider whether federal aid is best given to a state or municipal government in the interest of enhanced drug control, or directly to operating agencies.

I. Levels of government: The limited federal role

Drug policy in a federal system involves a series of decisions about allocating responsibility among levels of government, and a well-coordinated policy is thus a study of intergovernmental relations. The key questions are who should set policy, who should pay for it, and who should execute it among the many agencies of federal, state, and local government that claim an interest in drug control. Allocations of responsibility by level of government carry consequences that have a long-term importance. But little attention has been paid to level-of-government issues in current drug policy discussions, and the allocations of responsibilities that take place seem haphazardly determined.

The *National Drug Control Strategy* document published in 1989 contains only passing reference to mechanisms for coordinating the efforts of federal, state, and local governments. It discusses at greater length the problems presented by the multiple drug control activities of different federal agencies (Office of National Drug Control Policy, 1989, pp. 29–31). Yet the clear

Table 7.1. *Criminal justice function by level of government, United States, fiscal year 1986*

	Prisoners (%)	Jail inmates (%)	Police (%)
Federal	7	1	8
State	93	—	15
Local	—	99	77
Total	100	100	100
	(540,963)	(277,271)	(737,741)

Source: Zimring and Hawkins, 1991, p. 138 (prison and jail); U.S. Department of Justice, Bureau of Justice Statistics, 1987, p. 15 (police).

majority of all antidrug criminal justice resources are in the state and local governments, and so the nuts and bolts of coordinating federal, state, and local governments is essential to policy planning.

A disciplined analysis of the appropriate role for levels of government in drug policy will cover issues of tradition, of comparative advantage, and of coordination of function. We shall present in this section a checklist of inter-governmental issues under these three headings.

A peculiar tradition

The traditional division of authority in criminal justice is important to a discussion of drug control both because it reflects normative conceptions regarding the proper role of various levels of government and because it has produced institutional arrangements that a national-level drug control policy must either live with or seek to alter. The usual allocation of authority in criminal justice is one in which the federal government plays a distant secondary role to that of the state and local governments. The state governments usually assume responsibility for the penal law and the prison system, and the local governments are in charge of policing, prosecution, and jails. Table 7.1 illustrates the distribution of authority by level of government for prison inmates, jail inmates, and police officers for the fiscal year 1986. Over 90 percent of persons in prison in the United States are held in state prisons, and about 7 percent are in federal prisons. There is an even larger percentage of prisoners in local jails.

Measuring precisely the proportion of police at each level of government in the United States requires a series of problematic decisions about whether meat inspectors or state tax auditors should be classified as police. But the dominance of local government in positions defined as police jobs cannot be

Table 7.2. *Distribution of prisoners by drug and nondrug offenses, United States, 1986*

	Drug offenses (%)	Nondrug offenses (%)
Federal prison[a]	30	4
State prison	70	96
Total	100	100
	(49,000 est.)	(514,000)

[a] Drug estimates based on adding 10 percent to the 12,038 number based on a 91 percent sample.
Sources: U.S. Department of Justice, Bureau of Justice Statistics, 1987, Tables 6.25, 6.26, 6.55.

questioned, and local governments have a monopoly on the generalist police whose car and foot patrol activities are usually considered a core responsibility of the police. At the federal and state level, single-subject specialization is the rule rather than the exception and can lead to whole agencies with single topical concerns, such as the highway patrol or the U.S. Drug Enforcement Administration (DEA).

If drug control policy followed a typical pattern of criminal justice in the United States, decisions about the proper scope regarding the criminal law of drugs, as well as penalties, would be made at the state level; policing and prosecution would be the responsibility of local governments; and federal responsibilities would serve as a backup to state judgments about which drugs merit prohibition, as well as in areas of trans-state impact, such as border patrol, interstate transportation, and organized crime. The federal government has, however, played a less prominent role in drug control policy for most of the twentieth century. The Harrison Act of 1914 established federal standards for the criminality of drugs and a punishment scheme that has produced substantial federal criminal justice activity for three-quarters of a century. Table 7.2 demonstrates the special status of drugs by comparing the distribution of prison populations by drug and nondrug offenses for federal versus state prisons during 1986.

As Table 7.2 shows, about 30 percent of those in prison for drug offenses during 1986 were in federal prisons, a minority of all drug offenders but a concentration seven times as large as the proportion of nondrug offenders confined in federal prisons. A similar pattern of larger federal investment in drug rather than nondrug crime can be found in policing. The U.S. Drug Enforcement Administration is a separate police force at the federal level, the largest single-subject police force in national government (Office of National Drug Control Policy, 1990, p. 13). The federal agencies dealing with customs, air transport, immigration, and the FBI all have resources committed to drug control policy. Although it is difficult to estimate precisely the relative level of effort at the federal and local police levels, something approaching the thirty–seventy split that was observed in the prison system would not be a surprise.

The direct involvement of the federal government in drug law enforcement is therefore more substantial than in crime control generally. Is this simply a function of the mix of drug crime, including a larger number of offenses that present special problems for which only a federal police and prosecutorial presence will do? As we shall observe, there are a series of drug offenses for which a federal law enforcement presents a comparative advantage, including the importation of drugs across national boundaries and drug crimes involving multistate operations. But an analysis of the offenses for which convictions are obtained in the federal system suggests that these "special function" circumstances seem to be a minority of drug offenses at conviction in the federal criminal justice system. The sale and possession of modest amounts of drugs apparently in single locations are by far the dominant offenses prosecuted in the federal criminal justice system (Frase, 1980, p. 260).

The unusual concentration of national government resources in the drug area reflects more than a focus on transnational or interstate commerce in illicit drugs. Since the Harrison Act was passed, the national government has been a primary agency in the establishment and enforcement of prohibition, and it has continued to operate as a stakeholder in the enforcement of drug prohibitions for most of the twentieth century. The recent efforts of federal agencies to set national-level drug policy thus are not innovations.

But the proportionate federal share of federal, state, and local law enforcement efforts in drugs does not seem to reflect any clear judgment about functionally appropriate or historically stable allocations of responsibility. The principal determinant of whether the federal share of drug prisoners will be 30 percent (as it was in 1986) rather than 20 or 40 percent seems to be the level of federal effort expended, a unilateral decision of the national government.

The question of comparative advantage

What can be said about the apparent comparative advantages of federal versus local policing in the drug field, and of federal versus state and local prosecution and punishment? From a purely functional perspective, the advantages of federal law enforcement occur in the administration of policies against importation and other areas in which multinational or multistate activities extend beyond the ordinary scope of state and local law enforcement. There seem to be equivalent advantages favoring drug law enforcement at the local level where knowledge of local conditions, a police patrol presence, contacts in the community, or the capacity to relate shifts in drug-related phenomena to other changes in the community is required (see Haaga and Reuter, 1990). These community contacts all seem to favor stable, locally based, general-jurisdiction police agencies as the drug law enforcement of choice at the street level.

There is, in addition, a substantial deployment flexibility for general-jurisdiction police, so that resources can be readily shifted from drug to non-drug tasks in a way that single-subject police agencies such as the U.S. Drug Enforcement Administration cannot. In theory, general-jurisdiction officers can be shifted from a patrol function to antidrug activity to traffic control as needs and priorities change at the local level over time. When a single-subject police agency scales up or down, however, there is pressure to continue the new level of laborpower in subject-matter enforcement functions. Adding personnel to a single-subject police force can therefore have larger long-term functional consequences than can adding to laborpower levels in general-jurisdiction police agencies. There always are other functions to absorb laborpower in the general-jurisdiction setting.

At the present time, federal drug police are better able than are local police to develop and deploy specialists and to concentrate resources in a single geographic zone by shifting them from elsewhere in a national jurisdiction. In addition, federal drug police have historically enjoyed better pay and greater access to resources than local police have. This may result in the federal drug police's having more qualified personnel in both line and staff positions.

With respect to criminal prosecution, the only clear comparative advantages for federal prosecution are the larger resources and specialization available for drug cases. This may have special significance in complex cases and in cases in which witness relocation or multijurisdictional intelligence capacities play a special role. But also important is the larger federal resources available for drug cases in the current policy climate in which drug prosecutions are politically popular. When the penalties available under federal law are substantially larger than the maximum punishment mandated under state law, the larger threat of punishment gives federal prosecutors a superior means of securing witnesses' cooperation or plea bargains (Gershman, 1990).

In theory, if the federal advantage in law enforcement or prosecution is limited to a particular form of expertise, this could result in a technical assistance model in which state and local governments make substantive decisions and the federal government provides technical help. There are precedents for this kind of federal law enforcement assistance help, such as the federal fingerprint, criminal records, and stolen property registries in the FBI. But most of the federal–local collaborations in the drug control area mean federal policy dominance.

More significant for us than the details of an analysis based on comparative advantage is the novelty of this sort of analysis in a discussion of drug control policy in the United States. Our most important point is simply that coherent drug control policy requires sustained attention to the appropriate role of different levels of government in drug law enforcement. This is particularly relevant to drugs because the absence of a clear-cut traditional dominance in a single level of government in both law enforcement and prosecution generates more natural competition among levels of government for criminal justice functions. Responsibility for drug policy is more of an open question, and so calculations of comparative advantage may have practical importance. Any proposal for a shift in drug control responsibility that does not address issues of comparative advantage should be viewed with suspicion.

Separate questions. A second point worth emphasizing is that an adequate discussion of the allocation of responsibility among various levels of government must deal with three separate questions: (1) What share of the resources necessary to support particular drug control activities should come from federal, as opposed to state and local, government? (2) Which task capabilities should be part of federal law enforcement agencies? and (3) What share of particular activities in drug law enforcement should be performed by federal agencies? The distinction between financial and operational responsibility in drug control is new. Traditionally, drug enforcement activities were funded by the level of government that did the work. The federal drug law initiatives of 1986 and 1988 used models such as those found in education and road construction, in which federal funding and standards are combined with state operational responsibilities (see Pub. L. No. 100-690 §2021-41, 102 Stat. 4194 [1988]). This model of state assistance is having its initial trials in the 1990s.

Two separate questions must be asked about drug control functions in federal agencies. Analysts must first decide whether a particular activity is appropriate to the federal agency and then must determine the extent of this federal activity when federal, state, and local governments' competencies overlap. The question of whether federal drug law enforcement agencies ought to have any street-level buy-and-bust capacity is the sort of question that can be decided without an extended examination of current state and local resources. But determining the scale of federal efforts of this kind requires judgments about performance capabilities of federal versus local agencies that make the discussion as much one about the capacities of local as of federal law enforcement. This question of the scale of federal operations in drug control is a multibillion dollar issue in the 1990s.

Principles of coordination

Despite the rhetoric, the coordination of any law enforcement functions with federal, state, and local governments is not a setting in which the levels of government meet as equals. Federal laws are, by constitutional design, supreme, and so any doctrinal conflict between national government and state government on a legal issue will be resolved in favor of the national government. But supremacy in theory becomes supremacy in practice only if the national government wishes to invest its own resources in executing policy. For example, if a state government wishes to de-emphasize marijuana or even decriminalize it, the existing federal statutes will be sufficient to maintain the criminal status of the drug, but the state-level decriminalization will take hold if no federal resources are invested in enforcing the prohibition.

The state assistance legislation of the late 1980s attempts to coerce the states into complying with some federal standards as a condition of receiving federal aid, but this direct approach is limited by the fact that state governments, the recipients of the federal dollars, do not control drug policing or prosecution. There also are political pressures against making credible the threat of fund cutoffs. There has not yet been a real confrontation on this front.

It therefore is best to characterize the policy position of the national government in drug control as one of contingent supremacy, with the primary contingency being the willingness to commit independent federal resources. When federal agencies conflict with state and local governments on the priority that is to be given to a federal goal, the national government must enforce its own edicts. The clearest examples of this phenomenon concern the possession of marijuana in those jurisdictions that have sharply de-escalated criminal penalties, as well as the apparent conflict between the federal government and many state and local governments on the priority of eradicating the domestic marijuana supply in the national drug control policy. Backing up unpopular priorities might require a disproportionate investment of federal resources. But national and subnational drug control policies generally agree on most drug control priorities, so that there is a theoretical opportunity for joint action and coordination of activity. Models of joint activity now include strike forces (usually under federal policy dominance), federal fiscal aid to state government, and federally controlled efforts such as the high-impact initiatives announced in the 1989 *National Drug Control Strategy* for Washington, D. C., and extended to other jurisdictions in 1990.

When surveying the limited history of intergovernmental drug cooperation, one important contrast is between the horizontal and the vertical coordination of criminal justice tasks. The horizontal coordination of criminal justice functions involves agencies that perform parallel functions at different levels of government. For example, there is horizontal cooperation with the local police operating on a case in tandem with the DEA. Vertical models of cooperation or integration involve nonparallel criminal justice agencies in different levels of government working together. An example is the DEA's working with a local prosecutor on a state law case against narcotics defendants, or a federal prosecutor working with local police toward the same end. Horizontal cooperation is much more common than is vertical cooperation among levels of government in drug law enforcement. Indeed, there are few examples of pure vertical coordination in drug control or any other law enforcement area. Usually, some contact between the parallel agencies, for example, federal and local police, precedes or accompanies the contact between agencies at different vertical points in federal, versus local, criminal justice. The cultural gaps between different criminal justice agencies are at least as great, apparently as is the gap between different levels of government.

Principles for allocating resources. Even a $10 billion federal drug control effort faces problems of allocating limited resources that must be spread over a nation of 250 million, with thousands of political subdivisions. Three different strategies compete for use when the issue is allocating national-level resources; principles of proportion, need, and effort. A proportional strategy for allocating resources simply allocates laborpower or gives money to subfederal levels of government on a per capita basis. The usual mechanism for this is block grants of money. These grants in the drug control area are usually given to the states and then passed on to other levels of government through state mechanisms (see U.S. Senate Select Committee, 1990, pp. 124–7). Proportional formulas are much more common in allocating money than in allocating laborpower. Political pressures for pro rata allocation are powerful and inevitable when cash transfers are the mechanisms of intergovernmental assistance.

A competing principle is one of need, with a drug control policy providing resources to those areas that have the greatest drug problems. When it is enforcement resources rather than money being partitioned, need principles are more frequently used. The level of government that is the target of the need allocation is more frequently the city or the metropolitan area than state levels of government (see Office of National Drug Control Policy, 1989, pp. 129–30).

But new resources can be also allocated to reward efforts by state and local governments rather than pure need, and so federal resources are targeted to help those areas of state and local governments that are helping themselves most effectively. This deviation from a per capita formula comes most often when nonfinancial resources rather than grant-in-aid programs are the basis of distribution. What this can mean is that those making policy choices at the federal level might have to choose between inefficient real-world choices when the best solution would be cash grants to areas with special needs or meritorious local efforts. A cash grant may risk the aid formula by reverting to a per-person basis, whereas in-kind services may be less effective and more expensive than those that states and cities could produce with cash aid.

Federal drug leverage: Limits and implications. In financial markets, leverage is the process of using a high proportion of other people's money to support your own investment position. The federal drug control analogy to leverage is the minority share of federal funding in the recent drug war plans. What is called a national drug control strategy requires enforcement of criminal prohibitions that are federally funded at somewhere between 35 and 50 percent of the total resource expenditures. From a federal perspective, this sort of leverage sounds quite attractive – would that Social Security or agricultural support programs be so generously cofunded by other levels of government. But one drawback of such funding in drug control, as in other investments, is that diminished control over programs is associated with lower levels of federal government support.

If the federal government is providing 40 percent of all drug control funding, a doubling of the federal drug budget would only increase drug control activity to 140 percent of previous efforts if state and local efforts remained constant. This is a relatively modest increase in activity, but even the 40 percent figure is vulnerable to states' and localities' reducing their drug control expenditures to take account of the new federal expenditures. For example, doubling the number of persons in federal prisons for drug crime would raise the number of imprisoned drug offenders by only 30 percent if the states did not change their drug offender imprisonment policies (see Table 7.2). If the states did reallocate some of their scarce prison space to other crime categories, a federal expansion might have little or no net effect on total drug imprisonment.

In those circumstances, carrying over a federal drug war into a real expansion of total antidrug resources requires a great deal of federal jawboning as well as extra financial resources. If states and localities are satisfied with prior levels of effort, they can disinvest their own money in order to balance the larger federal spending. The federal government must find a method of disturbing a sense of equilibrium in state and local government so as to produce real increases in police, criminal adjudication, and prison resources directed at drug control.

Therefore, the federal government must put pressure on the states and localities if new federal money is to enlarge the total drug control investment. One tactic is requiring fund matchings or the maintenance of state and local efforts as a condition of federal financial aid. But because there is little federal dollar aid for policing and prisons, nonfinancial pressure is also a necessary aspect of pressuring nonfederal agencies to allow control efforts to increase, and the penchant for oratory that the first federal drug czar has displayed may be an important part of his successor's job as well if the federal government is to dominate drug control, despite its minority funding. In this light, crisis appeals by the U.S. president and the drug czar to the general public to regard drugs as a problem can be seen as a stratagem of intergovernmental relations.

II.   Branches of government: Program management and program labels

Not all governmental programs that address problems caused by drug use should be managed or controlled by the office that coordinates drug control strategy. If a drug nexus were a sufficient cause to assign program responsibility, the nation's drug control office would be running a panoply of enterprises ranging from urban renewal to foster care placement to drug interdiction to agricultural subsidies in drug-source countries. Thus, although there is no doubt that the health and custody problems of the newborns referred to as "crack babies" are drug related, it is quite another matter to argue that the control of government programs to help such children should be the responsibility of the governmental agency that coordinates drug control.

Intuitively, it would seem more suitable to classify crack babies as the primary responsibility of governmental agencies that usually deal with babies rather than those that deal with crack cocaine. This section will explore the rationales behind such an intuition, in search of criteria for determining which drug-related programs belong under the auspices of the drug control agency and which do not.

Four aspects of the problem of crack-damaged babies make it a poor candidate for administration by a drug control agency: (1) There are compelling nondrug values at risk; (2) the problem is closely linked to other issues that are not administered by a drug control agency; (3) responding to the problem requires skills and perspectives that are not associated with drug enforcement; and (4) responding to the problem may conflict with drug enforcement values that should be resolved in favor of the nondrug values.

The first argument against subsuming crack babies under the heading of drug administration is that there are nondrug values at risk in dealing with these infants that are more important than the drug law enforcement interests at issue. The compelling values we refer to are those of child welfare, the need to identify and protect babies at risk. Because this other-than-drug-control value is regarded as of controlling importance, the administration of the problem by other than a drug agency would be indicated.

Related to the dominant importance of child welfare is the fact that crack babies present a series of problems that are closely linked to issues that are not under the control of drug agencies. The crack baby problem is a fraternal if not identical twin to the problem of children born with fetal alcohol syndrome, and it is closely related to the problems posed by other newborns who are at special risk because of the combination of systemic illness and parental neglect. Any public policy that would treat crack babies as substantially different from newborns with fetal alcohol syndrome would probably have to do so based on a criterion other than child welfare. Yet any isolation of public policy toward crack children strengthens the probability that the criteria and programs administered under this rubric would not be consistent with the treatment of other high-risk infants.

Helping crack babies also calls for skills and perspectives that are not usually associated with a drug control agency. Expertise on child welfare, with specific reference to when prior neglect indicates an unacceptable risk of future endangerment; experience with foster care placement and administration; and the design of social services to monitor the quality of child care are not the skills or experience to be expected of a drug czar or czarina. The more that a program requires skills and perspectives greatly different from those associated with mainstream drug enforcement, the greater will be the case that the administrative responsibility for the program belongs outside a drug bureaucracy.

A final argument against drug agency control of crack baby policy is the likelihood of conflict between important child welfare values and the usual objectives of the drug control agency. As long as the child welfare objective is regarded as paramount, any potential conflict between drug enforcement and child welfare values argues for the outplacement of crack baby responsibility so as to avoid improper subordination of the child welfare values.

The medical literature suggests that babies born of cocaine-using mothers who have had continual prenatal care are disadvantaged when compared with babies born of non-drug-using mothers, but these children are probably vastly better off than are babies born of cocaine-using mothers who have had no prenatal care (see Chasnoff, 1988; Chasnoff et al., 1986; MacGregor et al., 1987). Policies that require physicians to report drug-abusing women risk the disadvantage of producing children likely to have received the benefit of less prenatal care and neonatal monitoring because pregnant drug-abusing women were deterred from seeking or sustaining programs of medical care. If the primary concern is child welfare, an open-door policy should be ex-

tended even to drug-abusing women. Conditioning prenatal care on abstinence only risks compounding the catastrophes for the children most at
risk.

Thus, an aggressive concern with child welfare justifies outreach programs
that identify and serve pregnant drug-using women without disclosing their
identities to enforcement agencies, programs that would tolerate repeated
violations of treatment agreements and conditions in the hopes that such re-
lapses could be overcome and a lower-risk newborn could result. But the
emphasis on privacy and the tolerance of relapse that the programs use to
recruit and hold pregnant women run against the drug treatment philosophy
of most drug enforcement agencies. Such strategies are certainly at odds with
the current philosophy of drug treatment programs as espoused by the *National Drug Control Strategy* (Office of National Drug Control Policy, 1989,
pp. 35–44).

A conflict between drug control and nondrug control values does not necessarily argue for placing program responsibility outside an office of drug
control. When the drug control values are considered paramount, the potential conflict with other program goals becomes an argument for locating administrative responsibility inside rather than outside an office of drug control
policy. In this connection, it can be said that the priority of values to be
served in the policy area should directly determine the sort of agency selected
to administer the policy.

The list of criteria explored in the crack baby example is illustrative but
by no means exhausts the issues that arise when considering the proper lo-
cation of administrative responsibility for drug-related programs. A decision
might turn on judgments about the institutional capacity of various administrative agencies to consider and balance a wide spectrum of considerations
as they may concern a drug-related problem. The State Department, for example, considers itself a better place to decide how the cooperation or non-
cooperation of foreign governments in drug matters can be balanced against
other considerations in determining American policy toward particular countries (see U.S. Senate Select Committee, 1988). The argument thus is that
drug control agencies give too much weight to drug issues. The capacity for
peripheral vision may be a significant advantage even if no single nondrug
interest is regarded as compelling.

The incomplete list of criteria just discussed suggests a number of areas in
which decision-making power on drug-related problems might best rest outside agencies of drug control. The manifold problems of needle sharing and
the transmission of AIDS are prime candidates for other than drug agency
coordination. The potential for conflict between minimizing the transmission
of AIDS and drug enforcement values is apparent when the policy options

include the distribution of clean needles to drug abusers under needle exchange programs. This is opposed by many drug enforcement groups because it expands the potential for intravenous drug use, by making needles more easily available (Tolchin, 1989). From a drug enforcement perspective, needle sharing also raises problems because the government provision of the means for injection seems to carry an official seal of approval for felonious drug behavior. This kind of dissonance makes needle sharing an awkward policy for a drug control agency. Even if such a policy makes sense, it should be housed elsewhere, probably in public health agencies.

With respect to protecting and reclaiming neighborhoods at risk from drug traffic, the case for other than drug control administration of programs rests first with the fact that identifying the best ways to deal with neighborhood programs may call on skills quite different from those needed for drug control. Further, the apparatus of drug law enforcement is one of a wide range of alternative resource investments that may be deployed in an effort to shore up neighborhoods. A drug control agency not only has drug control tools at its disposal; it also has a bias in favor of its drug control apparatus. It has been said that if the only tool one has is a hammer, an awful lot of problems will appear to call for nails. Efficient urban policy might require other tools.

Countervailing pressures

Placing the administration of drug-related programs beyond the control of drug enforcers carries both organizational and political costs that need to be considered. The primary organizational hazard in the outplacement of drug-related programs is the inconsistency or disharmony that can result when different antidrug initiatives are not subject to a centralized review. To bring all child-at-risk programs under a common management necessarily risks a lack of coordination among public programs for drug-affected children and other public programs directed at drug abusers. Placing a needle exchange program under the management of a public health agency risks the expenditure of public monies by one agency to distribute syringes to a population of drug users, while at the same time another agency may spend considerable resources to arrest drug users in possession of the publicly provided syringes.

If these problems were purely organizational, collaborative consultations among health and safety and law enforcement agencies might reduce both the overlap and the conflict. But to the extent that there are substantive clashes of priority between drug enforcement and other public policy goals, more than a committee meeting will be necessary to harmonize policy. The best solution currently available is to house a particular policy in the agency that serves the goals that should be paramount in relation to the particular problem at hand. Who makes that decision and at what point in the particular administrative process is an open question more likely to be decided in the political arena rather than as a theoretical issue of public administration.

There also are political pressures at work to recharacterize drug-related programs in ways that appear both logically and logistically awkward. Much as the crack baby presents problems that are common to a larger and a more diverse population of newborns at risk, program administrators frequently find that there is more "drug money" than "baby money" available in the political process and so relabel both programs and target populations to maximize their resource commitments.

What is wrong with calling the program an antidrug campaign if the resources available to crack-damaged newborns increase as a consequence? Even if the principles of program administration must be bent in the direction of drug enforcement priorities, it can be contended that the extra resources are doing more good for than harm to children. Further, selling social services as drug abuse prevention is seen by many as a way of competing for resources that would otherwise be monopolized by law enforcement and other mechanisms of drug supply reduction. So here is an inescapable aspect of realpolitik that must help determine the way in which programs are packaged, administered, and evaluated. The service provider can encounter circumstances in which it is necessary, in the phrase of one observer, "to rise above mere principle."

The two substantive problems with classifying welfare programs as drug control are inconsistency in welfare administration and inappropriate priorities. If the drug authorities are running the newborn program, fetal alcohol children might be neglected in a manner inconsistent with the general policies of child welfare, and punitive responses to program failures by mothers might put some babies at risk. The largest program area in which this sort of reclassification may take place is in publicly funded drug treatment programs.

III. The organizational strategy of federal effort

The preceding sections have considered the distribution of drug control responsibilities across different levels and branches of government. This section will carry that analysis further by looking at three linked questions relating to intergovernmental relations and drug control from the perspective of the federal government : (1) Whether federal budgets should consider expenditure patterns at all levels of government when making resource allocations; (2) the extent to which federal policy should attempt to control state and local drug control; and (3) whether state or local governments or other institutions should be the main recipients of federal monetary aid.

The issue of wide-angle balance

The drug control budget can be either $12 billion or more than twice that sum, depending on whether the focus is on the federal budget for such activity or on national expenditures by all branches and levels of government. Conventional budgeting at the federal level would focus on the smaller number and balance the expenditures among activities as if the political and strategic mission were the division of the federally funded share into antidrug activities.

Viewing the total level of expenditures as more than twice as much by taking into account on what states and localities are spending their resources can create a different sense of how federal funds need to be spent to balance the total drug control funding. Because law enforcement and prison are traditionally very large shares of the local and state governments' drug budgets, respectively, a higher fraction of the total than of the federal drug budget will be directed at criminal law enforcement and corrections. A wide-angle budgeting perspective raises the question of whether the federal authorities should compensate for an overemphasis of law enforcement activities by providing a smaller share of distinctively federal dollars for such activities.

In the "treatment versus interdiction" debate surrounding the federal drug budget in the late 1980s, the wide-versus-narrow funding perspective was not mentioned as a significant factor by the treatment advocates. Yet a wide-angle budgeting perspective would favor larger federal investment in areas of drug control not usually supported by the state. This is obviously so with expenditures for source-country agricultural payments and multinational drug eradication programs. But any drug control regime that regards treatment and health measures as important will also be pushed by a wide-angle perspective into larger commitments to these activities.

There are pressures, however, to make the allocation of resources at each level of government a separate microcosm in which competing agencies carve up available funds without reference to program choices at other levels of government. Political forces that oppose compensatory budgeting are usually strong, because the winning side in state and local funding battles is often the most potent political force at all levels of government.

When federal dollars are invested in politically less popular drug control tasks, these resources are both more important because they are a larger fraction of total spending in this direction and less effective because the states and cities are less likely to follow the federal lead. The policy dynamic is the same here whether we are examining federal antimarijuana initiatives in Northern California forests or support of unpopular treatment programs in urban areas. And the case for maintaining a wide-angle budget perspective seems beyond reproach even if some compensatory federal investments seem foolish. The federal drug coordinating agency should seek to balance more than just federal drug control efforts into a rationalized schema.

The desirability of state and local variation

Not all aspects of the public administration of drug control have escaped public notice. Haaga and Reuter presented the case for allowing local variation in drug control effort as a product of (1) the substantial variation in the nature and impact of drug problems, (2) the impossibility of federal control when most support and operational control is in local government, and (3) the experimental variations that should be encouraged, with federal resources available to evaluate their impact (Haaga and Reuter, 1990, p. 73).

If substantial levels of federal aid are not forthcoming, the debate about the desirability of variations in local drug control strategy is academic in the literal sense, because there is no mechanism to restrain variation. It would be possible, of course, to tie drug control conditions to state aid in other areas such as health care or highway construction. But any concerted effort to influence state and local drug enforcement will likely have a price tag in categorical federal aid. If large amounts of federal aid are to be a fact of drug control in the 1990s, the issue of tying that aid to particular standards of state and local performance should be addressed. Here we suggest that the case for uniformity of policy seems weak in the early 1990s not only because different places have different types of problems but also because there is little support for a single orthodox set of drug control strategies and priorities.

Federal aid can be conditioned on a minimum level of total drug control effort as well as on the provision of minimum levels of support for particular activities. But the current impetus to require particular sanction programs – as in driver's license revocation for drug offenders – or patterns of expenditure by function or by drug seems neither justified nor easy to enforce.

It is important to distinguish between earmarking federal funds for specific purposes and attempting to control the whole range of local drug control by conditioning aid on conformity. Insisting that federal funds be dedicated to a specific purpose seems a minimum condition of any program that has a principle beyond the bloc grant. It is when a dollar in aid seeks to control ten dollars in local effort that problems occur. But the enforcement of earmarking must reach beyond scrutiny of how just the federal dollars are spent, or else states and localities will be able to withdraw a dollar in local funds for every dollar's addition in federal aid. So some broader measure of effort will be necessary to enforce even the goals of earmarking funds to produce a policy emphasis. But desirable federal conditions should include only those necessary to achieve the impact of earmarking while forbidding only those local policies that directly clash with strong federal policies. This leaves ample room for state and local variations in levels of drug control, in methods of control, and in target substances.

The recipients of federal aid

The common core of federal financial aid programs is that the national government writes the checks, but there is considerable diversity in the institutions that can become the direct beneficiaries of federal aid programs, and active competition among potential beneficiaries. Federal funds can go either to the states or to county and city governments, or they can be given directly to public and private agencies that operate the services that the federal government wishes to support.

When bloc grants are the mechanism of federal financial aid, it is state and city governments that compete to be the primary recipient of such funds, and this is a battle that state governments usually win (U.S. Senate Select Committee, 1990, pp. 124–7). The arguments in favor of the state as the main recipient include the political importance of the state unit in the federal system and the administrative ease of depositing funds in that central repository for redistribution to municipal governments and operating agencies. The arguments against the state as the recipient usually suggest that cities are the more meaningful unit of governmental organization when speaking of the experience of drug problems.

Proponents of cities as aid recipients add that making the state the recipient adds another layer of bureaucracy to the distribution of funds at the same time that it invites political considerations rather than severity of drug problems to govern the all-important question of who gets what. As total federal drug aid approaches half a billion dollars, the debate over appropriate levels of government to receive and control the distribution of this money can be expected to intensify.

The pattern of drug control emerging in the early 1990s resembles the circumstances surrounding federal anticrime aid in previous decades. For general bloc grant assistance, it is the states rather than the cities at the receiving end (compare Cronin et al., 1981, pp. 86–90, with U.S. Senate Select Committee, 1990, pp. 124–7). But for special-emphasis programs directed at targeted areas, it is the cities that are the primary recipients (compare Cronin et al., 1981, pp. 96–9, with Office of National Drug Control Policy, 1989, pp. 129–30). The high-intensity drug programs suffer as a consolation prize in the battle for federal money because much of the aid is not in cash and is subject to significant program control by federal authority. This constrains the power of the recipient cities to direct the benefits of the federal aid.

A third set of aid recipients, programs directly involved in drug functions, can directly compete for federal aid only when the federal program earmarks levels of support for specific functions. The bloc grant is thus the natural enemy of categorical programs in which service agencies can compete for direct funding.

It is not realistic to debate whether existing bloc grant strategies of federal assistance should be directed at state government versus city government, as if the question were in doubt. Until cities elect senators, the likely recipients of bloc grants will be state governments. Instead, we think that the pattern of state dominance over bloc grants should be one element considered when deciding between federal bloc grant strategies of aid and alternative assistance strategies that are more selective in choosing the functions and programs to be supported. Distrust of the bureaucracy and politics that accompany bloc grants is more profitably channeled into a push away from the bloc grant mechanism rather than efforts to divert the same set of resources and structures to city government.

The details of the analysis of intergovernmental questions are important. But nothing in this chapter is more significant than the broad point we began by making: that the government organization of drug control has been a non-topic in the legislative and policy dialogue about drugs. As the scale of governmental involvement changes and increases, this pattern of neglect must end if conditions of even minimal rationality are to be obtained.

We shall discuss in the next chapter our doubts about the long-term future of unrestricted federal financial aid to state and local drug control programs, and we shall indicate that direct federal contributions to specific antidrug activities might have a longer life expectancy than do unrestricted bloc grants. But the political and economic forces that shape bloc grant programs in the states and localities make it highly unlikely that such programs can ever be self-reforming.

8

Memorandum to a new drug czar

Dear Sir or Madam:

First, our congratulations and best wishes on your appointment. Yours is a difficult and challenging job in the 1990s, and this memorandum is intended to help.

The Office of National Drug Control Policy was sired by the enormous importance of drugs as a national issue and congressional discontent with how the federal government's role in the drug war had been administered. In the 1988 legislation, the new federal drug control office was charged with producing no less than a national strategy to combat drug abuse, and one inevitable concomitant of such a national strategy was the increased focus on the federal government's responsibility for drug control policy and its outcomes. The first "drug czar" had as his principal responsibility the creation of a comprehensive drug control strategy (see Office of National Drug Control Policy, 1989). Each succeeding occupant of this office must necessarily evaluate the impact of the policies of his or her predecessors and propose policy changes. The first drug czar faced an empty canvas and correspondingly painted it with broad strokes. Large policies were announced and supported without assessment or evaluation.

The task of succeeding generations of leadership in the federal drug war will be less romantic but of substantial practical importance. Our advice to you is offered in two layers. First, we shall identify two major deficiencies in the *National Drug Control Strategy* of the Bennett administration. Second, we shall outline five policy perspectives that are designed to fit the demands for a national drug control policy in the United States in the 1990s and beyond. Our special concern here is the policy process. We shall speak not so much about what to do but about how to go about deciding the policy goals of drug control. But recent history teaches us that rational policy usually depends on a rational process for determining policy.

177

I. Two principles

The first and second editions of the the the *National Drug Control Strategy* ignore two basic foundations for a well-considered drug control policy. The next drug czar must come to know, first, that the consequences of different patterns of illicit drug use are an important element of drug control policy choice and, second, that priorities in policy goals are just as necessary to drug control as to any other area of public administration.

Consequences count

The importance of damage control as a drug policy goal would seem to be self-evident in an era when crack babies and needle-sharing AIDS carriers are nightly features on the television news. Not so. The current federal policy statement sees drug taking itself as the only focus of antidrug efforts, to the detriment of damage control.

The absence of an emphasis on reducing the harmful consequences of drug taking can be seen in both the basic organizational scheme of federal drug control policy and the quantitative goals that the Office of National Drug Control Policy submitted as performance targets for 1991 and 1999. Damage control is excluded from the basic architecture of the federal drug control strategy because the whole federal effort is divided into reducing the supply of illicit drugs in the United States and lowering the demand for such drugs (Office of National Drug Control Policy, 1989, pp. 12–14). The only index of social harm allowed in this dichotomous scheme is the measurement of the number of illicit drug takers and the quantities of drugs they ingest. Harmful consequences to users or the community may be one reason that drugs are outlawed, but a direct attack on the harmful outcomes associated with drugs is beyond the pale of current federal policy. The preservation of life and the maintenance of health are explicit goals of that policy only to the extent that bad outcomes like crack babies or overdose deaths can be avoided by cutting the supply of drugs or the number of people who wish to take them.

We trust that a new administrator of the National Transportation Safety board would become a laughingstock if the only safety policies he or she explored were to reduce the supply of automobiles and the demand for automobile travel. Certainly these two features of transportation in the United States are related to deaths and injuries from accidents, but so are many other things that can be touched by public policy. Some would object that it should not be federal policy to make drug use safe; rather, it should be discouraged. But nonusers, too, suffer when drugs cripple and kill. Not making the harmful consequences of drug use a separate focus would make sense only if nothing except the supply and demand for illicit drugs had an impact on the harms associated with drug abuse. This is not the case.

The same tilt away from loss reduction is evident in the quantified goals of federal drug policy over the coming decade. Of the nine goals identified in the *National Drug Control Strategy*, eight are solely concerned with either the supply of drugs or the demand for drugs (Office of National Drug Control Policy, 1989, pp. 93–98). Only one of the nine identified measures – trends over time in the number of hospital emergency room mentions of drugs by doctors or patients – concerns trends over time in the harmful consequences of drug taking. Even here, however, it appears that those who constructed the *National Drug Control Strategy* are more interested in the number of drug mentions in hospital emergency rooms as an index of the level of drug use over time rather than as a measure of drug-related health costs.

The following are a few of the things that are not counted when measuring the success of our current *National Drug Control Strategy:* overdose deaths, drug-related AIDS cases, damaged and addicted newborns, and drug-related homicides. This failure to make the reduction of the harmful consequences of drugs an independent policy goal is both disingenuous and wrong.

There is inconsistency akin to doublespeak in the current drug control rhetoric. When justifying the criminal prohibition of drugs like heroin and cocaine, the harmful consequences of these drugs occupies center stage. But when designating goals for drug control strategies, these harmful consequences and their reduction suddenly are insignificant. Thus if the criminal prohibition is based on the plight of crack babies, helping these children should be an independent priority of federal policy. Likewise, the failure to focus on harmful consequences when constructing quantitative goals for drug policy is not merely a stylistic matter. The way that we keep score in drug control has a great influence on where drug control resources are directed. When the special set of goals in the national strategy rates a decline in domestic marijuana production as more important than a smaller number of drug-related deaths and injuries, we witness the violation of a public trust.

Priorities matter

Because resources are scarce, an effective public policy depends on choosing carefully the goals that government is to pursue with limited resources. Not all drugs can be controlled by all means. Yet the current *National Drug Control Strategy* refuses to assign priority candidates for public effort among the wide spectrum of illicit drugs. The problem, we are repeatedly told, is all drugs, all drug users, and in no particular order. This lack of priority is closely connected to the *National Drug Control Strategy*'s inattention to the different consequences of taking different drugs.

If the central harm in drug taking is the moral and political nature of the act, this immoral defiance is spread evenly across the range of currently prohibited substances. If the death, injury, and disorganization caused by some drugs in some settings are peripheral matters for public policy, there will be no meaningful basis for choosing among drugs in the investment of treatment, prevention, and inhibition resources. Yet such a refusal to assign priority can have perverse consequences in the allocation of federal antidrug resources. We shall show in the next section that if the *National Drug Control Strategy* means what it says, the priority target for federal antidrug efforts should be not the plight of crack babies but the middle-class marijuana users in American suburbs and towns.

Marijuana as a test case

If the suppression of all forms of illegal drug use is entitled to equal priority, without respect to the harmful consequences of the drug, marijuana should be the priority target for federal drug control efforts and should command the majority of the fiscal and law enforcement resources to be deployed in the federal antidrug effort. The connection between the current *National Drug Control Strategy* and this conclusion should be spelled out in some detail because the result is a forceful demonstration of the erroneous nature of current strategic thinking.

Based on the premises of the *National Drug Control Strategy*, marijuana use should command the majority of federal antidrug funds because marijuana is by far the most widely used of the illicit drugs. According to the official measures of the National Institute on Drug Abuse (NIDA) household survey, more citizens admit to the use of marijuana than to that of all other illicit drugs combined (National Institute on Drug Abuse, 1988). If the use of each illicit drug is to be given equivalent negative weight, and if the social user is to be regarded as just as dangerous as the addict, then the allocation of antidrug resources should be determined by a head count of users. In this sort of plebiscite, marijuana wins hands down.

The quality of marijuana use in the United States also fits well with the priority targets of the *National Drug Control Strategy*. Casual nonaddicted users are regarded in that document as particularly threatening because they encourage the contagion of illicit drug use. Such casual users are a substantial majority of all confessed marijuana smokers. And marijuana smokers are, by and large, more vulnerable to federal drug countermeasures than are many of the users of harder drugs. Marijuana users are often students and employees in mainstream occupations. With that sort of stake in conformity, the deterrent force of sanctions such as the loss of a driver's license or federal student loans has considerably more bite than it does for the inner-city crack user with little prospect of automobile ownership or college enrollment. In addition, the peculiar chemistry of marijuana reinforces the vulnerability of the smoker because residues of marijuana's active ingredient can be detected by conventional drug tests up to twenty times longer than can substances such as cocaine, heroin, and alcohol. So according to the nonconsequential logic of the *National Drug Control Strategy*, marijuana smokers present a larger threat to the general society, are more vulnerable to the range of sanctions now imposed by the drug control policy, and are much easier to discover through urine testing programs than are other drug users.

The logic of this conclusion is impeccable, but the premises on which it is based are perverse. One problem is that a decrease in the number of casual users of marijuana in the United States may have no beneficial impact on the public health. Putting aside the moral uplift that can be associated with large numbers of people being deterred from possessing or using marijuana, a shift from marijuana to alcohol in equivalent doses would promise no improvements in health-related matters like automobile accidents, drug-related assaults, and the incidence of interpersonal violence. In fact, with respect to pregnancy complications and birth defects, dose-equivalent shifts of marijuana to alcohol could create a public health deficit.

Further, it is not obvious that the character-related drug user deficits that concern commentators like James Q. Wilson could be any smaller in circumstances of dose equivalence after a major shift from marijuana to alcohol (Tonry and Wilson, 1990, pp. 521–45). Thus it is only if persons frightened away from using marijuana minimized their total intake of available psychoactive substances that a campaign against marijuana could be expected to yield any palpable benefits to the public health.

From the standpoint of every significant social value except political compliance, marijuana is a relatively benign substance, and a major campaign to reduce its use would not produce obvious or substantial benefits. It might also be politically dangerous. Many citizens concerned about the violent rot of inner-city drug-impacted areas might have less charitable characterizations of a war on pot than "uncertain in benefits" when it became clear that anti-marijuana initiatives would come at the expense of resources devoted to either enforcement or treatment for cocaine and heroin. The political consensus that reinforces the current antidrug efforts would be sorely tested by the sort of enforcement priorities that would result if one took literally the premises of the *National Drug Control Strategy*.

One of the most powerful indications of the flaws in nonconsequential thinking about drug control is that the Office of National Drug Control Policy has never followed its own advice by targeting resources without making judgments about the harm potential of different drugs. There have been well-publicized and controversial, federally supported antimarijuana forays, but these were always low-budget loss leaders in a $10 billion drug war clearly focused on harder drugs. The next drug czar faces a choice between doing what his or her predecessors recommended or doing what his or her predecessors actually did. It will be necessary to reform the official rationale for federal drug control activity so that it is consistent with the real conduct norms of drug control.

Not the smallest reason that official drug control strategy should take account of mitigating the harmful consequences of drugs as a policy goal is to provide some framework for justifying the criminal prohibition of some (but not all) drugs of abuse. Something more than the tautological reasoning that illegal drugs are wrong because their use is forbidden by law seems necessary over the long run to justify a major investment in resources to patrol the border between licit and illicit intoxicating drugs. For most citizens, that something more is a sense that the secular damage associated with illegal drug taking is sufficient to justify public investments to deter and prevent widespread abuse. To base a policy of prohibition on such premises and then to ignore loss reduction as a drug control policy goal seems exactly the kind of inconsistency that the *National Drug Control Strategy* does not need.

II. Five practices

The following are five changes in the way drug policy is made that can immediately benefit the republic: two-track thinking, a focus on marginal cost and marginal benefit, attention to the lessons that can be learned from prior federal crime wars, priority for the maintenance of reentry channels for drug users, and the adoption of a chronic disease model of drug abuse as a social problem.

Two-track thinking and policy advice

The nation's drug czar has two functions: to serve as the chief rhetorical officer in the war on drugs and to be a drug control policy planner. These two functions involve two quite different types of discourse about drugs and drug countermeasures. We pointed out in Chapter 7 that federal lobbying to citizens and to states for extra investment in drug programs is necessary lest increased federal investments in the area be counterbalanced by decreased state and local spending. At least during periods of expansion in federal resource investment, proclaiming a drug emergency and cheerleading the investment of additional resources at all levels of government is the sort of task that calls forth hyperbole in problem statement, optimism that solutions are known and available, and a rhetoric of unconditional aspiration when stating public goals. The policy-planning process, by contrast, can function only in an atmosphere of pragmatic skepticism. The policy planner is sensitive to problem overstatements, unwilling to assume countermeasure effectiveness in the absence of evidence, and concerned about keeping the goals of federal policy from exceeding the outer boundaries of the achievable. The demands on the drug czar are thus simultaneously to be realist and idealist, booster and skeptic. And the problem is that when the rhetorical style of the drug warrior invades the policy-planning process, waste and false expectations must follow, as night follows day.

There are indications that just such a rhetorical infusion has taken place in both the Office of National Drug Control Policy and Congress. The severity of the drug abuse problem is assumed rather than investigated. The competition between the political parties has produced extravagant rhetoric on drug problems and unanimity on additional billions for countermeasures at a time when a political consensus on diminishing governmental investment in many other areas has been growing. Many observers attribute this spectacle of rhetoric driving policy to unspecified "political pressures" and devote little attention to systemic factors that may contribute to the overkill. We think that the dissonance built into the dual functions of the head of the Office of National Drug Control Policy is an important influence that requires attention and precaution. The very title of drug czar is hard to associate with a position of limited expectations and resources.

One possible solution to this problem would be to separate the functions of rhetorical leadership and administrative responsibility so that two different persons hold these two different jobs. Like a corporation president versus a chief operating officer, perhaps the drug war could be organized with a Chief Inside and Chief Outside performing functions that demand sharply different styles of discourse about the drug problem and governmental drug control responses. Some of this has happened already. There is almost certainly some delegation of policy-planning responsibilities down from the office of the director in the current administration of the program. But the separation of administrative and rhetorical responsibility will not work unless the drug czar becomes a figurehead with very limited operational authority. If the head of the office maintains substantial personal power, separating this person from the difficult operational choices and skeptical pragmatic style of drug policy planning may make things worse when hard decisions are made near the top of the administrative hierarchy. It is only if the drug czar's practical importance approaches that of the English monarchy that a separation of functions can serve as an effective countermeasure to rhetorical overkill in policy planning. We trust such figurehead status is not your ambition.

A more practical antidote to the drug czar's dual role is a policy-planning group that the director can respect and rely on. Such a group would participate in the policy-planning process and also provide perspectives on drug policy that will contrast with those that the drug czar will encounter (and encourage) on the rubber-chicken circuit. Probably such a policy group should not have many career government employees on it, and no political appointees. A wide spectrum of professional opinion could be represented. The group should be tough-minded, fiscally uninterested in federal drug policy, and committed to truth telling.

There is no evidence of this kind of pragmatic counsel, or of two-track policy thinking, in the public record of the Office of National Drug Control Policy under William Bennett. Instead, Bennett's skills and proclivities turned every public pronouncement into a rhetorical event. As long as the currency of U.S. drug control policy was rhetoric, Mr. Bennett did not see himself as needing independent expert tutorials. If a lack of balance between rhetoric and pragmatic judgment in the first two *National Drug Control Strategy* documents was a reflection of the first drug czar's abilities, the office might benefit if his successor were a somewhat less gifted rhetorician.

We view a policy-planning group with a fair amount of independence as a necessary teaching resource as long as the politics of drugs and drug control threaten to distort perspectives in the planning process. In drug control, there is every indication that this will be a long time.

Marginal-cost decision making

The debate about drug control in the United States too frequently is dichotomized so that observers are presented with a choice between two different kinds of drug policy, such as prohibition versus decriminalization, but little attention is paid to the differences in degree that will constitute the field of choice in drug control in the 1990s. We argued in Chapter 4 that the crucial questions of this decade and beyond are what level of resources should be invested in the criminal prohibition of various drugs and what mix of policies from the myriad available under the general rubric of drug prohibition should be selected.

We advance here two propositions of childlike simplicity: First, investment in drug control should be decided with attention to the marginal costs of the particular programs under review and the marginal benefits expected from them. Second, this kind of one-program-at-a-time, cost–benefit calculus should be the main drug policy arena of the next decade and beyond.

In the usual discussions of public administration, a college freshman would not expect extra credit for imposing this kind of framework on this kind of governmental planning. Yet most of the debate concerning drug control in the 1980s has treated prohibition policy as a package deal, a take-it-or-leave-it $25 billion proposition in which $5 billion nuances of program level or component mix are insignificant. An emphasis on drug control policy at the margin would be a welcome reform in the planning process for individual programs and an important paradigm shift in thinking about the scale of the entire drug control effort. For particular drug control programs, budget proposals should separately cost out different levels of program efforts, estimate the types of levels of marginal benefits projected from each spending level, and provide a basis for assessing programs' effects.

The rhetoric of program budgeting became a cliché in Washington a generation ago, but the sort of program accountability that we are discussing would be both novel and necessary in many parts of the *National Drug Control Strategy*. It is at the aggregate level that an emphasis on marginal cost and benefit could work its most significant transformation on drug control debate.

Each federal drug control budget is presented now as if it were a package-deal plebiscite on drug prohibition. There has been some debate on patterns of relative emphasis in Washington, with liberal Democrats supporting a relatively larger investment in treatment programs and law-and-order conservatives of both parties supporting more emphasis on policing and interdiction (Johnston, 1989). But this has been a debate about how to slice up an expanding pie, not about the wisdom or benefits of sharply increased investments in drug control. An emphasis on marginal cost and marginal benefits will push us toward a structured discussion of the appropriate scale of the drug control effort. When increasing drug control resources from $20 billion to $25 billion, are we getting our extra $5 billions' worth? Although the benefits of individual program elements of the drug war are frequently questioned, there has been no serious debate relating to the scale of the prohibition effort.

Our own enthusiasm for focusing on the scale of drug control is informed by our hunch that the antidrug effort as a whole and most of its component parts are experiencing diminishing marginal returns. We suspect that a detailed examination of the levels of effort for drug interdiction would reveal that resources could be saved by scaling back that enterprise without much impact on the availability of cocaine and heroin in American cities.

We see an enormous range of drug policies available under the general rubric of drug prohibition. The low-cost passive prohibition of marijuana in many jurisdictions produces some arrests for possession that fall out of the ordinary course of police street contacts, but no practical attempt to stop usage or interdict the noncommercial distribution of small amounts of the drug. The passive tolerance of hard-drug possession and use is probably also a police policy in some urban neighborhoods as long as violence and disorder do not erupt.

At the other extreme are the many undercover and buy-and-bust activities directed at disrupting retail sales of heroin and crack cocaine at much higher cost. There is at least as much contrast between these two forms of drug prohibition as there is between low-effort prohibition and formal decriminalization of drugs. Yet the within-prohibition choices available for a drug policy do not receive extensive attention in debates about decriminalization. We think that they should.

There is little evidence available on either the amount of street police resources currently directed to narcotics or the marginal impact of emphasis on narcotics versus other aspects of crime control. Our best guess is that many cities could redirect, without great loss, their police resources from drug control to general patrol or criminal investigation. But few of the data we need to make an informed assessment of this decision are available, because the question of the marginal effects of drug control has not been an important part of policy discussion. Indeed, we do not know the extent to which efforts in drug policing vary, let alone the difference in outcome associated with varying levels of resources. An important first step in rationalizing decision making is recognizing the significance of the question.

An emphasis on marginal cost and benefit can also help us refocus our thinking about treatment and prevention programs. Drug treatment is the one area in which the existing *National Drug Control Strategy* speaks of the necessity of program evaluation and in which there is some history of attempts to provide cost–benefit assessment (Office of National Drug Control Policy, 1989, pp. 35–44). But the recent debate on treatment resources seems to have suffered from the "share of the pie" nature of drug control program discussions. Such political debates seem to have assumed that the resources being misspent in areas such as interdiction should, once planners see the light, be redirected to other drug programs rather than AIDS research, deficit reduction, or child welfare.

In a similar vein, the proponents of drug prevention programs have concentrated on the importance of their favorite branch of the antidrug effort in competition with other drug control activities. We are far from certain that we would wish for the next dollar available to urban public schools being spent to augment drug prevention as opposed to other educational programs. But we are quite sure that drug prevention education programs should be competing with a broad array of educational program needs rather than just being earmarked for antidrug efforts. And these are questions that surface only when the expanding scale of antidrug efforts ceases to be treated as a given in policy debate.

Lessons from the war on crime

The current federal war on drugs was preceded twenty years ago by a federal war on crime that offers two important lessons for policy planners in the drug war. The political and bureaucratic cycles that produced the rise and fall of the Law Enforcement Assistance Administration (LEAA) are particularly important when considering the part of the federal drug effort that is targeted through state and local criminal justice agencies.

The federal crime war, like the later antidrug campaign, was established in response to the public fear that had been reflected in political campaigns. When the pressure mounted for the federal government to "do something," a multifront effort evolved, including grants to states and cities and comprehensive planning processes. At one point during the Nixon years, a group of eight high-impact anticrime program cities were the focus of the targeted federal aid programs (Cronin et al., 1981, pp. 96–9). Yet when the five areas were selected for the high-intensity drug-trafficking areas drug program in 1990, it was with no mention of the earlier program or its outcomes. Programs that seem to be carbon copies of earlier efforts were constructed in apparently innocent ignorance of their predecessors. In late-twentieth-century Washington, it appears that twenty years is a very long time indeed.

The two important lessons to be learned from the LEAA are that large-scale federal monetary assistance has a relatively short life expectancy but that national and state drug agencies established by federal initiative can survive and influence justice policy if they perform specific functions that local governments value. Financial aid to state and local government is chronically vulnerable to cost-cutting pressures in the federal government and thus has a relatively short life expectancy. The political appeal of federal money to help states and localities fight crime produced transfer payments that, at their peak, were substantially larger than federal drug bloc grants are now (compare Cronin et al., 1981, p. 112, with Office of National Drug Control Policy, 1990, pp. 58–62). But these grants lacked specific missions or large constituencies in the states and localities. The tug-of-war between the Democrats (who wished the cities to receive war-on-crime funds) and the Republicans (who preferred the states to be given bloc grants) produced an eventual stalemate as the bloc grant formula prevailed but then rather quickly turned into revenue sharing and all but disappeared.

Some would hold that this short cycle of federal bloc grant funding was a product of the particular historical context of the LEAA. But three successive national administrations – Ford's, Carter's, and Reagan's – presided over the disappearance of significant financial federal aid for local crime control. In retrospect, it seems likely that each of the three would have attempted to curtail the federal fund flow in the absence of an initiative by its predecessors. Further, once inroads against federal aid had been made, no strong countervailing political or bureaucratic campaigns produced significant opposition. Bloc grant funding therefore seemed vulnerable to attack at almost any time and under widely divergent political sponsorship, and the cutbacks, once achieved, were almost inevitably not restored.

Will drug control prove different? The political sex appeal of federal money to combat state and local drug problems is substantial, but no more substantial than street crime was as a priority target of the 1970s. Program monies that become drug control supplements to policing, courts, and corrections have rather diffuse impacts, lack a unique mission, and thus show vulnerability to the hungry budget cutter. Federal programs that support unique drug program activities may prove a hardier breed because the particular function will be seen to depend on federal funds.

The insecurity surrounding federal cash grants can make the vulnerability of such funding programs into a self-fulfilling prophecy. If states and localities doubt the long-term viability of federal grants, little program innovation will accompany the money, and funds will be blended into the support of the usual spectrum of governmental activities. The diffuse impact of the funds – itself in some part a product of insecurity – then becomes part of the rationale for cutting back the program of aid.

This segment of the history of the war on crime preaches caution about the long-term survival of general bloc grant formulas and suggests a survival strategy for federal aid that includes earmarking funds and identifying unique programs that would have a great share of total support from federal initiatives and a clear federal identity. Aside from very special law enforcement activities such as strike forces, the best candidates for local programs that can predominantly be funded by federal initiatives are drug treatment and prevention. But the bloc grant is a natural enemy of this kind of resource concentration of federal funds. Ultimately, we would argue, the bloc grant to states and localities becomes its own worst enemy by ensuring the conditions that make unlikely the continued cost sharing of state and local government burdens.

While federal financial aid to state law enforcement was marching down the trail to insignificance, some of the information systems, coordinating activities, and research and technology efforts of the federal crime war enjoyed a longer survival in their own right and affected how criminal justice systems are administered by states and localities. Although information and technology may sound like largely neutral contributions to a criminal justice process, the greater visibility of criminal justice decision making created by information systems may well be a significant factor in the increased use of imprisonment in state and local criminal justice (Zimring and Hawkins, 1991, pp. 173–5).

The lesson in fashioning the federal role now is to do market research in those information processing, training, and planning exercises that states and localities are anxious to receive. Once such operations are in place and accepted, turning them to the service of the missions of the federal drug control office may prove easy. It turns out that prosecutor-management systems and

Bureau of Justice Statistics reports have not only had a longer career in the policy arena than criminal justice bloc grants have, but they may also have better served the goals of those who in the 1970s and 1980s wished to preside over a toughening of state and local criminal justice.

The necessary open door

In the long term, we think that a drug control consensus in the United States will depend on policies that can be viewed as including the interests of the drug users. Balancing condemnation of sin with the positive prospect of the sinner's redemption is, of course, more American than apple pie, and it is a particular need for drug control policy in the 1990s.

As we stated in Chapter 5, there is a tension between the image of drug using and drug users that facilitates the prevention of drug abuse and that best fits active treatment and rehabilitation programs. Prevention programs aim to stigmatize drug use and the drug user. Indeed, the wrongfulness of the drug user and the ominousness of the drug experiment are repeated themes in antidrug campaigns, from the fatal glass of beer to reefer madness to crack frenzy. The prevention perspective emphasizes the danger of first use and the irreversibility of the damage done by drugs.

Drug treatment lives on hope. A treatment program therefore must sell a potentially positive future to the drug user to motivate treatment, and it depends on an image of affirmative change in order to gain political and financial support. Investments in repair and redemption are necessary not only for drug treatment but also for the whole of drug policy. What we call an open-door policy is one premised on the assumption that drug users can be reintegrated into the social and economic mainstream of American life. This should limit the stigma imposed on users in the prevention and criminal justice branches of drug policy.

An open-door policy of limited stigma for drug users is required by justice, advisable for social policy reasons, and justified by the known facts on drug use and its long-term consequences. For this reason, a strong emphasis on publicly funded treatment opportunities is an element indispensable to a just drug policy. There are two reasons that limited stigma for illegal drug users is required by considerations of justice. With respect to young persons, we argued in Chapter 5 that notions of irresponsibility that make us view children as victims of the allure of drugs should limit the punitive responses available when they are convicted of drug use. To a lesser extent, all illicit drug users habituated while young might claim some diminution of blame on that account, although the extent of this is limited by the contingent and reversible image of drug habits that animates an open-door approach.

The second jurisprudential limit on punishing drug users is the requirement of proportionality vis-à-vis other convicted persons. Even if the harm-to-community aspects of drug use are emphasized, it is difficult to argue that the convicted drug user merits as much penal confinement as does a convicted burglar or the drunk driver whose behavior presents a more direct and palpable prospect of injuring other community members. Just as the moral damage of some drug use might justify some criminal punishment, the limit of intended and achieved social harm in the drug possession offense should serve as a retributive limit to criminal punishment.

The social policy argument for an open-door drug policy has both positive and negative features. On the positive side, emphasis on the reclamation of drug users encourages trust by relatives and friends of drug users. The prospect of rehabilitation also boosts morale for criminal justice and treatment personnel: Nobody wants to work with hopeless cases. And the savings in economic and social terms are substantial whenever drug takers cross back into the social mainstream.

The negative reason to require an open-door drug policy is the devastating impact that a permanent stigma would carry for minority group members in urban ghetto areas. The decline in cocaine use among the general population has produced a concentration of cocaine use in the urban ghetto to match the historically large concentration of heroin there. The costs in these community areas of erecting a permanent barrier to the entry of many young adults into jobs and job training because of a drug history would be great. In many community areas, the legitimacy of a drug control policy may depend on the willingness of those who administer it to readmit former drug users into the social and economic mainstream.

The facts, as well, favor a hopeful perspective on the integration of drug users into a social mainstream. To be sure, the exit from illicit drug use is a process that seems to encompass multiple instances of recidivism on the path to drug abstinence. But this is true for tobacco and alcohol dependence as well, yet treatment programs produce high rates of eventual recovery among populations that persist in trying to quit. Many persons habituated to every known drug of abuse have shifted back toward the social mainstream. Although there is always the fear that "this drug is different" when the pharmacological agent is new, there is no evidence currently available to suggest that crack cocaine habits are impregnable.

Once it is recognized that the reintegration of drug users is linked by many people to the legitimacy of an antidrug program, we can understand the large symbolic stake that some groups hold for treatment on demand for drug abusers. This concept allows the observer to view drug control as a government program that has drug users as its beneficiaries. The absence of such an open door, however, would make millions of drug users into the unconditional enemy of government policy. This, in turn, would make many people unwilling to enlist in a drug war.

We stop short of asserting that a drug policy based on permanent stigma and exclusion could never work, for this is not known. But unqualified anti-drug crusades run unnecessary risks of rejection by small but important sub-publics. An open-door drug policy thus seems both just and prudent.

A chronic-disease perspective

Those who see a "drug-free America" as a serious policy goal both misunderstand the nature of drug problems in the United States and leave our drug control policies vulnerable to charlatanism and distortion. A chronic-disease perspective on drug abuse is a constructive response to this utopian rhetoric, a view that the appetite for licit and illicit mood-altering substances is a permanent part of American life insusceptible by its nature to a complete cure. Rather, like arthritis, although the costs and discomforts of drug abuse will vary substantially over time, the underlying condition should never be expected to disappear.

We think that this conception of drug abuse as a chronic disease is more than a campaign slogan; it can be useful as a policy tool as well. Seeing the appetite for and use of mood-altering substances as a permanent part of American character helps us focus on the achievable goals of drug control policy. As long as a drug-free America is the policy goal, there is no reason to discriminate between relatively benign and relatively costly drugs, nor should much effort and resources be directed at moderating the harmful consequences currently associated with drug use. In a drug-free America, pregnancies that risk substantial impairment to the newborn will not happen and therefore need not be treated on a continuing basis. In a United States in which drug abuse is a permanent problem, the reduction of harmful consequences becomes an obviously necessary goal of public policy.

Recognizing the chronic nature of America's drug problems will not only focus on appropriate countermeasures; it will also expose the false promises of those who tempt us with cures. The comparison with medical practice is instructive: By far the largest branch of medical fraud in Western society is that group of charlatans who promises cures for chronic conditions. Whether the presumed agent is copper bracelets, secret vitamin compounds, or a laying-on of hands, the operative attraction of the medical quack is the promise to cure once and for all what mainstream medical science diagnoses as chronic.

When patients know that their condition is chronic, they have found an antidote to the fraudulent appeal of the quack. As soon as they accept that a cure is not available, they have acquired an immunity to fraud and an easy way of identifying it. Because quacks are irresistibly drawn to promising cures, consumers who know that they are chronically ill have a litmus test for fakery. We think that parallel processes are at work in drug control and that recognition of the permanent vulnerability of American society to drug abuse provides an important insurance policy against overstatement and fraud in drug control.

One other virtue of a chronic-disease perspective is that it compels a long-term view of drug problems and policy. If drug problems are chronic, drug policies must be long range. The recognition of chronicity also makes observers sensitive to the extensive history of drug abuse and drug control in ways that make their current policy choices more informed. To know that this year's drug and this year's drug problem fit into a historical mosaic of drug problems is to generate doubts that this year's problem drug is without precedent, that lessons learned about the control of other substances will not apply. Drug problems will be our permanent companions in the United States, just as we have been coping with drug problems in every period of our history.

There may be, we should hasten to add, a bright side to the recognized chronicity of American drug problems. One medical prescription for long life is to "get yourself a chronic disease and manage it well." This formula is a truth that applies to drug control as well. A temperate and realistic drug control policy may carry with it larger social benefits. That is, it can teach the interdependence of subsocieties in the American future, and the wisdom of investment in disadvantaged segments of that society as a protection that can be justified on selfish grounds. Certainly the drug problem was the only issue in the late Ronald Reagan and early George Bush years that focused public attention on the plight of the urban ghetto. In this sense, the public's fear of the contagion of drugs can be a basis for supporting necessary social programs.

We do not mean to suggest that the primary rationale for public investment in urban problems should be drug control. It is ludicrous for programs such as Medicare and Aid to Families with Dependent Children to be justified on the basis that they are "needed by poorer families if they are to remain a bulwark against a life of drug use" (Office of the National Drug Control Policy, 1990, p. 9). But the right kind of drug control programs can work well with education programs, family support, and the provision of economic opportunity. And if drugs provide an occasion for learning in the 1990s that "no man is an island," the lesson may still have a positive effect.

Recognizing the long-range nature of America's engagement with drug abuse reminds us that our drug problems can be survived. This is history's most cheerful and most important lesson. Drug problems have been part of our development for more than two centuries. A long history of coping provides evidence of a social capacity to muddle through to the American future.

Appendix: Estimates of illicit drug use – a survey of methods

This appendix discusses a variety of methods being developed to estimate the extent of illicit drug use in the United States. The construction of such indices is of central importance to the evaluation of drug control measures because of the need to find some way of measuring illicit drug use as the target dependent variable of government programs. We shall examine the current measures under five headings: production and sales figures; health indices, including morbidity and mortality rates and hospital admissions; indices derived from surveys covering such things as drug use and drug problems; criminal justice statistics relating to drug convictions, parole violations, and the like; and data relating to drug tests in the civilian sector.

Some of the measures that we will consider can be used as evaluation tools in more than one way. For example, statistics regarding drug overdose deaths can be significant not just as an index of trends in drug use but also because public policies have the reduction of such deaths as their primary target. But all of the indices discussed in this appendix have also been used as part of an attempt to measure variations in the level of citizen drug use.

I. Production and sales

One important distinction between licit and illicit drugs concerns the availability of information from governmental regulatory and fiscal agencies that provide a sensitive and accurate index of consumption levels of licit drugs. By contrast, accurate measures of the production and consumption of illegal drugs are not available. The effectiveness of a legal prohibition on the production and consumption of the proscribed drugs is problematic, in part, because prohibition is remarkably effective in restricting the amount of reliable information available regarding the production, distribution, and consumption of illicit drugs.

The Food and Drug Administration (FDA) as well as the Department of Commerce's Census of Manufactures provide data regarding the production of prescription and over-the-counter drugs. In the case of "schedule drugs," sensitive, audited measures of the volume of consumption have been available for some time. For alcohol and tobacco – legally allowed substances subject to extensive state and federal taxation – accurate statistics relating to production and importation for domestic consumption have also been available, usually by state, for a long time. Although these may underestimate production and consumption because they do not encompass data relating to substances on which taxes are evaded, this shortfall is thought to be modest and, in relation to alcohol, is probably declining over time.

It may be regarded as somewhat ironic that much of our historical information about alcohol use in the United States is available only because of the taxes levied on it. Thus, we have a great deal more information about the consumption of grain alcohol in some areas than we do about the consumption of grain. There is further irony in the fact that two of the periods for which we lack reliable estimates of domestic alcohol consumption are those in the mid-nineteenth and early twentieth centuries – the periods of prohibitions – when it was the subject of the greatest concern.

II. Health indicators

Mortality

Drug-related health statistics are derived from registers of death or from health authority and hospital records of reported injuries or illnesses associated with the use of drugs. With respect to deaths, some data are available because particular causes of death, such as cirrhosis of the liver, are recorded on death certificates. In other cases, data relating to the presence or absence of alcohol or other drugs in the blood may be recorded, although this is not done routinely.

When drug-related syndromes are identified as the cause of death, a statistical time series would be a good measure of one major problem caused by drugs, if the assessments were reliable and the extent of the testing were either constant or in proportions that were known over time. Cirrhosis deaths are in fact used to measure alcoholism transnationally. More recently, there has been some recording of cases in which, on the basis of toxicological examination, drug use involving alcohol, opiates, cocaine, barbiturates, or amphetamines has been cited as a primary or secondary cause of death if organ failure resulted from specific levels of toxicity.

There are two issues with respect to deaths identified as drug related in this way: First is the problem of distinguishing cases of suicide in which the deceased subjects intended to end their lives and would have tried to do so by some other means had drugs not been available, from those cases in which death resulted from an accidental overdose. Second is the fact that there will be variations over time both in the type and proportion of cases subjected to analysis and in the degrees of care with which the analyses were carried out and conclusions are drawn from them.

There is a second category of postmortem examination that generates data on patterns of drug use: cases in which tests are carried out on deceased persons for the purpose of determining the presence or absence of alcohol or other substances in the blood. In many areas, these tests are performed nearly routinely, as in the case of traffic fatalities or other special circumstances, such as accidents, homicides, and suicides, in which postmortem examinations are performed. Such data provide some indication of the correlation between particular drug use and accident-causing activity. Used in carefully constructed case control studies, they offer a good deal of information about the causal relationship between particular levels of drug use and accident fatalities (Donelson, 1988). However, when nonlethal levels of drugs are present in the blood of deceased persons, the causal role of psychoactive substances in the blood in relation to fatalities is an open question.

Delayed mortality

A special set of problems exist when there is a long delay between the use or exposure to a substance and death as a consequence. When thirty or forty years can elapse between the beginning of exposure to an agent and the onset of a fatal condition, it is, of course, more difficult to determine causation. Beyond that, however, the long gaps invite emotional conclusions that perhaps fatal consequences can be avoided and a tendency by the public to think of causation as a less-direct consequence of the time gap. Some of the most significant health risks of widely used drugs have long gestation periods, including cancer and heart disease for tobacco, and cirrhosis and throat cancer for alcohol. We lack studies of long exposure to many other drugs that might reveal similar patterns of delayed mortality.

Although there is always some tendency to discount mortality risks that surface after long delays, one change in social and governmental attitudes in the United States over the past few decades is the serious attention now paid to these delayed risks. The attention paid to the cigarette–cancer association is only one example of the increased social awareness of delayed risk phenomena. Others include the long-term risk of exposure to asbestos and toxic chemicals. What level of discount can be applied to the cost of lives to be lost in the far future? It seems likely to us that the aging of the U.S. population, as well as advances in medical science, has reduced that discount in recent years, so that delayed mortality and morbidity are now regarded as significant.

Morbidity

Death data are not the only health statistics that are currently used to measure the prevalence and consequences of drug use. Public health statistical measures of drug involvement include the number of hospital emergency admissions in which drug use is mentioned by the patient, as well as estimates by health authorities of the numbers of specific incidents such as accidents or live births in which the use of a particular drug causes health problems.

The most important currently used measure of drug-related morbidity is the Drug Abuse Warning Network (DAWN) that compiles statistics concerning the frequency with which illegal drug use is mentioned by patients admitted to hospital emergency rooms. This measure is the only health-related statistic included among the nine measures that the Federal Drug Control Office proposes to use as a quantified measure of the extent of the drug problem in the United States (Office of National Drug Control Policy, 1990, pp. 117–21). Other relevant morbidity statistics include estimates of babies born with grave problems associated with the maternal use of cocaine, alcohol, and other drugs; estimates of nonfatal traffic and other accidents involving high levels of alcohol or drugs; and estimates of aggregate morbidity-related time lost from work attributable to substances such as tobacco and alcohol.

Data on morbidity associated with illegal drugs are frequently used to measure the prevalence of drug use as well as to measure the problems associated with such use. Thus, the upward trend in mentions of cocaine use is cited in the current *National Drug Control Strategy* more as a measure of levels of cocaine use in the United States than of fluctuations in particular problems associated with that use (Office of National Drug Control Policy, 1990, p. 120). Estimates of the number of "crack babies" are also used as a barometer of crack cocaine use in particular urban areas.

There are many difficulties associated with using existing morbidity measures as data in trends in the general population's use of a substance. The utilization of hospital emergency rooms varies greatly by social class and demographic zone, so that the use of the DAWN network measures mention only the proportion of the population that uses emergency rooms. There are other problems with the softness and variability of identifying drug use by means of most of the current morbidity measures. Whether the users of emergency rooms think that a particular drug is the cause of their medical emergency depends in part on the current reputation of that drug. Further, the degree to which medical personnel seek drug-related explanations of the problems that they see probably has a dramatic effect on the number of use mentions that turn up in the system. Thus, drug mentions in emergency room settings probably increase more than does drug use during periods of intensifying concern about the impact of a particular drug.

There is evidence of this phenomenon in the recent history of the DAWN program. Between 1985 and 1988 the mention of cocaine by emergency room patients went up 360 percent (Office of National Drug Control Policy, 1990, p. 120), whereas survey research data estimate that the number of persons reporting cocaine use in the United States fell by almost half (Office of National Drug Control Policy, 1989, p. 1). Thus, either cocaine use became six times as injurious as previously reported, or the growing salience of cocaine as an issue in many communities increased the extent to which the drug was mentioned. This phenomenon was not restricted to cocaine. Between 1985 and 1988, mentions of marijuana use more than doubled in the DAWN data, but the survey research suggested that marijuana use was down 36 percent (Office of National Drug Control Policy, 1989, pp. 1, 96).

The mention of drug use by patients who may feel at risk of criminal prosecution may also vary with the intensity of government antidrug activity. Making emergency room patients more fearful of reporting drug involvement cuts down the number of drug mentions in hospital emergency rooms, without necessarily reflecting any less use of the drug in the community. Thus, the assertion that "reductions in drug-related medical emergencies would be a good indicator of national anti-drug success in the years ahead" (Office of National Drug Control Policy, 1989, p. 96) is true only as long as "success" can refer to either reduced use or reduced mention.

There is reason to suppose that statistical reports of syndromes like crack babies and fetal alcohol disabilities also are sensitive to the level of concern in the general and medical communities about a particular problem. As medical concern about the impact of cocaine use on the users' babies broadens, the extent to which neonatal difficulties are attributed to cocaine use in high-risk maternal and infant health populations will probably increase as well. This has certainly been the pattern with respect to identified instances of fetal alcohol syndrome. In an analogous circumstance, in the wake of public and professional concern about child abuse, there have been far more instances of reported or suspected child abuse than any measures of child death or children at risk could possibly explain.

Under the circumstances, data on drug morbidity are problematic if not supported by objective measures used in a constant fashion over time. And most of the currently used measures of drug-related morbidity lack both objective indicators and measurement methods that have been used in a consistent fashion over time.

III. Survey indicators

Survey research can be used in two different ways to establish levels of drug use: by asking samples of the population what kinds of drugs they have taken and under what circumstances, and to measure the seriousness of drug problems by asking samples of the population their opinion regarding how much of a problem drug taking is in their community or in the nation as a whole. Each type of survey research has been regularly conducted for at least two decades, and the accumulated information of each data set sheds some light on drug use as a social problem in recent American experience.

Self-report measures

One way to find out how many Americans are using drugs is to ask them. For those drugs that are presently classified as illicit, this type of survey depends on a species of self-incrimination. But self-incrimination has a venerable pedigree in social surveys: Adolescents and adults have been asked for profiles of their criminal behavior for almost half a century in the United States, beginning with the studies by Austin Porterfield (1943, 1946) and Wallerstein and Wyle (1947). For as long as adolescents have been surveyed about deviant behavior, smoking and drinking have been a significant part of the behavior about which pollsters have sought information. Items relating to drugs other than tobacco and alcohol were added to youth surveys in the 1960s. In the 1970s two separate types of survey targeted specifically at drug use were initiated and have continued to the present day.

The National Commission on Marijuana and Drug Abuse began a survey of household drug use in 1971 that sought information from household members about their use of heroin, cocaine, marijuana, and other psychoactive substances currently classified as illicit. These surveys have been periodically repeated since the early 1970s and are currently administered by the National Institute on Drug Abuse on a sample of just under ten thousand people.

A second series of self-report surveys have been administered to high school seniors in selected American high schools since 1970. These surveys have included questions about alcohol use and a range of generally prohibited substances, including heroin, cocaine, marijuana, the amphetamines, and some barbiturates. In addition, other youth surveys aimed more generally at self-reports of delinquency have periodically sought information from a sample of young persons about their alcohol and drug abuse.

Each of these types of survey provides an incomplete representation of the United States population. The household samples miss those members of the American population that do not live in standard households, and they may undercount adolescents and young adults who live in the household infrequently and are less likely than adults to respond to the surveys. The high school senior samples miss the approximately one-third of all American adolescents who do not stay at public school to the point of graduation and who are likely to be at a higher-than-average risk of drug use. Other surveys of

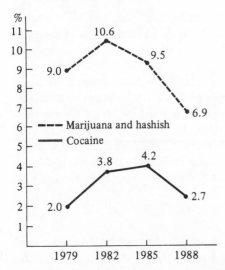

Figure A.1. Trends in the percentage of adults (aged 26 and older) reporting use of cocaine or marijuana in the past year. (From U.S. Department of Health and Human Services, *National Household Survey on Drug Abuse: Highlights*, 1988, p. 66.)

adolescents sample more broadly among youth by educational attainment but undercount the hardest-to-find youths in the most socially marginal groups that, according to official statistics, tend to have higher levels of contact with the criminal justice system and higher rates of alcohol and drug involvement.

Apart from problems associated with sampling, self-reports of alcohol and drug use depend for their reliability on the respondents' willingness to report candidly the types and levels of their drug use. But even in regard to licit substances such as alcohol, Americans are notorious underreporters of the frequency and quantity of their ingestion. This is easy to detect in the case of alcohol because independent measures of consumption are available, but it is probably also true across the board for psychoactive substance consumption.

In regard to illicit drugs, it has long been noted that heroin use is underreported both in absolute terms and relative to the use of other illicit drugs. How accurately the levels of use of other illicit drugs are reported is the subject of differing views among social scientists. Moreover, there are some indications that willingness to report the use of some illicit substances varies over time as the intensity of social disapproval of illicit drug use waxes and wanes.

Figure A.1 shows trends in the percentage of adults reporting having used either cocaine or marijuana in the last year, between 1979 and 1988. Because this is a survey of all households, the poll took samples from a relatively slowly changing population, whereas by contrast, a cohort of high school seniors changes completely every year. So Figure A.1 tells the story of changes in drug use among the same people over time, and the trend most recently is down.

There are reasons to suppose, however, that more than decreases in drug use are measured in the National Institute on Drug Abuse polls. Heroin use is notoriously underreported in all surveys, as is much behavior that carries a social stigma and legal risk. For this reason, trends over time in self-reported drug use may reflect the changing social status of illegal drugs as well as their decreasing use. Because both decreasing use and increased stigma produce the same pattern in poll responses, the two phenomena can be confused.

Drug attitudes

Three things should be said about the index of citizen attitudes toward the seriousness of the drug problem in the United States: It is important; it is volatile; and trends in this indicator are not linked in any obvious way with the statistics on drug use. The importance of citizen attitudes toward the drug problem need not be belabored. The major determinants of drug law enforcement are political, and public opinion is a major influence on the political priority of drug countermeasures at federal, state, and community levels.

The volatility of public opinion in regard to drugs as a problem owes little to the changing popularity or unpopularity of Colombian drug cartels or street-level American retail drug dealers. Public hostility to illegal drugs and those who deal in them is a constant feature of survey research results. But the priority that citizens assign to drug problems is subject to quite rapid changes. Thus, the Gallup organization reported that the proportion of Americans that considered drugs to be the country's most important problem declined dramatically from about two-thirds to less than one-tenth of the population over the period from September 1989 to November 1990 (*Gallup Poll Monthly Newsletter*, 1990, p. 26). Part of this sort of fluctuation occurs because the public assessment of other problems changes over time. In the case of the 1990 decline in the perceived importance of the drug problem, publicity given to the federal budget deficit and also the savings and loan failures are no doubt a part of the explanation of the diminished salience of drugs. But if the intensity of public concern drives policy, it is precisely the changes wrought by shifts in public concern regarding other problems that may have drug policy significance.

Certainly, there is no obvious correlation between levels of drug consumption as measured by surveys and fluctuations in public concern about drug problems. Thus, the decline over the mid- and late 1980s in the reported use of all major categories of drugs was in fact accompanied by an intensified concern about drugs as a societal problem. Instead, perceptions of the seriousness of the drug problem seem to be more closely related to publicity about "the threat that drugs pose," in a manner that suggests that public anxieties about drugs can feed on themselves as long as other problems do not supplant drugs in the competition for air time and other forms of media attention. In any event, much more needs to be known about changes in public attitudes toward the drug problem as both a dependent and an independent variable in American drug policy.

IV. Criminal justice data

The wide variety of measures available in criminal justice statistics relating to drugs generally tell us more about the impact of drugs on the criminal justice system than about trends in drug use in society at large. Data are available on arrests for drug use by type of drug over time, on many of the resources invested in drug cases by police and prosecutors, on drug convictions, and on the proportion of jail and prison space occupied by drug case defendants. None of these measures clearly reflects changes in civilian drug taking, because the emphasis placed on drug prosecutions by criminal justice officials can have a dramatic impact on the volume of drug cases that is wholly independent of variations in citizen drug use.

One relatively new measure of drug involvement in criminal justice seems more independent of shifts in criminal justice resources than are any previous standard measures. The National Institute of Justice's Drug Use Forecasting (DUF) system uses urine tests carried out on persons just arrested for felonies as a measure of change in the propensity of arrested felons to have used drugs, over time and in different cities. When the data on arrests exclude those arrested for drug-related offenses, this seems to provide a good, independent measure of the degree to which a city's robbers and burglars are using particular drugs. However, because robbers and burglars are by no means a cross section of a city's population, one cannot extrapolate from DUF rates and drug usage trends to the general city population.

Nevertheless, for many purposes, drug use patterns among criminally active segments of the population may be more important than general civilian rates. They certainly constitute data worth collecting and analyzing. The system has already disclosed substantial variations from city to city in the usage of particular drugs by felony arrestees. It remains to be discovered whether these intercity variations are associated with different levels of crime and violence cross sectionally, or over time when changes occur in a single city.

V. Broad-sample drug tests

One 1980s innovation in drug control shows promise also as a means of measuring variations in citizen drug use. As the military, some governmental agencies, and employers come to test applicants or current employees routinely for drug use, aggregated statistics on drug test results of large groups became available as an index of drug-using patterns.

The percentage of navy recruits or IBM sales trainee applicants who test positive for cocaine or marijuana use is a drug use indicator with several advantages over survey research results, criminal justice drug testing, and health statistics on morbidity or mortality. The principal advantage of the drug test over survey research is that it provides an objective indicator of whether a drug use pattern is present. It may be an exaggeration to say that drug tests do not lie, but the veridicality of the results of drug-testing procedures far exceeds the credibility of unaudited citizen self-reports of drug use.

Drug tests of broad segments of the population are superior to those of persons arrested for felony crimes because they profile a broader cross section of the population. Moreover, they do not test for drug use at a peak period of distress and dysfunction in an individual's life. The National Institute of Justice's Drug Use Forecasting (DUF) system, which collects data from arrestees in the central booking facility in selected cities, tests an atypical sample of persons during atypical periods in the lives of each member of the sample.

Both the objective nature of the drug tests and the breadth of the samples of the subjects give the civilian sector tests an advantage over hospital emergency room admissions, medical examiners' reports, and other health indicators of patterns of drug use. We have already seen that a considerable degree of subjective judgment influences the attribution of death, disease, and hospital admissions to drug causes. Drug test results, by contrast, use unchanging chemical standards. Further, drug test results among broad population sectors reflect the prevalence of recent drug use among healthy and normal segments of the population. The potential uses for aggregate test profiles as drug use indicators include the measurement of trends in specific drug use over time; the comparison of drug use patterns in different geographic regions, for example, by comparing the drug test profiles of army recruits in the Northeast with those of army recruits in the South; and the study of variations in drug-present patterns as a function of gender, age, ethnicity, and other individual characteristics.

The principal use to date of aggregate test results has been to determine trends over time in the tests of military recruits and military personnel. The falling rates of positive testing for cocaine and marijuana use among military recruits and personnel have been read as evidence of the declining use of those drugs throughout the general population. There are, however, two problems associated with inferring a drop in general drug use from a drop in positive findings among tested populations. First, many of the populations that present themselves for drug tests are self-selected, and the self-selection process may change in response to drug testing. As would-be military recruits or computer salespersons learn of the tests' existence and their capacity, drug users may postpone applying, and applicants may postpone drug use. They not only can defer drug testing, but they also may opt out altogether. The subpopulations at risk for testing have special incentives to behave in ways that distort their drug use profiles from those of the general population.

For this reason, drug tests carried out on active service military personnel may provide a better index of fluctuations in drug use than do drug test results on those seeking to enlist in a military force. It is much easier and less expensive for a would-be recruit with a history of drug taking to defer a test than it would be for a serving member of the armed forces to resign from the service.

A second problem with inferring declining drug use from a decline in positive test profiles is that subjects who would test positive may develop methods of cheating or avoiding tests as test regimes become institutionalized. The folklore on this topic includes urine-sample switches, identity switches, record sabotage, corruption, and a variety of other species of adaptive response. As such adaptations occur, they will produce the kind of pattern of drop in positive results that would ordinarily be taken as evidence of a drop in civilian drug use. Because it is not currently possible to obtain objective evidence of the extent to which various drug test programs have been compromised, the reliability of their results as general population drug use indicators is questionable.

When all these problems in relation to drug testing are taken into account, there is ample reason for caution in determining policy on the basis of trends in drug test results. Nevertheless, a balanced program of research into drug use would place more emphasis on drug test result data, as opposed to unaudited survey research data, than is the case in the current national drug control strategy. In the document outlining that strategy, the National Institute on Drug Abuse, *National Household Survey* is described as "the best instrument now available for measuring the dimensions of drug use by the American public." By contrast, the principal function of drug testing is seen as being to "deter employee drug use" because of the possibility of "disqualification from employment" for those who test positive (Office of National Drug Control Policy, 1989, pp. 56, 81).

References

Aaron, P., and David Musto (1981). "Temperance and Prohibition in America: A Historical Overview." In Mark H. Moore and Dean R. Gerstein (eds.) *Alcohol and Public Policy: Beyond the Shadow of Prohibition.* Washington, DC: National Academy Press.

American Psychiatric Association (1987). *Diagnostic and Statistical Manual of Mental Disorders* (DSM-III-R). Washington, DC: American Psychiatric Association.

Anglin, M. Douglas, and George Speckart (1983). "Methadone Maintenance in California: A Decade's Experience." In L. Brill and C. Winier (eds.) *The Yearbook of Substance Use and Abuse.* New York: Human Sciences Press.

(1987). "Narcotics Use and Crime: A Multisample, Multimethod Analysis." University of California at Los Angeles, Department of Psychology. Mimeo.

Ashley, Richard (1975). *Cocaine: Its History, Uses and Effects.* New York: St. Martin's Press.

Bakalar, James B., and Lester Grinspoon (1984). *Drug Control in a Free Society.* Cambridge, England: Cambridge University Press.

Barker, Sir Ernest (1915). *Political Thought in England, 1848–1914.* London: Butterworth.

Barnes, Deborah M. (1988). "Drugs: Running the Numbers." *Science* 240:1729–31.

Barrie, J. M. (1912). *My Lady Nicotine.* New York: Cassell.

Bartels, Robert (1973). "Better Living through Legislation: The Control of Mindaltering Drugs." *University of Kansas Law Review* 21:439–92.

Beecher, Lyman (1843). *Six Sermons on the Nature, Occasions, Signs, Evils, and Remedy of Intemperance.* (10th ed.) New York: American Tract Society.

Blum, Richard H. (1969a). "A History of Opium." In Richard H. Blum and Associates, *Society and Drugs.* San Francisco: Jossey-Bass.

(1969b). "On the Presence of Demons." In Richard H. Blum and Associates, *Drugs I, Society and Drugs.* San Francisco: Jossey-Bass.

Brecher, Edward M. (1972). *Licit and Illicit Drugs.* Boston: Little, Brown.

Buckley, William F. (1985). "Legalize Dope." *Washington Post,* April 1, 1985.

Burke, Edmund (1803/1890). *Works.* Vol. 6. London: George Bell & Sons.

Burnham, J. C. (1968–9). "New Perspectives on the Prohibition 'Experiment' of the 1920s." *Journal of Social History* 2:51–68.

Bush, George (1989). Inaugural Address. *New York Times,* January 21, 1989.

Chaiken, Jan M., and Marisa R. Chaiken (1990). "Drugs and Predatory Crime." In

Michael Tonry and James Q. Wilson (eds.) *Crime and Justice. A Review of Research*. Vol. 13: *Drugs and Crime*. Chicago: University of Chicago Press.

Chambliss, William (1967). "Types of Deviance and the Effectiveness of Legal Sanctions." *Wisconsin Law Review* 2:703–19.

Chasnoff, Ira J. (1988). "Newborn Infants with Drug Withdrawal Symptoms." *Pediatrics in Review* 9:273.

Chasnoff, Ira J., Kayreen A. Burns, William J. Burns, and Sidney H. Schnoll (1986). "Prenatal Drug Exposure: Effects on Neonatal and Infant Growth and Development." *Neurobehavioral Toxicology and Teratology* 8:357–62.

Clark, Norman H. (1976) *Deliver Us from Evil: An Interpretation of American Prohibition*. New York: Norton.

Clayton, Richard R. (1985). "Cocaine Use in the United States: 'In a Blizzard or Just Being Snowed?' " In N. J. Kozel and E. H. Adams (eds.) *Cocaine Use in America: Epidemiologic and Clinical Perspectives*. NIDA Research Monograph 61. Rockville, MD: National Institute on Drug Abuse.

Cohen, Stanley (1972). *Folk Devils and Moral Panics*. London: MacGibbon & Kee.

Courtwright, David T. (1982). *Dark Paradise: Opiate Addiction in America Before 1940*. Cambridge, MA: Harvard University Press.

Criminal Law Reporter (1988). Anti-Drug Abuse Act of 1988 (selected sections). Vol. 44, no. 5, pp. 3001–29.

Cronin, Thomas E., Tania Z. Cronin, and Michael E. Milakovich (1981). *United States v. Crime in the Streets*. Bloomington: Indiana University Press.

Culyer, A. J. (1973). "Should Social Policy Concern Itself with Drug Abuse?" *Public Finance Quarterly* 1(4):449–56.

Donelson, Alan C. (1988). "The Alcohol-Crash Problem." In Michael D. Laurence, John R. Snortum, and Franklin E. Zimring (eds.) *Social Control of the Drinking Driver*. Chicago: University of Chicago Press.

Dubowski, Kurt M. (1987). "Drug-Use Testing: Scientific Perspectives." *Nova Law Review* 11(2):415–552.

Elsberg, Robert (1990). Chairman's Report of Subcommittee on Marijuana Laws in Minutes of Meeting of the Criminal Justice Committee, Governor's Policy Council on Drugs and Alcohol Abuse, Sacramento, CA, June 8. Mimeo.

Englemann, Larry (1979). *Intemperance: The Lost War Against Liquor*. New York: Free Press.

Fagan, Jeffrey (1990). "Intoxication and Aggression." In Michael Tonry and James Q. Wilson (eds.) *Crime and Justice. A Review of Research*. Vol. 13: *Drugs and Crime*. Chicago: University of Chicago Press.

Fisher, Irving (1930). *The "Noble Experiment."* New York: Alcohol Information Committee.

Fort, Joel (1969). "A World View of Drugs." In Richard H. Blum and Associates, *Drugs I, Society and Drugs*. San Francisco: Jossey-Bass.

Frase, Richard S. (1980). "The Decision to File Federal Criminal Charges: A Quantitative Study of Prosecutorial Discretion." *University of Chicago Law Review* 47:246.

Friedman, Milton (1987). *The Essence of Friedman*. Edited by Kurt R. Leube. Stanford, CA: Hoover Institute Press.

Gallup Poll Monthly Newsletter (November 1990).

Gershman, Bennett L. (1990). 'Prosecutorial Discretion Under Federal Sentencing Guidelines." *New York Law Journal*, April 20, 1990.

Great Britain, Home Office (1968). *Cannabis: Report by the Advisory Committee on Drug Dependence*. London: Her Majesty's Stationery Office.

Great Britain, Home Office, Department of Health and Social Security (1975). *Report of the Committee on Mentally Abnormal Offenders*. London: Her Majesty's Stationery Office.

Greenwood, Peter W., with Allan Abrahamse (1982). *Selective Incapacitation*. Santa Monica, CA: Rand Corporation.

Grinspoon, Lester, and James Bakalar (1976). *Cocaine: A Drug and Its Social Evolution*. New York: Basic Books.

Gusfield, Joseph R. (1976). *Symbolic Crusade: Status Politics and the American Temperance Movement*. Champaign–Urbana: University of Illinois Press.

Haaga, John G., and Peter Reuter (1990). "The Limits of the Czar's Ukase: Drug Policy at the Local Level." *Yale Law and Policy Review* 8:36–74.

Haller, Mark (1968). Introduction to John Landesco, *Organized Crime in Chicago*. Chicago: University of Chicago Press.

Hamowy, Ronald (ed.) (1987). *Dealing with Drugs: Consequences of Government Control*. Lexington, MA: Heath.

Hart, H. L. A. (1963). *Law, Liberty and Morality*. Stanford, CA: Stanford University Press.

Harwood, Henrick J., Diane M. Napolitano, Patricia L. Kristiansen, and James J. Collins (1984). *Economic Costs to Society of Alcohol and Drug Abuse and Mental Illness: 1980*. Research Triangle Park, NC: Research Triangle Institute.

Hegel, Georg Wilhelm Friedrich (1956). *The Philosophy of History*. New York: Dover.

Hofstadter, Richard (1955). *The Age of Reform: From Bryan to F. D. R.* New York: Knopf.

Hudner, Karen (1987). "Urine Testing for Drugs." *Nova Law Review* 11(2):553–62.

Institute of Judicial Administration, American Bar Association, Juvenile Justice Standards Project (1982). *Standards Relating to Noncriminal Misbehavior*. Cambridge, MA: Ballinger.

Jellinek, E. M. (1947). "Recent Trends in Alcoholism and Alcohol Consumption." *Quarterly Journal of Studies in Alcohol* 7:1–43.

Johnston, David (1989). "Bush's Drug Strategy Is Criticized as Failing to Seek View of Cities." *New York Times*, September 16, 1989.

Jordan, Thomas E. (1987). *Victorian Childhood: Themes and Variations*. Albany: State University of New York Press.

Kaplan, John (1970). *Marijuana – The New Prohibition*. New York: World Publishing.

(1983). *The Hardest Drug: Heroin and Public Policy*. Chicago: University of Chicago Press.

(1988). "Taking Drugs Seriously." *The Public Interest* 92:32–50.

Kerr, K. Austin (1985). *Organized for Prohibition: A New History of the Anti-Saloon League*. New Haven, CT: Yale University Press.

Kozel, Nicholas J., and Edgar H. Adams (1985). *Cocaine Use in America: Epidemiologic and Clinical Perspectives*. NIDA Research Monograph 61. Rockville, MD: National Institute on Drug Abuse.

Kyvig, David E. (1979). *Repealing National Prohibition.* Chicago: University of Chicago Press.

Landesco, John (1968). *Organized Crime in Chicago.* Chicago: University of Chicago Press.

Larkin, Jack (1988). *The Reshaping of Everyday Life 1790–1840.* New York: Harper & Row.

Lender, M. E., and James Kirby Martin (1987). *Drinking in America: A History.* Rev. and expanded ed. New York: Free Press.

Macaulay, Thomas Babington (1849). *The History of England.* Vol. 1. Boston: Phillips Sampsons.

McBay, Arthur J. (1987). "Efficient Drug Testing: Addressing the Basic Issues." *Nova Law Review* 11(2):647–52.

MacGregor, Scott, N., Louis G. Keith, Ira J. Chasnoff, Marvin A. Rosner, Gay M. Chisum, Patricia Shaw, and John P. Minogue (1987). "Cocaine Use During Pregnancy: Adverse Perinatal Outcome." Paper presented at the seventh annual meeting of the Society of Perinatal Obstetricians, Lake Buena Vista, FL, February 5–7.

McLaughlin, Gerald T. (1973). "Cocaine: The History and Regulation of a Dangerous Drug." *Cornell Law Review* 58:537–73.

Mayor's Committee on Marijuana (1944/1966). "The Marijuana Problem in the City of New York." In David Soloman (ed.) *The Marijuana Papers.* New York: Bobbs-Merill.

Mencken, H. L. (1943). *Heathen Days.* New York: Knopf.

Michaels, Robert J. (1987). "The Market for Heroin Before and After Legalizaton." In Ronald Hamowy (ed.) *Dealing with Drugs: Consequences of Government Control.* Lexington, MA: Heath.

Miike, Lawrence, and Maria Hewitt (1988) "Accuracy and Reliability of Urine Drug Tests." *University of Kansas Law Review* 36(4):641–82.

Mill, John Stuart (1859/1910). "On Liberty." In *Utilitarianism, Liberty and Representative Government.* New York: Dutton.

Morris, Norval, and Gordon Hawkins (1970). *The Honest Politician's Guide to Crime Control.* Chicago: University of Chicago Press.

(1977). *Letter to the President on Crime Control.* Chicago: University of Chicago Press.

Mosher, James F. (1977). "The Prohibition of Youthful Drinking: A Need for Reform." *Contemporary Drug Problems* 6:397–436.

(1980). "The History of Youthful-Drinking Laws: Implications for Current Policy." In Henry Wechsler (ed.) *Minimum Drinking-Age Laws.* Lexington, MA: Heath.

Musto, David F. (1987). *The American Disease: Origins of Narcotics Control.* Expanded ed. New York: Oxford University Press.

Nadelmann, Ethan A. (1988). "The Case for Legalization." *The Public Interest* 92:3–31.

(1989). "Drug Prohibition in the United States: Costs, Consequences, and Alternatives." *Science* 247:939–47.

National Commission on Law Observance and Enforcement (Wickersham Commission) (1931). *Report on the Enforcement of the Prohibition Laws of the United States.* Washington, DC: U.S. Government Printing Office.

National Commission on Marijuana and Drug Abuse (1972). *First Report: Marijuana: A Signal of Misunderstanding.* Washington, DC: U.S. Government Printing Office.

(1973). *Second Report: Drug Use in America: Problem in Perspective.* Washington, DC: U.S. Government Printing Office.

National Institute on Drug Abuse (1988). *National Household Survey on Drug Abuse.* Washington, DC: U.S. Government Printing Office.

Nixon, Richard (1971). "Special Message to the Congress on Drug Abuse Prevention and Control, June 17, 1971." In *U.S. President. Public Papers of the Presidents of the United States, Richard Nixon, 1971.* Washington, DC: U.S. Government Printing Office.

Office of National Drug Control Policy (1989). *National Drug Control Strategy.* Washington, DC: U.S. Government Printing Office.

(1990). *National Drug Control Strategy.* Washington, DC: U.S. Government Printing Office.

Packe, Michael St. John (1954). *The Life of John Stuart Mill.* London: Secker & Warburg.

Packer, Herbert L. (1968). *The Limits of the Criminal Sanction.* Stanford, CA: Stanford University Press.

Peterson, Mark A., and Harriet B. Braiker, with Suzanne M. Polich (1980). *Doing Crime: A Survey of California Prison Inmates.* Santa Monica, CA: Rand Corporation.

Porterfield, Austin L. (1943). "Delinquency and the Outcome in Court and College." *American Journal of Sociology* 49:199–208.

(1946). *Youth in Trouble.* Fort Worth, TX: Leo Potishman Foundation.

President's Commission on Law Enforcement and Administration of Justice (1967). *Task Force Report: Narcotics and Drug Abuse.* Washington, DC: U.S. Government Printing Office.

President's Commission on Organized Crime (1986). *Report to the President and Attorney General. America's Habit: Drug Abuse, Drug Trafficking, and Organized Crime.* Washington, DC: U.S. Government Printing Office.

Quinton, Anthony (1978). *The Politics of Imperfection.* London: Faber & Faber.

Reagan, Ronald (1982). "Radio Address to the Nation on Federal Drug Policy, October 2, 1982." In *U.S. President. Public Papers of the Presidents of the United States, Ronald Reagan, 1982.* Washington, DC: U.S. Government Printing Office.

Reuter, Peter (1984). "The (Continued) Vitality of Mythical Numbers." *The Public Interest* 75:135–47.

Robinson, Richard (1950). *Definition.* Oxford, England: Oxford University Press.

Rorabaugh, W. J. (1979). *The Alcoholic Republic.* New York: Oxford University Press.

Rush, Benjamin (1814). *An Inquiry into the Effects of Ardent Spirits upon the Human Body.* Reprinted in Yandell Henderson (1934) *A New Deal in Liquor: A Plea for Dilution.* New York: Doubleday, Doran.

Ruskin, John (1851/1874). *The Stones of Venice.* Vol. 3. London: Smith, Elder.

Santayana, George (1906). *The Life of Reason.* Vol. 1. New York: Scribner.

Schelling, Thomas (1967). "Economic Analysis of Organized Crime." In U.S. President's Commission on Law Enforcement and Administration of Justice, *Task*

Force Report: Organized Crime. Washington, DC: U.S. Government Printing Office.

Scott, J. M. (1969). *The White Poppy: A History of Opium*. London: Heinemann.

Silverman, Lester P., and Nancy L. Sprull (1977). "Urban Crime and the Price of Heroin." *Journal of Urban Economics* 14:80–103.

Sinclair, Andrew (1964). *Era of Excess: A Social History of the Prohibition Movement*. New York: Harper & Row.

Singer, Max (1971). "The Vitality of Mythical Numbers." *The Public Interest* 23:3–9.

Skolnick, Arlene (1975). "The Limits of Childhood: Conception of Child Development and Social Context." *Law and Contemporary Problems* 39:38–78.

Special Committee of Investigation (appointed March 25, 1918, by the secretary of the treasury) (1919). *Traffic in Narcotic Drugs*. Washington, DC: U.S. Government Printing Office.

Speckart, George, and M. Douglas Anglin (1985). "Narcotics and Crime: An Analysis of Existing Evidence for a Causal Relationship." *Behavioral Sciences and the Law* 3:259–82.

Stephen, James Fitzjames (1873/1967). *Liberty, Equality and Fraternity*. Edited by R. J. White. Cambridge, England: Cambridge University Press.

Stryker, Jeff (1989). "IV Drug Use and AIDS: Public Policy and Dirty Needles." *Journal of Health Policies, Policy and Law* 14:719–40.

Symposium (1988). "The Great Drug Debate." *The Public Interest* 92:3–65.

Szasz, Thomas (1987). "The Morality of Drug Controls." In R. Hamowy (ed.) *Dealing with Drugs: Consequences of Government Control*. Lexington, MA: Heath.

Tolchin, Martin (1989). "Two Bush Aides at Odds on Giving Needles to Addicts." *New York Times*, March 11.

Tonry, Michael, and James Q. Wilson (eds.) (1990). *Drugs and Crime*. Chicago: University of Chicago Press.

Towns, Charles B. (1912) "The Injury of Tobacco." *Century*, 83:766–72.

Trebach, Arnold S. (1982). *The Heroin Solution*. New Haven, CT: Yale University Press.

U.S. Bureau of Alcohol, Tobacco, and Firearms (1989). *Monthly Statistical Release for Tobacco Products: September 1989*.

U.S. Congress (1937). House Committee on Ways and Means, 75th Cong., 1st sess. Hearings on H.R. 6385 (Taxation of Marijuana).

U.S. Department of Health and Human Services (1988). *National Household Survey on Drug Abuse: Highlights*. Rockville, MD: National Institute on Drug Abuse.

U.S. Department of Justice, Bureau of Justice Statistics (1987). *Sourcebook of Criminal Justice Statistics*. Washington, DC: U.S. Government Printing Office.

U.S. Department of Justice, Bureau of Prisons (1936). *Federal Offenders 1934–1935*. Fort Leavenworth, KS: Federal Prison Industries Press.

U.S. Department of Justice, Office of Justice Programs, National Institute of Justice (1990). *Research Action. March 1990*. Washington, D.C.: U.S. Government Printing Office.

U.S. News & World Report (June 1951). Interview with H. J. Anslinger, "Teen-Age Dope Addicts: New Problems."

U.S. Senate Select Committee on Narcotics Abuse and Control (1988). *U.S. Foreign*

Policy and International Narcotics Control. Washington, DC: U.S. Government Printing Office.

(1990) *Annual Report for the Year 1990*. Washington, DC: U.S. Government Printing Office.

U.S. Senate Subcommittee to Investigate Juvenile Delinquency of the Committee on the Judiciary (1969). Hearings on Narcotics Legislation, 91st Cong., 1st sess., September 17.

van den Haag, Ernest (1985). "Legalize Those Drugs We Can't Control." *Wall Street Journal*, August 8.

Vidal, Gore (1972). *Homage to Daniel Shays: Collected Essays 1952–1972*. New York: Random House.

Wallerstein, James S., and Clement J. Wyle (1947). "Our Law-abiding Law-Breakers." *Probation* 25:197–218.

Walton, Robert P. (1938). *Marijuana: America's New Drug Problem*. Philadelphia: Lippincott.

Warburton, Clark (1932). *The Economic Results of Prohibition*. New York: Columbia University Press.

Webb, Beatrice, and Sydney Webb (1903). *The History of Liquor Licensing in England*. London: Longman Group.

Weintraub, Bernard (1989). "President Offers Strategy for U.S. on Drug Control." *New York Times*, September 6.

White, R. J. (1967). "Editor's Introduction." In James Fitzjames Stephen, *Liberty, Equality and Fraternity*. Cambridge, England: Cambridge University Press.

Williams, Allan F., Robert F. Rich, Paul L. Zador, and Leon S. Robertson (1975). "The Legal Minimum Drinking Age and Fatal Motor Vehicle Crashes." *Journal of Legal Studies* 4:219–39.

Wilson, James Q. (1990a). "Against the Legalization of Drugs." *Commentary* 89:21–28.

(1990b). "Drugs and Crime." In Michael Tonry and James Q. Wilson (eds.) *Drugs and Crime*. Vol. 13: *Crime and Justice: A Review of Research*. Chicago: University of Chicago Press.

Wittgenstein, Ludwig (1968). *Philosophical Investigations*. 3rd ed. New York: Macmillan.

Yanagita, Tomoji (1973). "An Experimental Framework for Evaluation of Dependence Liability of Various Types of Drugs in Monkeys." *Bulletin on Narcotics* 25(4):57–64.

Yolles, Stanley (1970). "Statement for the National Institute of Mental Health." Presented to Subcommittee on Public Health and Welfare of the Interstate and Foreign Commerce Committee, U.S. House of Representatives, 91st Cong., 2nd sess., February 4.

Zeisel, Hans (1968). *Say It with Figures*. 5th ed. New York: Harper & Row.

Zelizer, Vivian A. (1985). *Pricing the Priceless Child: The Changing Social Value of Children*. New York: Basic Books.

Zimring, Franklin E. (1978). *Confronting Youth Crime*. New York: Holmes & Meier.

(1982). *The Changing Legal World of Adolescence*. New York: Free Press.

(1984). "Kids, Groups and Crime: Some Implications of a Well-Known Secret."

In Gordon Hawkins and Franklin E. Zimring (eds.) *The Pursuit of Criminal Justice*. Chicago: University of Chicago Press.

Zimring, Franklin E., and Gordon Hawkins (1973). *Deterrence: The Legal Threat in Crime Control*. Chicago: University of Chicago Press.

(1987). *The Citizen's Guide to Gun Control*. New York: Macmillan.

(1991). *The Scale of Imprisonment*. Chicago: University of Chicago Press.

Zinberg, Norman E., and John A. Robertson (1972). *Drugs and the Public*. New York: Simon & Schuster.

Index

213